Gerald —

I'm optimistic you enjoy my 1st book + this one. I know you're passionate about civility + gratitude is a similar trait.

Congratulations on all your success ... working at Tesla, Sivel + Sharp, + being a great guy! You are an excellent role model for veterans on all they can accomplish.

Russ

Our Gratitude Mission

Also written by Russ Terry:

My Gratitude Journal

Copyright © 2015 Russ Terry

All rights reserved.

ISBN: 1519668899
ISBN-13: 978-1519668899

Our Gratitude Mission

15 People, 365 Days, Infinite Transformations

Russ Terry

Acknowledgements

First and foremost, I have to thank my super smart friend, mentor & fellow Coach – Jenn Festa Giordano – for having the idea for this book. She said it during one of our many catchup sessions, which by the way are a great thing to do. I am also quite grateful to my wonderful Mom – Diane Terry – who instilled gratitude in me as a kid when she often said, with conviction, "PMA – Positive Mental Attitude." I am very appreciative too to our intelligent and insightful editor, Diane Liewehr. (What a great first name she has, right?) Her feedback was immensely helpful, she caught many things I missed and she was an excellent sounding board for me in various decisions I made about the book. I am also grateful to our proofreader, Korland Simmons. Like our editor, he had many value-added insights and edits. The two of them made this book even better from a grammar, punctuation and flow standpoint!

I am of course very grateful to ALL the authors in the book. This was a huge undertaking, with a lot of work, plus some twists and turns along the way. I am proud to be partnering with them on this project. Last but not least, I want to express gratitude to the 800+ people (as of fall, 2015) who have a copy of my first book, *My Gratitude Journal*. The success of that assured me that gratitude is something a lot of people are interested in and want to learn more about.

Introduction

I am excited – and of course grateful – that you spent your hard-earned money on our book. We are proud of it and I have been waiting a long time to share the inspirational stories of gratitude in here. As the leader of this mission, it's been my honor to partner with the 15 incredible people who have opened their lives to us in *Our Gratitude Mission*.

At the start of each chapter, we will share info – their age, where they live and where they are from. (By the way, since they're sharing theirs, I should tell you mine too! I am 44.) It is so cool to see the diversity we have in terms of age, race, gender, geographic location, marital status, sexual orientation and more. Some authors have a formal "Baseline" at the start, indicating their mindset at the beginning of this journey. Others weave it into their chapter informally. At the end of each, I give my "Terry's Take": quick insight on the wisdom they shared, them as a person and/or my interaction with them.

The book is about gratitude, but there are also many Self Development pointers in here. If you're looking to Live Your Best Life, this is an excellent tool to work with. Our hope is that, as a result of reading *Our Gratitude Mission,* YOU are inspired to go down your own gratitude path, whatever that means for you. Also, look out for the follow-up to this – *Our Gratitude Mission 2* – which contains even MORE inspiring folks who went on this year-long journey of being grateful. Last but not least, I hope to write a FOURTH gratitude book in by 2018, focused on KIDS and how they can be more grateful. Look for my contact info at the end if you're a parent of a child who is game to go on a Gratitude Mission. Your kid could be in book #4!

Our Gratitude Mission

Table of Contents

1: Schelo Doirin – Light of the World	8
2: Mari Ryan – My Journey in Journaling	26
3: Kadia Saraf – Living my Truth is my Birthright	52
4: Deidra Clark – I've Got a New Attitude!	72
5: Diane Liewehr – Living Life Consciously	92
6: Marian Ruiz-Diaz – Don't Worry, Be Thankful	122
7: Peter Franklin – And For This, I am Grateful	150
8: Donna Newman-Robinson – I Have a T-shirt For That Too!	178
9: Toqeer Kazmi – The Journey Begins	194
10: Marguerite Pierce – My Gratitude Shift	216
11: Tracy K. Pierce – Fitting Life Puzzle Pieces Together Through Gratitude	246
12: Mark Ferrante – With Change to Spare	268
13: Nydia Givens – I Did Not Die: Gratitude 365 Enjoying the Journey	282
14: Alex Long – 365 Blessings	308
15: Domonique Lewis – The Key is Within Us	332

Our Gratitude Mission

Chapter 1

Schelomith Doirin

Light of the World

Age: 22

Hometown: Miami, FL

Current City: Miami, FL

Our Gratitude Mission

April 21, 2014
Baseline

Prior to embarking on this gratitude mission, I began writing in a journal that was given to me many years ago. I realized that whenever I wrote out my dreams and thoughts, I had a much better day. It's as if the burdens that I woke up with melted on the pages and dried with the ink. When Russ shared with me that he wanted to put a second book together, I wasn't too sure if I wanted to participate in it. I remembered the sense of freedom that writing brings, but I thought to myself, "There couldn't possibly be 365 things to be thankful for!" After days of contemplating, and asking others around me for advice, I came to the decision that this would be a great journey to partake in.

I began this journey on March 1st, 2014. I spent most of the day hanging out with a new friend of mine, and that night I wrote about my first gratitude experience. I realized how easy it is to overlook the things and people you are truly grateful for. Writing about friendship that night was the push I needed to start this journey right! After that I realized how many great and promising things are going on in my life. I moved from Miami, FL to Wayne, NJ for a year of school, and I've been meeting the most positive and loving people along the way. Why not document everything?

At this point in life there are many things I am looking forward to. Within the next year, my plans are to learn more within my fields of study - Finance and African Studies - and by the end of 2014 I want to apply for the Peace Corps, where I can use the things I am learning toward a project in another country. My hope is for my grateful nature to grow deeper within me and influence the people I encounter. This gratitude journal is a constant reminder to look at the brighter side of things and that even in my worst days, there's always something exceptional to thank God for.

Dedicated to my siblings: David D, Ruth, Noadia, Venise, and Nethania, and to my best friends, the Noel family

"To the outside world, we all grow old, but not to brothers and sisters. We know each other as we always were. We know each other's hearts. We share private family jokes. We remember family feuds and secrets, family grief and joys. We live outside the touch of time." – Clara Ortega

"The comfort zone is a beautiful place, but nothing ever grows there." - Unknown

My gratitude process first began in May 2013. I was in college at the time and felt as though I was in a bubble. My decisions were unknowingly controlled by the remote I called friends, from the places I visited to the songs that I listened to. At this point in my life, I was actually stressed out by and heavily influenced by the very positive people around me. The saying "Show me who your friends are and I'll tell you who you are" couldn't be more accurate. Although I've always surrounded myself with great and uplifting individuals that I wanted to resemble in some way, by doing so I was suppressing my true personality and leadership potential. I needed a break from my comfort zone and concluded that the best place to begin my growth was at my roots in Africa.

My trip to Africa lasted about five and a half weeks. I went with four other students and two professors from my school, Florida International University. We visited Senegal and Gambia, two countries with the same people and customs, but different languages due to their colonization. The people were friendly and helpful and spent most of their free time with their families and neighbors.

Our Gratitude Mission

I immediately spotted major cultural differences while living there. For example, it is traditional to wait for everyone to join the table for dinner before eating. There they would eat from the same plate, they were only allowed to use their right hands, and for most dishes utensils weren't needed. Another tradition I enjoyed was the naming ceremony. This was a celebration that shut down an entire neighborhood a week after every child was born. Friends, family members and neighbors all dressed up to hear the baby's name and welcome the child with songs, prayers and monetary offerings. Although I have always understood the importance of being family-oriented, it surprised me to see how the community members invested so much time and detail in each other's lives. It was truly a life-changing experience for me and I value every lesson learned abroad.

Upon my return, I did my best to maintain the grateful nature I adopted. I spent more time with the people I love, while focusing on developing my character and personality all over again. I came back a different person. I understand now that the Western culture is not invariably the best and that there are simpler ways of living that can bring me satisfaction. Experiencing Africa informed me that I had a misconception of gratitude. I originally didn't understand the depths of the term. But I now know that if I am grateful for something or someone, I should show it through my words and actions. I also realized how much I took the things around me for granted. Having access to electricity, Wi-Fi, air conditioning, clean water, etc. are all luxuries. It took a trip like this for me to recognize the importance of thanking God for both what I have and also what I don't have.

I began to organize myself better after the trip. I set daily to-do lists and held myself accountable for more of my words and actions. I trusted myself and I trusted God more for the direction I was headed.

To do list:
- ***Stop complaining. Viewing your glass as half full in every situation will give you the best insight on the events taking place around you. When you're in a disagreement, stop for a minute. Breathe. And think about things from the other person's point of view.***
- ***Train your mind, Schelomith. Speak things in and out of existence firstly through your thoughts and next with your words.***
- ***Keep in mind that not everyone is having as good of a day as you might be. Therefore your attitude and selfishness may actually worsen their situation.***
- ***Smile more. It's contagious.***
- ***Do a nice gesture for a stranger. There's always an opportunity for this. If something physical cannot be demonstrated, then strike up a conversation with someone waiting in line with you. You never know who you might meet and inspire.***
- ***Treat everyone like a potential new friend.***

After spending a few weeks in Miami I reminded myself that my journey had just begun. I soon packed my bags and moved to a small town in New Jersey, where I attended a school that was only one-fifth of the size of my university back home. This is where I met Russell Terry.

An Alumni Brother of Alpha Kappa Psi heard him speak at a fraternity event and recommended I contact him to speak at the school. We wanted to bring someone in that would inspire students to become better leaders and of course encourage them to join the new fraternity chapter we were establishing at William Paterson University. After weeks of emailing each other we finally met. I could sense his inspirational spirit even through the messages and I knew that this was someone I wanted to stay connected with long after his workshop was over. He spoke to a room full of students about the importance of transforming themselves from a manager to a leader. I left that room motivated to challenge my leadership skills and take on more roles in hopes to grow into an influential icon. Russ also expressed the idea of me participating in a gratitude mission he was putting together. I promised to give it some thought and after a few days of careful consideration and prayer, I decided to give it a try.

"Let us be grateful to the people who make us happy; they are the charming gardeners who make our souls blossom." - Marcel Proust

Here are some of the many noteworthy gratitude entries from my year of being grateful:

April 24, 2014
My hands; I can type on the computer, flip the pages of this book, drive, grab, feel and hold the hands of my loved ones.

April 26, 2014
My health; I have been maintaining a healthier lifestyle by exercising and eating more nutritious options. Doing this has allowed me to look and feel better. I am more confident and energetic. I hope to keep this standard of living.

May 1, 2014
My mind; I can store memories. I can understand, reflect, visualize and challenge myself daily. My mind is a sponge.

May 9, 2014
Thank God for the time I have spent in New Jersey. This has been the biggest investment of my life so far. Through taking on more responsibilities I have grown and discovered my likes, dislikes, pet peeves, strengths and

weaknesses. My life has transformed for the better. I am confident in the woman I have become and all that I have to offer the world.

July 2, 2014
For the first time in as long as I can remember, my younger sister asked me for advice about something personal. Occasionally, I would mention that I am thankful for her presence in my life, but she doesn't express those same sentiments to me. She would rather speak to my friends about what's going on in her life before approaching me. I have shared with her that it hurts for me to see that. I've spent a long time praying for our relationship and that she would begin to understand things from an adult perspective and I see it's starting to work. A conversation like that has shown me that she is beginning to grow up, and values my advice. We may not be like the sisters on television, but I am optimistic that things will improve between us.

July 15, 2014
My family and I had the opportunity to drive to an island in Florida today to celebrate my parents' 25th wedding anniversary. I am very fortunate to have them as an example of what a healthy relationship looks like. I cannot recall hearing my parents argue or say anything negative about the other around my siblings and me. They demonstrate their love through their daily sacrifices to raise their six children and also through their support for one another. Physically and emotionally, they rely on each other's words and actions to carry them throughout the day.

For years my father has stated that if something were to happen to his wife, expect for him to be gone soon after because he cannot live in this world without her. I used to laugh and remind him that other people enjoy his presence too. However, he is certain that no one can care for him like his wife does. It's an admirable mindset to carry and I'm sure my mother feels the same way.

Our Gratitude Mission

I am undeniably spoiled to experience the wildly romantic displays of affection my father exhibits daily. This man breaks the stereotype of a black father in America. He teaches. He loves. He supports. He sacrifices. He gives. He's selfless. He's kind. He's humble. He's faithful – and prides himself in that. He's trusting. He's there.

Although the qualities my father carries are difficult to come across, they are not unheard of in modern America. These are the character traits I hope to carry and search for in a man.

My mother is also an instrumental figure in my life. Writing about her altruistic heart is enough to fill this book. But with both parents in mind I will leave it at this:

They say the apple doesn't fall far from the tree. If you are the tree, what type of fruit would you like to bear? Character doesn't reconstruct itself overnight. The transformations you undergo in your 20s prepare you for your 30s, your 30s for your 40s, and so on. Begin to focus on the apples you'd like to produce in the near or distant future. These are the apples that will uphold your legacy. Then when the apples are ripe they can confidently say, "I fell from a pretty good tree."

I am grateful that I did.

August 3, 2014
Today I spent all day with a friend of mine that moved back into town. Gina's story is not a typical one. She lost both parents soon after she started college and has been forced to bounce around since then. I've witnessed her deal with difficult situations. But still she stands. She is a key person in my life. She has taught me the importance of picking yourself up when all seems dreary and destitute. She is the epitome of optimism. The more time I spend with

her, the more my character improves without hindrance. I know from the depths of my heart that our friendship will continue to grow and, just as iron sharpens iron, we will continue sharpening each other's minds.

August 28, 2014
I had a dream last night that I gave a speech to a large audience about the importance of viewing the decisions we make in life as an investment. The things we listen to, spend money on, spend time on, what we eat, whether we exercise or not, the friends around us, the work we put in, the relationships we get into, the amount of time spent reading, heck the amount of time spent on social media! All of these choices impact the next stages we experience in our lives.

Ask yourselves today: what am I investing in? And what specific benefits are coming from these investments? When I spend time with my friends, has this person contributed to my physical, mental, spiritual or emotional growth? Are they honest with me? What about the events I spend money on? Do I feel accomplished or fulfilled at the end of it like I hoped I would or am I left trying to convince myself it was a good night? I am grateful I had such a great, vivid and insightful dream!

"Today is the oldest you've ever been, and the youngest you'll ever be again." – Eleanor Roosevelt

Now is the time to start investing in yourself.

September 3, 2014
I am thankful for the small victories in life. Everything we accomplish, whether large or minute, contributes to our character development. I realized today that my small victories include keeping my composure at work, obeying my parents even when they ask me for ten things at once, improving my listening

skills, breaking a bad habit or even first recognizing that I have a bad habit. These accomplishments are things I knew I needed to change when the year began.

As the year progresses, I often take the time to reflect on my development. It's mind blowing to see how a million little steps can take me farther than 1,000 big steps.

Take time to think about where you used to be and where you are now. Are you so focused on taking massive steps and neglecting the little meaningful ones? If yes, then write a list of 10 small things you'd like to transform within yourself in the coming weeks. Once you have mastered them, seek 10 more habits that can be changed. I guarantee you will not only find something to keep working on, but more importantly also something to be proud of.

December 3, 2014
"Two people are better off than one, for they can help each other succeed. If one person falls, the other can reach out and help. But someone who falls alone is in trouble. Likewise, two people lying close together can keep each other warm. But how can one be warm alone? A person standing alone can be attacked and defeated, but two can stand back-to-back and conquer. Three are even better, for a triple-braided cord is not easily broken." - Ecclesiastes 4:9-12

Having a strong support system is imperative for our personal growth. Although we go through fluctuations in life, we're all enduring this journey together. Maintaining transparent relationships with people we hold dear will alleviate our pain during our most vulnerable moments. I am so grateful for the team of like-minded, loving, and graceful individuals that I call my friends. I can walk with boldness and certainty, not because I'm impervious to pain, but because I cannot be broken as long as my friends and family are close by my side. My hope is that everyone can find a group of confidants that make them feel the same way.

December 28, 2014

I am grateful to be crowned sister of the year! This is a title bestowed by my youngest sister Nethania to show her appreciation to the sister that stood out the most to her throughout the year. She explained that I've been helpful with her school work and acknowledged my effort to be more present in her life. This title reminds me that my efforts are not done in vain. I don't care too much for the recognition; I simply want her to learn from me. I'd like for her to grasp the little life lessons I throw into our conversations. To see her grow into a powerful, loving, caring, and giving woman that knows her worth is all the reward I desire. I will continue to work hard as her older sister to set an example of the traits every woman should possess.

December 29, 2014

Every year my siblings and I have a secret Santa exchange for the holidays. It usually takes place a few days after Christmas to avoid the havoc in the stores. This year I knew that my gift would probably be the easiest because I have been in such a grateful mood lately. My sister Noadia was my secret Santa; she gave me perfume and a voucher to play water sports near South Beach here in Miami. I am grateful for the gifts that she gave me, but more so for the ability to give. I drew my brother, David's, name and after observing him for the past few months I decided to give him a ticket to California for his spring break. He's currently in grad school and has been working diligently toward his goal of becoming a pediatrician. He deserves this trip for all of his hard work as a student and as my only brother. I am thrilled to grant him this gift.

Our Gratitude Mission

January 13, 2015
I am grateful for the ability to learn. It is the first week of classes and although I don't believe school defines my success, I am aware of the opposition I may face as a young black woman without a degree. So I'll sacrifice my time and energy to the books as "proof" that I can learn. I intend to be ahead of the game this semester. I'd like to improve on my time management skills and work ethic within the next few months. The benefit of these improvements will hopefully be the ability to advance in my career field.

January 14, 2015
Today makes it two years since my friend Phillip died. I avoid both speaking and writing about it and I no longer visit his Facebook page. At one point I wished that my memories of him would become faint and eventually feel like just a dream. Nonetheless on days like this, and on his birthday, I have found myself on his Facebook page once more. This is because his sister has been flooding my newsfeed with pictures and words of him.

Although my heart is still troubled by the suicide, I constantly remind myself of the words my friend Joel gave me that night I called him crying. He reminded me that I did my best as a friend, and that at 19 years young I couldn't have known what was going to happen. Whenever I was in his presence I displayed genuine concern for his well-being. I always supported his dreams. I prayed for him fervently and wished the best for him. But I guess it wasn't enough, was it?

A few days prior to his death he reached out to me. As we caught up through text messages, I sensed that something was odd about him, so I acknowledged my concern. "Why? Don't worry I'm good," he replied. It eased me a little to hear this response. I couldn't shake off this feeling but nevertheless I moved on with the conversation.

I relived this moment several times after his death. I used to wonder what could've happened if I persisted with the conversations but the thoughts of "should've, would've, could've" have ceased since then. Suicide survivors carry a stigma. Often when a suicide occurs, people look at the friends and family of the deceased and blame the death on our lack of attention to detail. My high school friends and I were ashamed of what happened on our watch. Yet I soon discovered that the more I spoke about it, the more others would open up about their battles with depression. Many in this stage don't understand the damage suicide would do to the people around them.

All I wanted was for my friend to have a life filled with joy. The people around you want the same. It may not be easy to admit sometimes but the situations we are currently facing have all occurred at some point in time. There's nothing new under the sun. Someone has gone through it and someone has gone THROUGH it. And so can you.

I yearn for everyone to see themselves the way God does. I long for them to come to the realization that He has granted us purpose-filled lives. I cry as I write this journal entry tonight knowing that a large number of people will never be able to fully express their insecurities to those they call friends. This is the way we overcome our hardships -- by opening up. When someone expresses signs of solitude, I'll be sure to always take it seriously. I vow to listen, offer help and be nonjudgmental in sensitive moments like this. Ignoring it does not make the problem go away.

So was it enough? Were my love, and our love and support, all substantial enough to have lifted him out of that pit? I think the answer is yes. I cannot erase the past but I now recognize the signs of depression better. Suicide used to be a foreign concept to me. However, now that I am enduring the pain of losing a loved one to it, I see the importance of praying for discernment so that this may never occur again.

Our Gratitude Mission

"Trust in the Lord with all your heart and do not rely on your own insight. In all your ways acknowledge Him and He will make your paths straight." – Proverbs 3:5-6

January 20, 2015
I am grateful for another successful Walk My Shoes (WMS) meeting today.

Soon after Phillip died one of my closest friends, Sainte Fanie, founded Walk My Shoes, an organization that vowed to focus on the personal and educational development of students in both Miami and Haiti. One of the biggest collaborative projects WMS has is called Healing Art, which is a summer program that pairs high school students with college mentors. We trust that with the proper guidance, any student can thrive in life. In addition, we sponsor the education of an orphan in Haiti and hold various events throughout the year to exhibit the beauty of our Haitian culture.

I am excited to see the direction the organization is going in and I am grateful to be a part of such a remarkable team.

February 28, 2015
Today I ran my first 5K obstacle course. This was the most physically challenging thing I have ever done. But I did it. We did it. I say "we" because although I was the only one from my original team that did the 5K instead of the 15K, I ended the race with an entirely new team of supporters. From the very first wall I climbed, there were people around me that I didn't know pushing me to overcome it and more people on the other side to catch me if I fell. I started the race thinking, "I'm going to do this for myself, so that I can say I accomplished something physically challenging." But as I went on, I realized it's all about the journey, not necessarily the destination. Not only did I think about myself, but I considered others around me. I had moments when my new team breezed through certain obstacles that I struggled with, however they didn't leave me behind. And we JUST met! In the moments that I was strong and they struggled, I was also glad to reach out a hand.

So I thought to myself today: if only everyone in the world carried this mindset. We all have goals. We're all going through this obstacle called life together so why not reach out a hand to those around you whether you know them or not? If your neighbor falls, help them up and push them to keep going. If they struggle with something, support them in their efforts to overcome it. Those motivating words, pats on the back, high fives, they make a difference in the next person's life.

My Thoughts after my Year of Gratitude:

My year of gratitude was full of life and laughter. I recall beginning my year thinking that there was no way I could find 365 things to be grateful for, however I soon realized that the number is actually incalculable. Yes, at times I was grateful for my bag of chips or my new haircut, but I also had in-depth journal entries in which I elaborated on the power of a positive mind. Even when faced with intense resistance that should have contributed to me drawing to the conclusion that life sucks, I decided to take control of my future by maintaining a "glass half full" mentality.

I am currently in the final stretch of my undergraduate studies. With only a few months of school remaining, I hope to start a business prior to my graduation, secure a position with a great company promptly after, and position myself for an early retirement. The gratitude mission has taught me that by actively choosing to be optimistic I ensure that no matter where life takes me, my day will always end on a great note. Being that I am the youngest author in this book, and only in my early 20s, I can securely say that this mission has prepared me for the many trials adulthood brings. My intentions are to spread this mentality with whoever is willing to develop so that they may discover more of themselves and become a blessing in the lives of others.

Our Gratitude Mission

"You are the light of the world—like a city on a hilltop that cannot be hidden. No one lights a lamp and then puts it under a basket. Instead, a lamp is placed on a stand, where it gives light to everyone in the house."
Matthew 5: 14-15

Terry's Take

I am so incredibly inspired by Schelo. I have said this before (in *My Gratitude Journal*), but I feel so passionately about it that I am saying it again: make sure you have college students in your life, regardless of your age, socio-economic status, or anything really. Today's youth are tomorrow's future. They are smart, optimistic, and know a heck of a lot of things we don't!

I am infinitely grateful to have met Schelo and partnered with her on *Our Gratitude Mission*. It warms my heart to see the nice things she said about me in here. I love speaking with her on the phone, or seeing her when we are in the same city, because she is such a great person AND is going to accomplish amazing stuff in this world. I am sorry that she had to experience the loss of a friend to suicide, especially at such a young age, but I am optimistic that, because she shared her story in our book, it will help others prevent additional deaths.

I could not think of a better person than Schelo, our youngest author, to kick off this book for all of you.

OK now on to the rest of the wise authors!

Our Gratitude Mission

Chapter 2

Mari Ryan

My Journey in Journaling

Age: 45

Hometown: Greenwich, CT

Current City: Holland, OH (near Toledo)

Our Gratitude Mission

A little more than a year ago, I left my job of 14 years that provided me financial security and comfort in what I was used to. I sought out a newer, simpler life and I found it; or so I thought. I moved away from friends and family and started a new job and life in the Midwest. Some may call it running away. I call it facing reality. Facing the reality of all I had hidden and been through in the past 25 years. Facing much of what I had deeply buried as I quickly moved through life.

Although I had many times of uncertainty during this life change, I also faced times of clarity. I was able to find faith again, to find happiness again and to find me again. I have been able to reflect on what I have, what I have been through and what I have to look forward to. I have never felt happiness like I do now and am now able to take the time to be grateful for everything and every opportunity I have had, something I had been unable to do in a life that was centered on wealth, success and superficial things. This journey with Russ is about remembering every single day what I have forgotten for so many years.

Time and time again throughout my life, people have said to me, "You are so strong" or "I wouldn't have been able to get through what you have been through" or "How did you turn out so normal?" Sure, I have been through each of the top most stressful events – death of a loved one, divorce, moving, loss of job, illness, etc. Some were more difficult than others, some more tragic and some more impactful. Many people may think I have been through my share of life challenges. To others, they have seen more. I am not stronger than anyone else. Everyone copes and gets through in the best way they can. For me, my ways of coping were not coping. They were masking, until this past year.

On the surface, my life looked pretty good. By the age of 40, I had a very high paying job. I owned my own home, drove a nice car, had traveled the world and had a ton of friends and a great social life. I was divorced and had no kids so I wasn't living the perfect life, but I was living the life that many probably would not have complained about. But deep down, under that façade, I was miserable. I had forgotten what it meant to really live. I had focused on the material and forgotten about the real. I had missed out on the things in life that really meant the most. I needed to make a change. I needed to stop and figure things out. And that is just what I did.

For 25 years, my life was overshadowed by a horrible event that happened on a cold, rainy day in October 1989. It was the day of my grandfather's funeral. I was a sophomore in college when my maternal grandfather passed away. Upon my grandfather's death, my mother drove the four hours to be with my grandmother before the rest of the family was to arrive. On the day of the funeral, my father, two brothers and I arrived at my grandmother's house to meet them beforehand. Rather than finding two women dressed in black and ready to go, we found two women bludgeoned to death. It was no random crime, nothing had been taken and the police described it as something like urban legend: a story so gruesome and evil, it could not possibly be real. But it was. Instead of a funeral for my grandfather that day, we had a triple funeral a few weeks later.

After the funerals, I went back to school. I graduated, got married, got a job, moved to a new town, got divorced, got married again (and ultimately got divorced again). Life had gone on. Through the years, as the murders remained unsolved, I kept in touch with the investigators. However, that contact was infrequent and inconsistent. At times there seemed to be leads but those leads never went anywhere. So the case remained opened and a mystery to all. I generally was more frustrated with the investigation than I was hopeful, yet I could easily put it aside.

Our Gratitude Mission

Fast forward to two years ago, when I was living my seemingly great life and working at one of the top, most recognizable accounting firms in the world. I had lived abroad with my job, working in an international role. I had been with the firm for more than 10 years so I was somewhat comfortable. Yet my job was killing me. My hours were crazy and not sustainable. My workload was unmanageable. I was quickly becoming unable to keep up with my work and my performance was suffering as a result. This was around the time I met Russ.

Russ was also with the firm and we started working closely together to send one of his Directors to Singapore. It was a messy assignment with many issues, so we communicated a lot. In our first conversation, I soon realized that speaking with him seemed easy, and I knew our connection would extend beyond our respective roles in the firm. As the stress of my work situation was slowly smothering me, Russ was amidst a huge change. He was leaving the firm to become a Life Coach. I was sad to see Russ leave but I was so excited for him and his new journey and, selfishly, I was excited for what this meant for me. As my leadership saw me struggling, they recommended an internal life coach for me. I had a few sessions with her but also sought out coaching from Russ externally.

Russ and I had our first coaching session in August 2012. Initially, our sessions mostly focused on my job. I was terribly unhappy. My job had consumed my life. I cried every day over the stress of not being able to keep up. I was on a very fast downward spiral and, despite my cries for help with my workload, I was not seeing any relief. Even worse than the high volume of work: knowing that my performance was slipping. I had always been high performing and to know I was barely meeting the expectations of my role was killing me. Through my sessions with Russ, I knew I needed to make a change. Russ didn't tell me what to do. Russ coached me to come to this realization on my own.

His probing questions unleashed the 'aha' moments that would drive me to my decision to leave the firm – which is exactly what I did.

Early in 2013, I resigned from the firm after almost 14 years. It was a mutual separation and the firm and my leadership treated me well through my transition and my eventual termination. Now I was unemployed and had to figure out what I wanted to do. I had worked in a few different capacities through my career so I needed to decide if I wanted to stay in a capacity I had experience in or try something completely new. But first, I needed some decompression time. No longer was I swimming in 1,000 unread emails. There were no more 10pm or 5am conference calls. I didn't really know what to do with myself.

I remained unemployed for seven months. During that time, I decompressed, I reconnected with friends and I looked for another job. What I didn't do was appreciate the time I had. Unlike most, I was in a financial situation where I could take my time to find a new role and ensure it was one that I was going to be happy about. I applied for more than 200 positions. I had more interviews than I could count, including three out of state, plus in person interviews and countless web-based/Skype-like interviews. I enjoyed my time off but, during it, I wasn't grateful for what I had. I couldn't see the gift I had right in front of me – which means I didn't really take advantage of it. I had a schedule tighter than when I was working and never really stopped to enjoy my freedom.

As luck would have it, I was being considered for two roles, both out of state: one with a very large, well known company on the west coast and one with a smaller, relatively well known company in the Midwest. After much consideration, I took the role in the Midwest – suburban Toledo, Ohio to be exact. Some of my friends thought I was crazy not to pick the west coast role but I had my reasons. I had been the small fish in a huge company before. The opportunity in the Midwest promised to allow me to make a difference in the organization. Not to mention the cost of living in the Midwest was vastly lower than on the west coast. This was more in line with what I was looking for. So off I went to my new life.

I began my job in November 2013. From the day I accepted the offer to the day I moved was a quick three weeks, so the transition was fast. I had a house to sell in Florida, I needed to find accommodations in Ohio, I had to find a way to get my three animals and me to my new home and I needed to manage all that comes with moving 1,200 miles away -- all while starting a brand new job. It was a stressful time, to say the least. I thought my house would sell right away. I found the house I wanted to buy and the builder agreed to let me rent it until I sold my Florida home and could use the money from that on the purchase of the one in Ohio. But after a month in my new home, my old house still hadn't sold and the builder was getting anxious. My new job was OK but there were some immediate red flags with my new boss. I chalked this up to the transition to a new job; after all, it had been the first time I had started with a new company in almost 15 years.

By February 2014, things seemed to be falling apart. I still hadn't sold my home, the builder in the house I was renting was threatening to evict me, my concerns with my boss were proving to be real and I was living through the worst winter the area had ever seen. What had I done? I left everything I knew for this. I was alone, concerned about my finances, concerned about my job and wondering if I had made the right choice. Sure, I had met a few friends. But I spent more time Netflix binging than I did seeing humans. I could not see anything positive at this point. Everything was crumbling.

Then March happened.

It was the first week in March when Russ asked for participants for his book. I immediately jumped at the opportunity. At the exact same time, just when I didn't know what to do about my house, I received a viable offer on my Florida home. With that, I was able to fend off the builder and ultimately purchase the home I am now in. On March 6th, 2014, I began my gratitude journaling. On March 6th, 2014, I closed on my houses. Things finally seemed to be coming into place.

Journaling what I was grateful for was rather simple in the beginning. I could easily think of lists of things I was grateful for and sometimes even wanted to write ahead! I'm not sure, however, that I was really appreciating what I said I was appreciative of. It was easy to find things – something I had done that day, foods I had eaten, a show I had watched. However, very soon after I started my journaling, when I thought things for me had taken a turn in the right direction, they took a turn back for the worse and journaling became the way I was going to get through a very trying year, one which taught me about myself, about my friends and family and about life itself.

I had been so excited to start my new job. When I was in the interview process, I learned that the organization I would ultimately come to work for was looking for someone to come in and build one of their key functions that had little to no structure. There was high visibility on the function and because this was something I had done before, I could really come in and be the hero by simply doing what I knew and loved. Even though I was new, I had so many ideas and aspirations. I was going to be a rock star.

From my first day, I could tell things were quite disorganized. I was somewhat reserved with my opinions though since I had just started. I took in as much as I could. I didn't have the best onboarding plan – minimal training and knowledge transfer. My boss Rebecca (not her real name) seemed to be all over the place. She was very busy between meetings and did not seem to have much time to spend with me. The other team member, Stephen, was a temp who had only been in the role for 6 months and would be transitioning out of it as I was brought in to replace him. He was fantastic and did everything he could to help me out. But his knowledge was somewhat limited and only as good as what he had been taught. I leaned on Stephen a lot in the beginning, knowing he would soon be moving on. So in the first few months, I tried to take in as much as I could. Where I could give my opinion on something, I did gingerly. Even though I had been brought in for my industry expertise, I quickly picked up on the sense that Rebecca did not really want to hear my thoughts. Her background was in a different industry and she had been asked to come in and clean up this function with minimal knowledge. By the time I arrived, she had spent almost a year redesigning the function and was set in how she thought things would best work. It seemed my ideas were too late.

Since this had been the first time I had started with a new company in close to 15 years, I thought my uneasiness in the beginning was simply due to growing pains of starting somewhere unknown. There were a few moments early on that caused me to raise an eyebrow but the real red flags were truly raised about three months into my new job. I couldn't figure Rebecca out. Her mood swings were unpredictable. It seemed like the smallest things made her tremendously angry. When she arrived in the morning, I learned it was best not to speak to her. I had to pick and choose and prioritize what I spoke to Rebecca about. At this time, I was not yet journaling. I was also very new to the role and the geographic area and had very few friends. The co-workers I spoke to were just that, co-workers. I was starting to feel very alone. I had my friends from back in Florida and my family but when I would tell my stories and express my concerns, they seemed trivial. Perhaps I was making a big deal out of nothing?

At the time it didn't seem trivial however, I was (what felt like) a million miles away from my friends and family. I was in a new job that I was, in essence, tied to for two years because the company paid to move me and I signed a relocation repayment agreement. I didn't know what I was going to do. I began to isolate myself. Fortunately for me, the winter weather kept me inside so I was able to use that as an excuse not to venture out. I had met a few people through work who invited me to dinner or movies but I was always able to find a reason not to go.

Things continued to worsen at work. I became fearful of reading my emails, regularly expecting blasphemous responses from Rebecca, which had become the norm. I was doing everything in my power to ensure that I was not making mistakes and doing everything I thought she wanted me to do. But regardless, she would often say things such as, "You did this wrong," "This isn't right" and "You can do better." She was breaking me down and it was taking a significant toll on me emotionally, personally and professionally. But somehow, where and when I needed to hold it together, I was able to. Where and when I needed to let it out, I could. And did.

It was during this time that I realized the importance of my journaling. I had overcome the obstacles of moving and buying and selling a home but my employment situation was volatile. My journaling, which was easy in the beginning, became more meaningful and more heartfelt. It wasn't just about what I was grateful for, it was about what I was grateful for and why. Sure, Cheetos may have made me happy on any given day, but I came to a point where I was thinking about why Cheetos made me happy. Through these thoughts, memories were often brought up. Sometimes good ones, sometimes memories that helped give me insight into something about myself. So while I enjoy Cheetos, I remembered a time when my mom brought Cheetos in to me at school with my lunch. A nice memory in and of itself, but it was also a reminder of what a great mom I had and how much she did for me. Writing down one small item opened up the door for so much more.

Back at work, the worst of the worst happened just eight months after I started working at my new job. There had been some pretty bad incidents between Rebecca and me up until now but this one took the cake. It was a very public verbal shaming by Rebecca over leftover sandwiches. I'm not kidding! From the sandwiches, it turned into an attack on my abilities. I wanted to scream at her but I didn't. I calmly suffered through it all. One of my co-workers turned friend, Vicki Viers, saw it all. We had started to build a friendship over the last few months as she had outside visibility into my situation. As things worsened, Vicki had become my confidant. We both came in early which gave us time to catch up. Vicki became the first person I went to when I was feeling angry or the tears were flowing. Vicki was the first person to make sure I was OK in this situation after experiencing what had just happened.

My other co-worker turned friend, Karen Bonner, knew something was terribly wrong as I went flying by in tears. Karen knew less of my situation and hadn't had the firsthand experiences. She only knew what I had selectively shared with her. Given Karen's role, I hadn't shared as much with her as I had with Vicki (yet) as I didn't want to put her in an awkward place.

Karen came after me and on her advice, I calmed down and called my director and ultimately went to Human Resources (HR). Upon my return to my desk after these conversations, I was confronted by the many coworkers who had heard the exchanges and were disgusted by what they had just witnessed. From their reactions, I felt supported and vindicated that I had not overreacted. Not only had I not overreacted, I had reacted a way I never had before.

Rewind a year and beyond and this situation would have been a completely different story. From the moment I had a concern or issue, I would have had the ear of HR and/or Rebecca's boss, my director. That is not to say I had not had any conversations with either in my current situation, but they were very different discussions. The 'old' me would have had a conversation every time something that didn't seem right happened. Those conversations would have gone like this: "Rebecca did this to me," "Rebecca did that to me," or "What are you going to do about this?" These discussions would have been complaining and whining and unproductive. I likely would have also threatened to leave or just left. Granted, I had a significant repayment that would have been due back to the company if I did leave, but that wouldn't have mattered in the past. I would have figured out the money. I would have been much more reactive.

Instead, I chose to take a less aggressive route. I reached out to my director and HR for advice (even prior to the incident mentioned above). I looked for ways to remedy the situation without further breaking the relationship between Rebecca and me. I reached out to other leaders as well, leaders who had long tenure with the company who might give me better insight into the culture or ways that I might be able to manage Rebecca better and improve our working relationship. I did whatever I could to make it work.

And I leaned on Vicki and Karen. The old me of the past would have held all this in. Minimally, I may have shared some of my frustrations with friends or family, but I never would have relied on friendships to help me through the situation. I relied on Vicki and Karen. They were the only two who were keeping me sane. I had a level of comfort and support in them, knowing I could tell them anything and they would give me their thoughts. If I was overreacting, they told me. If I needed advice, they gave it to me.

I also felt for Rebecca. I knew she was having some personal issues that were spilling into her professional life. I reminded myself of the pressure she was under from leadership and the stress that was causing her. I knew that this role was not what she had signed up for and she was not happy being in it. My feeling for her was sorrow. I was sorry to see that someone could be so miserable at times. She could be happy and very nice. She had it in her. There were days where she was very pleasant. She could be fun and sometimes showed a great sense of humor. But those times were few and far between. I couldn't imagine what it must be like going through life just waking up and being miserable most of the time.

Why didn't I hate her? The old me would have. She was terrible to me and, in my opinion, was out to ruin me. She gave me misery and made me question myself and my decision to take this job. She made coming to work difficult and left me hoping either she would leave or I would find another job. I should have hated her. But instead I prayed for her. I also knew it was the journaling that got me to this place. Journaling made me think and feel in ways I had not before. It brought me to a place of peace I had not been in for a long time.

In August, Stephen, who had moved on to a different company, let me know of a role opening up at his new employer. Stephen, Vicki and I had maintained a friendship over the period, having dinner on occasion and communicating frequently. Stephen had experienced some of what I had been going through, having worked for Rebecca himself. He knew much of what had been going on and he, Vicki and Karen all offered great support and insights.

I procrastinated in applying for the job and once I did, the hiring team was unsure if they wanted to consider me. I had only been in my current role for eight months and that was a concern to them. I probably would not have gotten an interview if it weren't for Vicki. She knew one of the Directors on that team, met that woman for dinner, shared with her enough information on my situation and asked that they just have a phone conversation with me. And that they did.

After a month of interviewing, I found out I was one of the two finalists for the role. However, I was lacking a key requirement for the position, which the other candidate had. That person got the offer and as fate would have it, he was someone that I had hired and had worked for me many years earlier in Florida. Being in a small industry, I found out that he had been offered other roles from other companies but seemed to be playing games and never actually accepted the jobs.

For five months this individual played games and finally the offer was rescinded. I was back in the picture. Another month of interviewing and some internal politics and I still did not know if I had the role. That carrot of getting out of my situation had been dangled in front of me and the thought of not getting the job was becoming hard to imagine. Vicki, Karen and Stephen all kept me sane. It was Karen who encouraged me and helped me draft a message to the hiring VP which I believe ultimately landed me the role.

In February 2015, I left that job that tested me and challenged me and began in my new role. From the moment I started, the company and its employees were welcoming and encouraging and it felt like home. If it were not for Vicki, Karen and Stephen, I do not believe I would be where I am today. Their support, their encouragement and their help got me there. My ability to open up to them, to look to them for support and allow them to help me was also a big factor in my transformation. My journaling gave me that ability.

It was exactly June 2, 2014 that I realized the effects of my journaling. I had been writing in my journal for almost three months at that point. I knew the journaling had caused me to think about what I was grateful for every day and, as I mentioned, it was easy for me to find things to be grateful for. Quite often my gratitude involved my friends and family, food and nature. But on June 2nd when I was driving into work, I was staring into a beautiful sunrise when it hit me. This is my entry from that day:

> 6/2/2014 – I am very grateful that I now take the time to stop and smell the flowers. Each day, remembering to be grateful for something is at the forefront of my mind. I have become conscious that often my gratitude is for nature, a sunset, a sunrise, the trees, the flowers, the deer, and the bunnies. But this is not an obsession I have with nature. This is because I have changed. Not only have I changed my job and my location, but I have changed my priorities and how I look at life! Two years ago, I was too busy and consumed in my job to be aware of anything that was going on around me. I never had time to breathe and certainly not time to relax. Now I do. Now I can appreciate everything I was missing. I have become more aware of everything around me. I'm learning to live my life again.

While my gratitude journey taught me much, in the core of my learnings, it taught me to slow down. As a New Yorker by birth, slow has never been in my blood. I have always moved fast. I never saw what was around me. I never really appreciated everything I had. I took almost everything around me for granted. Moving fast caused me problems. It caused me to jump to conclusions. It caused me to make mistakes. When I began to slow down, it seemed my world changed.

The first thing I began to notice was the world around me. Repeatedly, my journal entries detailed the beauty of nature. Having just moved back to the Midwest, I was experiencing the seasons again for the first time in 10 years. I had been in Florida for the years prior and in that time, I never appreciated living in the sunshine state. I'm certain if I had been journaling while I was there, I would have come to love what so many do about Florida. But because I was just moving through life, I didn't appreciate the palm trees, the sunshine, the beaches and the beautiful sunsets. To me, my memories are of heat and humidity, and endless days of stifling temperatures and frizzy hair. Today, I see all the beauty around me. Whether it's the rain, the snow or the sun, I see it. And it makes me happy. These are just a few of the many entries I have about the beauty I now see:

> 5/11/2014 – The morning sun and moon. There is nothing more beautiful than seeing the sun rise and the moon high in the sky early in the morning while driving into work. It makes Mondays much more pleasant!

> 5/18/2014 – The change of seasons. I spent most of my life in locations that had four seasons. However, for the last 10 years, I have been living in Florida and have forgotten the beauty of spring. I love seeing the trees and flowers all blooming and everything turning bright green against the blue sky. I don't think that I realized how much I missed it until I began to relive it.

> 6/4/2014 – I have flowers! I moved into my house in December at the start of what would be the worst winter on record in Toledo. I had no idea what the landscaping on my house would look like in the spring. Today I came home to beautiful pink roses that had bloomed.

> 9/13/14 – I love rainy mornings. Even though I only got four hours of sleep last night, the sound of rain this morning is so peaceful it makes me forget everything else.

Our Gratitude Mission

> 10/8/14 – The moon. Words cannot describe how beautiful it was this morning. It was huge and I felt like I could reach out and touch it!

The second noticeable change in slowing down is how I handle things in life in general. I no longer jump to conclusions, I no longer make judgments, I no longer react and overreact and I am a lot calmer than I ever knew I could be. Stopping and smelling the flowers - literally and figuratively - is a given effect of my journaling clearly documented throughout my year. Stopping and remembering what I do have and not focusing on what I don't has given me a change in my mindset and how I view things as they happen. Case in point, my 44th birthday this year: I generally don't like to make a huge deal of my birthday, but it is my birthday so I do take some advantage of the extra attention that I get. When a water crisis happened the day before my birthday and caused all sorts of chaos in the area, my birthday celebrations were cancelled and overshadowed by what was going on in town. I would normally be annoyed by this. It was MY birthday and this water crisis was quite the inconvenience. But instead, my mind turned to the gratitude I had for living in a place where normally I had access to water, something hundreds of thousands do not have every day. This was truly a first world problem and rather than it being all about me, it needed to be more about those who had a real need and remembering those who could only wish they had such a problem. On my birthday I wrote:

> 8/3/14 – Today is my 44th birthday and I intended on posting about the things I am grateful for this birthday. However, yesterday I awoke to the news that dangerously high levels of toxins had been detected in the water in my area. Initial reports said no drinking, no boiling and no contact with the water for humans and animals, which meant no showering! While we have now been told it is OK

to shower in cold water, the rest of the water warnings still remain in place. Quickly, chaos broke out yesterday. Water went quickly, and there were stories of fights over water and price gouging, stories of people taking advantage of the Red Cross, and of people buying more water than they would need, taking it away from those who do. Restaurants are closed, movie theaters are closed. The zoo is even closed. We have no answers and now there is a panic. Through that, though, I have experienced incredible demonstrations of humanity. In my search for water in the wee hours of the morning, I encountered strangers who directed me to where I could find water, unsolicited help, people banding together and helping each other, people helping the elderly by bringing water to those without transportation. Strangers who would never speak to one another in the course of a normal day are conversing, sharing stories, sharing ways to help and ways to get help…conversations that would have never happened if we were not all coming together through this emergency. I found water this morning and for that I am grateful. But I am mostly grateful and thankful for the human kindness I experienced today.

Slowing down also lets me think through situations and gives me a perspective that I otherwise would not normally have. As I said earlier, I no longer make judgments or jump to conclusions about situations. Road rage was not an uncommon reaction for me. If someone cut me off or was driving erratically or tailgating me, it would set me off. I would become annoyed and angry and if it was in the morning, this could often set my mood for the day. But today, I cannot let things like this bother me, perhaps the person had an emergency, perhaps they were having a bad day. Who was I to judge their situation when I knew nothing about it? This became my normal mindset once I starting journaling.

Another benefit and big change that I can only attribute to the journaling is slowing down in my actions. Multitasking has always been a way for me. I rarely sit still. I like to get a lot done in a short period of time. My mind rarely slows and there is always something for me to do. I'm not necessarily talking about always having to be involved in social activities and being on the move in that sense. I'm talking about "personal work." There always seem to be chores. I'm clean to a fault, my bills all need to be paid immediately and everything must be in its place. Prior to this year, that meant that when I would do things around the house, I often tried to do more than one thing at a time, which often meant dropping things, breaking objects and in some cases, hurting myself. I had on more than one occasion, quickly tried to do something – like get up on a chair – while not really thinking about it and the result often was not good. I have broken lights, dishes, put holes in walls and ruined personal items as a result. But that is no longer the case. Perhaps I have taken some pressure off myself, perhaps by recognizing all that is around me, I have realized that there are things more important in life than being able to carry 15 grocery bags in at once. Whatever the reason, the result is well worth it.

Slowing down in how I handle situations has been a significant change. No more are the days when the small things seem like the end of the world. I can easily take a bad situation and find the good in it. I am able to manage my emotions and my reactions and think before I act. As I already mentioned, this played a huge part in how I handled my work situation. I am proud of how I responded and I have heard repeatedly from friends that they would have blown a fuse and not been able to handle it as well as I did. It has also helped in several other personal situations, including an issue with the least favorite part of the home I love, my basement.

On September 10th, I walked past the stairs to my basement and noticed a reflection at the bottom of the stairs going down to it. Catching my eye, I took a second look and all I saw was water. I have owned homes with basements before but I have never had to deal with a flood. It was about 5am when I noticed it and at first I didn't know what to do. After some internal discussions in my head, I decided I should call the insurance company. The insurance company put me in touch with the restoration company who was out within an hour. After draining the basement, they told me that both of my sump pumps - the main one and the backup - had burned out and I was going to need to replace them. They recommended a plumber who came out and put in two shiny new sump pumps. Given my house was not even a year old, it was surprising to everyone that the sump pumps would both fail. But they did and the only thing I could do was replace them. A year ago, I would have raised hell with the builder over this. But what was the point? Where would that get me? Here is my entry from that day:

> 9/10/14 – I am so grateful for calmness I have learned in life. Today my basement flooded. It was a disaster. In my prior life, I would be completely stressed and overly dramatic about the situation. Today, I was calm and handled the incident as it came. Even the restoration worker commented on how I carried myself in that trying time.

A day later, as my home was engulfed by the not so quiet hum of the 12 industrial drying fans in the basement, I received a call from the insurance company telling me that I did not have flood insurance on my policy and the flood would not be covered. I inquired about coverage and the cost and quickly added it. Although I was unsure of why I did not have the coverage to begin with, what good would it do me at this point to argue with my agent? You bet I would have a year ago, but on this day, my thoughts turned more to how much I love my home and being grateful for being in a position in life to have such a lovely place to live - something many people don't have.

Fast forward to November, and it's the day before Thanksgiving. When I got home from work, I caught that same reflection. I couldn't believe it! My basement had flooded once again. There had not been any rain and I had two brand new sump pumps so how was this possible? So I went through the same exercise again - restoration company, plumber, and insurance company - and within a few hours my basement was on its way to being dry again. While it put a damper on my Thanksgiving Day, it couldn't put a damper on my spirit.

Slowing down has also given me time to stop and think about myself – what I have, what I have been through, where I am and where I want to go. It is not that I didn't have thoughts in these areas before. However, I think when you start writing down your gratitude and it becomes something that you think about in every moment in your life, your perspective changes. With gratitude at the forefront of my mind, I have become introspective and have been able to identify some areas in my life where what I experienced 25 years ago is still causing an impact. I can see where my actions have often been a result of what I have been through. I've also realized that it's quite normal that what happened would still have an effect on me.

Another significant change I experienced through this journey had to do with my friends and family. I don't have a large family and I haven't been particularly close with them over the years. On the flip side, I have always had a huge circle of friends. But similarly, I wouldn't say I had friends I was very close with. I would speak with my friends and family on a regular basis. I would go out with friends all the time. But that was all surface. I had a bond with very few people who I felt I could tell everything. They were my go-to people to talk to when I was happy or sad or needed a shoulder to cry on.

Through my transformation, I recognized that this was a direct effect of the tragic loss of my mother so many years ago. I also realized that's a factor in my single status. I have been too afraid to get close to people. Too afraid they will disappear and I will have to feel that sense of loss again.

However, when I started to write about what I was grateful for, my friends and family were regularly coming to mind. I began to see that I needed them. They were reaching out to me and I wasn't necessarily reciprocating. I was protecting myself by not allowing them to be close and not allowing myself to build the bonds. I was taking them for granted. Here are a few examples of my gratitude for my friends and family:

> 3/30/14 – Friends who don't give up. One of my new friends in OH regularly asks me to do things with her. I'm kind of a homebody and often don't go. But she still asks! If I were the one asking and kept getting turned down, I would have given up by now. Well I finally broke down and agreed to go out and we went shopping and had dinner and saw a movie and I had the best time ever! That teaches me how wrong it is to want to stay at home all the time.

> 5/6/2014 – Friends and family. This is the first time in six months that I returned to Florida after moving away. I have been overwhelmed by the number of people who took time out of their days and rearranged their scheduled to catch up with me.

> 7/19/2014 – Friends who push me beyond what I think I can do and finding the strength and ability to do it.

8/24/14 – My niece and nephews. I hadn't seen my niece for three years and had never met my 2 year old twin nephews. I am so grateful to reconnect with my family and have the opportunity to spend time with them and get to know them.

8/25/14 – My sister-in-law. Today is her birthday and with every second I spend with her, I am reminded what an amazing mother, wife, sister and person she is. I am grateful for the love and joy she brings to everyone around her every day.

10/9/14 – The friends I have made in the past year. I have great friends in all the places I have lived but I can honestly say nothing compares to the two that I have met here – Vicki and Karen. They are always here for me, no matter what.

11/9/14 – Spending time with my good friends. It's not often you meet friends who you just immediately connect with and know they will be friends for life – friends who you are immediately comfortable with and feel like you can share everything with. I have been very fortunate to find two since I moved here. A month ago, my gratitude was for the friendship. Today, it's for spending time with them!

12/7/14 – Meeting new people. Yesterday I met a wonderful new group of people for our chocolate making party. We had a wonderful time filled with joking and laughter. The people I have met here are so genuine and caring and easy to get along with. I can see that I have some new long term friends in these women.

12/24/14 – For my friend Vicki who invited me to her sister's home for Christmas Eve

12/25/14 – For my friend Karen who invited me to her sister's home for Christmas and who had more presents for me than I could ever imagine and made me feel like I was part of the family. I was very sad to not be home and they took away my sadness and loneliness.

Over the last year, I have seen my own growth in my abilities to give in my relationships. In the beginning of the year, I preferred to just hang out with myself. I kept to myself. A good weekend was one at home alone. This transformation was one of the first I saw through my journey in journaling. It began with the recognition that I had two people, Vicki and Karen, in my new world, and they were not going to give up on me. With Vicki it started as a casual work relationship that evolved into a strong friendship. Karen was the first person I ever went out with after moving to the area. She was inclusive of me with her friends and regularly invited me to go out and spend time with her, her friends and her family. They both began to include me in their world. Even when I declined their invites, they still continued to invite me. There was something that clicked in me at some point that made me realize that I had two people who wanted to be a part of my life who weren't going to give up. When I was alone and things weren't going well, they were there for me. As I started to gingerly open myself up to them, the results were unexpected. Vicki and Karen have become two of the closest friends I have ever had. We regularly spend time together, we spend holidays together, and we have fun together. I know they are there for me and I am there for them. They supported me every step of the way when I was struggling at work. They do not judge me. I can laugh with them or cry with them and no matter what we do when we are together we always have a great time.

This ability to let Vicki and Karen into my life has also led to an improved relationship with my family. For many years, I have had a surface relationship with my family. I would see them every couple years, if that. Quite often, when I saw them, there were arguments and fights and it wasn't always the most pleasant of get-togethers. And that was my fault. For years, I held a large amount of anger toward some of my family members. Much of that anger was my own judgement of certain situations. It was my assumptions of what happened and how certain things were handled. However, when I allowed myself to open up to my family, the doors opened. We have been able to work through many of my misconceptions and judgments – as well as the ones they had toward me. The result is a relationship with my family that is better than I could have ever imagined!

In the past year, I visited my family twice in six months. That's twice more than I visited in the last five years. I also visited with some of my extended family who I haven't seen for more than 10 years. I still have some work to do in this area, but I am so grateful that this past year has allowed me to reconnect with them and given me a second chance with my family.

Overall, there are not enough pages in a book or words in a dictionary to explain how documenting my gratitude daily has affected my life. Today, I am in a place that, a year ago, I never imagined I could be. I have a new job, I have great friends, I am now close with my family and every day I am able to reflect on the positive and marvel in every blessing I have received. All these improvements are no coincidence. I truly believe that when you can find gratitude in your daily life, you can find true happiness. That happiness spills into everything you do and everyone you touch. It is contagious. Positive thoughts do truly bring positive actions.

Terry's Take

Of the 15 authors, Mari is the one I have known the longest. I am so grateful we are both out of what was a toxic work environment for us individually, although the firm overall is a great place to work. (Not trying to burn any bridges here!) That seems like a lifetime ago. I am proud that we have each created an incredible new life for ourselves ... lives that would not have happened if not for the challenging job situations we went through that motivated us to take action. I always say I am grateful for what I experienced. It made me stronger, and I know Mari is too.

What she went through personally 25 years ago is something I would not wish on my worst enemy. I cannot tell you what it is like when a colleague, friend and client says in regular conversation "the murders." I bet most people have not had to face such a horrific loss of immediate family members. I know Mari says in her chapter that others have told her this, but it is worth repeating: She is so incredibly strong! Knowing her story makes me want to run downstairs, wake up my Mom, hug her and tell her how much I love her. I am on vacation with her as I write this. Hopefully it inspires you to do the same!

Our Gratitude Mission

Chapter 3

Kadia Saraf

Living my Truth is my Birthright

Age: 38

Hometown: Tel Aviv, Israel

Current City: New York, NY

Our Gratitude Mission

My name is Kadia. Woman. Actor. Warrior. Free Spirit. Yogi. Independent Mom. Courageous. Vulnerable. Strong. Inspired. Empowered. Beautiful. Loved. Go-Getter. Divine. Runner. Early Bird. Dancer. Justice Seeker. Daydreamer. Here again.

I was born to two hippie-hearted parents who were young and carefree. My father was a musician and my mother a flower girl. That's how I remember it. I recall memories from very early on in my childhood of me playing in nature, making toys out of everything. I remember dancing and being surrounded by music. And ... I remember darkness. I didn't know what that darkness meant but I remember how it felt. I have always been surrounded by crisis in my life. I grew up in two countries, Switzerland and Israel, and had a loving family and nature-filled childhood, which I wouldn't change for the world. I did however grow up in a household with one addicted parent and another living a life with the sole purpose of holding the family together and protecting my brother and me. I thank God that my family is healthy and wholesome today; we all went through recovery as a family and are very close to each other.

I was an outsider as a child. I had a few good friends but the rest of the kids would bully me. I don't like using the word bully too often because it has such a bad connotation. Don't get me wrong... it was very bad. I wouldn't want any child to feel what I felt. But it did shape who I am today. It taught me resilience and strength. My survival skills were heightened and my compassion for others deepened. Naturally, I grew up with guards and the need to be in the spotlight to give people legitimate reasons to love me. So, I pursued every possible diploma and award there was, thinking that it would officially make me lovable and worthy. I did enjoy learning new things and achieving goals, but I pursued it with a toxic motive: to fill my void with the attention those achievements would give me. It wasn't working. I felt empty and kept jumping from one thing to the next. The only thing that always felt right to me was acting. Eventually, I had a breakthrough to stop jumping around, and instead follow my passion and become an actor, for me.

I carried a lot of negativity into my adulthood and attracted those kinds of people into my life as well. I felt like I was cursed because I constantly had negative scenarios go through my mind. I became physically ill with asthma, so severe that in order to breathe I would finish an entire inhaler a day, which caused weakness and made my heart beat really fast. I had no motivation - I was just stuck. People told me that I constantly complained and always saw the worst-case scenario. I eventually realized that doing these things was not conducive to my health.

I entered one unhealthy relationship after the next, and was constantly worried about people's opinion of me and being alone. Becoming a mother eased those feelings and made my heart bigger but also my shoulders heavier. Slowly and safely I started opening up to the idea that abuse and misery do not belong in my life. It wasn't an overnight revelation. It took time to "peel the onion" and it was a painful process. But slowly I got to know me: who I am, my greatness, my worthiness and most important my love for myself.

In 2012, I made a conscious decision to change my life. I left a marriage that made me unhappy, and changed my profession to match my lifelong passion. I became an actor and immersed myself in yoga and the process of "onion peeling," which allowed me to shed off layers that didn't serve my growth and happiness.

Soon after that, I started working with affirmation lists and boards that focused on positive goals that I wanted, as opposed to ones I didn't want. That turned into daily prayer and meditation and that into occasionally documenting the things and people I was grateful for. I ran every morning, rain or shine and like Forrest Gump, I haven't stopped since. Within three months I had no more difficulty breathing – there were no traces of asthma. It was transformative. I was surrounded with love and more opportunities to grow. Amazing people started flowing into my life from the most unexpected places. But I still felt like I was not giving it my all. I knew in my heart that the only way to commit to it fully was to write every day, on both the good and the bad days. There is always something to find to be grateful for and it's my decision which part of the glass I want to focus on, the "empty" or the "full." I choose the "full."

■■■

This last year has been the most transformative yet. The most apparent change is that my own inner voice finally became louder and clearer than the voices of others. I've always been one to get things done and try new things; courage was never missing from my life. But everything I did was always accompanied by guilt and a big question mark marquee, representing my self-doubt. This year many things have changed thanks to the discovery of myself or better yet re-discovery. Following my dreams and living my truth is my birthright. The Universe wants me to share my gifts with the world. The Universe wants us all to follow our truth. I started making changes: I purged situations and people from my life that held me back and also made conscious choices about what I will spend my time on. I started taking weekly classes at my home-based acting studio. I kept up my workout regimen and improved every physical goal I had: running, yoga and on-camera combat skills. Now I am ready to climb even higher. I am ready to do the best work at what I'm great at, now I am ready to have healthy, loving relationships, now I am ready to succeed. Now is the time. Now.

My life already started changing thanks to the gratitude mission. When we ask the Universe for something we want, the Universe can only respond when we articulate our intentions in a positive manner, and one that knows that our wish must benefit others as well. I've noticed that since I became part of this, the act of expressing gratitude peels layers of crap off me, allowing me to be truthful to myself. Things started happening to me, good things! And the most exciting part is, I became happier and held less resentment. I've noticed that my thoughts have changed from negative and dramatic to positive and optimistic. I started placing more trust in the Universe and its plan for me.

My most empowering experience was the unending support of my women's tribe. After my divorce I decided to spend more time on my own and improve my relationship with myself. Although it was a blessing by itself, I've noticed that my relationships with other women became deeper. This is something I wasn't used to having, because my relationships with women were always of a competitive and unsupportive nature. Slowly I started forming a community of empowering and inspiring women around me that I call "my tribe." I would have to be a poet to verbally describe their strength, depth and greatness. I was reminded about where I come from and that it's safe to go back to my roots, my instincts, intuition, movement, and my natural sense of self, all of which was already engraved in my soul's memory. It's a recovery… a journey back to my truth.

My relationship with my family has improved too. I am open and honest with everyone without feeling the sense of guilt. I used to feel guilty when I spoke to loved ones when I knew that what I was saying wasn't going to make them happy. I felt like I was walking on eggshells and felt insecure in my own words. The gratitude path has helped me accept and love myself in a way that I am now more comfortable expressing the truth in direct yet kind ways.

Wait. The guilt hasn't completely disappeared. Walking the journey of gratitude is not an instant fix that removes my shortcomings within one year. I still hold guilt, but with the help of my tools I can work through it, acknowledge it, accept it and then take action. And when I don't recognize it, I have my family and tribe to remind me. After all we can't do the work alone. We need our community like we need the sun.

Although it was hard, I've come to a place where I'm comfortable saying "no." In the past, if I said "no" it was always accompanied by explanations as to why not. None of that is necessary today. I say "no" mostly with a kind smile and that's it.

What's also changed is that I no longer say "sorry" when it is not needed, and I do say it where it is necessary. I've learned the difference between the two and that I don't actually have to be sorry when I say "no" to someone. It's my prerogative and my business as to why.

I never anticipated these changes when I started this path. I honestly thought that I'd be walking on air with a constant smile on my face, an image that certainly annoyed me. It is indeed one of the outcomes, I do smile more, but because my eyes are open and I recognize beauty, which I didn't before. What surprised me the most is the fact that the changes worked like a snowball. One thing led to another and the outcome was larger than I expected. I've noticed that my life in general started to evolve and deepen. I saw and felt deeper within, not just around me.

I don't give up my morning routines since they directly affect the rest of my day. For the last year I have been more adamant in starting my day with meditating, writing my affirmations and gratitudes and then saying a few powerful prayers. This has been my ritual and it's been good to me.

One of the most amazing changes is the fact that I don't stress about the little things anymore. I was always stressing when something didn't go the way I had planned it and it sent me into a tailspin without exception. Now when it happens I ask myself: Is this change a matter of life and death? If the answer is no, I just let it unfold in front of me and adjust myself to what is. I can't control my surroundings, but I can control my response to them. After the brief moment of initial panic, I get excited to see what the Universe has planned for me, so it's a win-win situation.

Not only have I benefited from documenting my daily gratitude, but my children have also.

I am a mother of three and physically raise them on my own. It can become very hectic in our household, so I have tools for them to use when it becomes too much, too much for me mostly. When they fight, we now gather together and each child says what he or she likes about each family member. We all take turns to point out the good in each other, which leads to a complete truce.

They also found an affinity for coloring mandalas (spiritual and ritual symbols in Indian religions, representing the Universe), which is incredibly meditative for them and for me. We have a daily affirmation calendar by the kitchen and every morning they take turns to read the day's affirmation. I have noticed that they are more grateful for things they receive and for time we spend together. Nothing will make me happier than to know that my children are grateful for their life and for the abundance in their life and for them to be truly happy and content with it.

• •

My Top Ten Entries of this Year

04/26/14 – When I was much younger I was great at short distance races! My sprints were fierce. And I approached life the same way: Short sprints in life and on to the next race. Today I reached a place where my endurance is better than ever. I commit to a distance and stick to it no matter what. That reflects on my life too. I made a commitment to be a great actor and it never felt so right! Today I am so grateful for being able to do what I truly love.

Our Gratitude Mission

05/11/14 – Today is Mother's Day! How can I not express gratitude on this day? I am grateful to have been born to my mother Verena, who is my biggest supporter no matter how crazy my goals are. She is the one I will dedicate my Oscar to! When I became a mother I came to understand what she went through and how she felt all these years. It's the hardest job on the planet, and it never ends. I am grateful for my three beautiful children, Rain, Noa and Shia, who make me want to run far and dance with joy at the same time. My shoulders have grown heavier, my nerves thinner but my heart has grown bigger. Thank you, God, for blessing me by making me a nurturer.

08/13/14 – On this journey of gratitude journaling I find myself struggling on some days to find a person or thing to be grateful for. It's not always on a lit marquee. On some days it's loud and clear but on others it's not crystal clear. I know that no matter how I feel, if I try hard enough, and on most days it won't take much, I can find something to be grateful for. I've learned to look at the full half of the glass. I've discovered that magic is brewing on days like today. Today is a day in which I worked hard, took actions and planted seeds and just because they have not yet come to fruition, it doesn't necessarily mean that nothing is moving in the Universe. I've learned to appreciate and cherish silent days when nothing seems to happen. My grandmother always tells me that the best dishes are cooked on low fire, so today I am grateful for moments that combine uncertainty and faith; moments which are filled with wonder and excitement.

9/4/14 – Today marks a beginning of a new chapter in my career. I have signed a contract with a new manager and new agent, both of whom believe in me and my success. I am so elated to have found a team so great.

09/13/14 – There is nothing more rewarding than to be surrounded by empowering women who make change in this world. I hosted a clothing swap party, which turned out to be a success and inspiration for all. I love my community and will continue to contribute. Today I am grateful for the women in my life.

10/12/14 – I often struggle with letting go. Letting go of control, letting go of overthinking and letting go of stressing about the results of the actions I take. It's as if I am thinking that the world will fall apart if I don't hold all the pieces together. But I know better, I know that my Higher Power is the only one who can keep me sane and put everything where it belongs. The moment I let go of that illusion of control I suddenly feel a sense of lightness and hope. Today I did just that. I made a conscious decision to let go. I can control my actions but not the outcome and the sooner I get it the sooner I allow the Universe to do its work. Today I am grateful for not always getting what I want but always getting what I need.

1/27/15 – Snow day, bad tire, and hectic day. I drove to pick up my kids from school before the snowstorm hit us. Midway I got a flat tire. I could barely see the road ahead of me and started to panic inside. But I didn't. What used to be "Why me?" "I'm being punished" or "FML" is now "There's a situation, thank God we are all safe and whole. What's the next step to solve this?" I approached it like any other challenge. So yes, I was stuck with a flat tire with my kids in the middle of a fierce snowstorm, but the moment I approached it with a solution-minded attitude, it all worked out fine. On a day that everything goes wrong it's a good opportunity to take a moment and acknowledge what is working. I am grateful that we are all safe and the only thing that broke was the tire.

2/2/15 – I got to work, write, work out, love, live, laugh, compliment and help someone today. It was productive but not too stressful. I am realizing that my stress level must be lowered because I can't take it when it's too much. One day at a time. Today I am grateful for this day, being alive and healthy.

3/11/15 – I often get stressed out when a day is filled with errands and a long checklist. Today I chose to take it one task at a time. I pretended as if I didn't have anything else other than that specific task and managed to tackle it without stress while being fully present. Once done, I moved on to the next task as if it was just added to my list. I don't always move through my day that way, but when I do, I feel light and I definitely smile more. Today I am grateful for the added smiles.

4/16/15 – Today is the last day of my Gratitude Journal year. After my morning meditation I tried to compare today's feeling to how I felt on the morning of the first day of my Gratitude Journal year. I found that I had the same kind of excitement, for what's yet to come and for acknowledging all of the abundance I am already blessed with. It's all already within me.

I've had many experiences during this year and was fortunate to be able to document them. Today may be the end of a year but also the beginning of a new one.

Pivotal Events in my Year

My Health

This year I celebrated three years of breathing without struggle. In 2010 I was stricken by this horrible phenomenon called asthma. The kind that is constant. I had to take a breath after every two spoken words. I couldn't breathe. I went to several doctors, and underwent all kinds of tests and eventually was given the news that I will have to be on medication for the rest of my life in order to control it. I wouldn't accept it. I even told my doctor that I would prove him wrong. I knew in my gut that asthma is a symptom of stress in my case. So I decided to make changes, both personal and professional, which were at first painful but ended up making me a happy – and healthy – woman.

I fought through my illness by running and working toward achieving my dreams. Asthma – gone. Every time I breathe with awareness, I am overwhelmed with a gush of gratitude for that simple ability to breathe. I am constantly reminded of the memory of those tough times, and that my health and well-being is in my hands. I must take care of myself and be picky with whom and what I surround myself.

I am in better shape than I've ever been, I am more at ease with my own body and I have achieved, in my yoga practice, milestones that I'd set at the beginning of the year.

My Career

At the start of my gratitude journey I felt a bit lost and unfocused. I had just begun to work with teacher Mary Boyer and was signed with an agency that wasn't a good fit for me. I felt frustrated, filled with passion but no platform to express it.

Beginning my day with affirmations and gratitude helped open up more opportunities and instead of stressing about the "HOWs" I just decided to start my day with a goal and work toward it. I am one that is hard to surprise. But I was constantly amazed by the sources from which the opportunities came.

Soon after, I signed with a new Talent Agency and new management and things started rolling. This entire year was preparing me for what's coming. I met amazing people, worked on my craft and kept going. This is one of the most important topics for me. I was born to do this and spent my childhood on stage performing. There isn't a day that goes by that I don't dream about acting and performing. That's when you know what your destiny is. In the course of the last year I have come to accept that and pursue this dream with all I've got. I've also noticed that certain people in my life, whom I love dearly, have distanced themselves from me in the process. This is the year when I found out who really is my friend and whom I can trust with my dream. Not many of those are left but many new friends who share a similar dream have come into my life. The moment I became aware of who I am and accepted myself, I started making smarter decisions including whom to keep close and from whom to detach with love. Michael Levine once said: "If you want success, you must fire your flaky friends," which means you must surround yourself with like-minded and like-hearted people and distance, even if just for a little while, from those who hold you back with actions, words and even negative thoughts and judgments. The good news, Michael said, is that those friends can re-apply later on "when they get their act together."

From the moment I made that switch in my thinking and my actions, everything started falling into place. I didn't feel stuck and hopeless anymore. My life is uncertain, and yet I feel happy and safe.

My Struggles and how I deal with them

See my "My Top Ten Entries of This Year" from earlier in the chapter for examples of my struggles and how I overcome them.

Every morning I wake into a new day by writing my affirmations and gratitude. I then meditate for a little while and step off my bed with the right foot to remind me to be compassionate. I am aware that there are no mistakes or wrong paths because every time I got lost, took a different path, thought that I wasted my time doing something or failed at a relationship, I ended up meeting someone new who changed the course of my path. So in a way, I had more pivotal experiences when things didn't work out the way I wanted them to.

Breaking old habits and patterns that were ours for a couple of decades cannot happen in one therapy session or a seminar or even in one year. It takes a long time to break patterns and replace them with new positive ones. So often I was hard on myself when old habits were rising to the surface and determining my actions. Today, I accept that they will still come up from time to time and that today, I have the tools to deal with them. I know that I come back to my breath, count to ten or even a hundred if need be. That gives me time to observe my situation from a clear place, ego placed aside and leading with my truth.

••

Favorite expressions of Gratitude

A grateful heart is a magnet for miracles.

This expression reminds me to focus on what I have. That alone will open my eyes and ears wider to recognize miracles that I otherwise wouldn't see because I'm busy frowning.

"Everything has its wonders, even darkness and silence, and I learn whatever state I may be in, therein to be content." ~ Helen Keller

Waiting for everything to be perfect to find contentment will be an endless wait. Finding contentment in the imperfect and in uncertainty … that's where the light is.

Thank you for not always giving me what I want, but always giving me what I need.

I used to dislike this expression because I felt like I knew what I needed. Today I understand that I don't know everything and I don't know what the big picture looks like. In retrospect I am grateful for all those times I didn't get what I wanted.

Whatever hour God has blessed you with, take it with a grateful hand.

I used to believe that everyone else is lucky and blessed and I stand last in line. Every single time crisis struck me I said, "Here we go again" or "Of course that should happen to me." I was used to it. I never for a moment thought that good things could happen to me too. Best case scenario is just as likely as worst case scenario.

"Nothing is either good or bad. It's thinking that makes it so." ~ Shakespeare

Another lesson I have learned is that my attitude determines how I act. Our experiences are our own projections. So why make it negative when I can make it positive?

Thank you for waking me into another day.

I say this every single morning. I am grateful for opening my eyes, for seeing the sun, listening to birds chirping and for the opportunity to follow my dreams.

The most powerful prayer is "Thank you."

My father taught me this one early on. But I was so resistant and always found more to want. I didn't see that I had exactly what I wanted, and I was where I needed to be.

Thank you for my health.

Another one I say every morning! I am so blessed to have my physical and mental health. It's everything.

When you put one foot on the past and one foot on the future you pee on the present.

That was always one that made me giggle. My dad has his ways to send messages. There's a reason why present is called just that. The Now is a gift.

"When you complain, you make yourself a victim. Leave the situation, change the situation or accept. All else is madness." ~ Eckhart Tolle

This is the story of my life. This one expression made my life change from being a martyr to happy. Just like the serenity prayer: God grant me the serenity to accept the things I cannot change, courage to change the things I can and the wisdom to know the difference. If I can change it, I change it. If I can't, I accept it. I stopped being a victim.

Lessons I have learned

- I am always provided for at any given moment.
- My thoughts, words and actions cause an energetic tsunami and affect everyone around me and in the world.
- I am worthy of happiness, success, and abundance.
- The way I start my day determines how the rest of it will look.
- I don't owe explanations to anyone about my decisions and thinking process.
- Sharing my gratitude with people makes them feel important.
- Best case scenario is just as likely, if not more likely, to happen than worst case scenario.

Open Letter

In the process of eliminating layers of thoughts and feelings that didn't serve my growth, I put together a goodbye letter to those feelings:

Dear Control, Low Self-Esteem, Self-Criticism and Fear of Abandonment,

I want to take a moment and thank you for serving me in times of need. I have had so many events and instances where your availability helped and saved me. Perhaps not always, but at least I felt a sense of security and familiarity with you around.

Our Gratitude Mission

Now that I have grown to love myself and accept my life and my greatness in this life, I no longer need your services.

Control, I take responsibility for my actions and let go of those that aren't mine to control. I accept that my view is not the only view. Therefore I no longer need you to hold on to results and others' actions.

Low Self-Esteem, I have discovered that it was all fake; it was all in my head! None of the things I thought about myself was actually real. So ciao.

Self-Criticism, although I still sometimes want to get your opinion on things, I find that I trust myself much more today. I am still working on forgiving myself as easily as I forgive others but I got this one from here on out.

Fear of Abandonment, oh my oh my, we had a long run together. You still cling on to me, I know it's hard to let go, but I am ready. I have this new guy his name is God and he will never abandon me. Ever. I got him. I got me. Everything else will come and go as needed.

Thank you for your services, good luck with everything.

Goodbye,

Kadia

••

Final Thoughts

I am grateful! I'm grateful for this book, for Russ and for the entire team -- everyone shares their passions, fears and love for life in such a courageous way. I am grateful for the roof over my head, the abundance of food in my fridge, for my car that safely takes me from one point to another, for fresh running water and for my warm bed. I am grateful for the social media platform that connects us like-minded people every single day and creates such change and connection in the world. I am grateful for my body and mind and the health I am blessed with and for the courage and drive I have when I wake up every morning. I am grateful for my parents: My dad who is an open-minded, free spirited man who always encourages me to keep an open heart and be in the state of creation every day. I am so grateful for my mother who supports everything that I do, puts her heart into my crazy adventures and is my biggest fan. I want to make her proud. And I am grateful for my children: Rain, Noa and Shia who are my rock and true North, who remind me that teaching is not just done with words but mostly by leading by example of courage and action.

Terry's Take

I love Kadia's chapter! She makes me laugh AND makes me think. Her letter near the end of the chapter is inspiring and hilarious. Kadia is the only one of the authors who is here in the United States that I haven't met in person yet. I think it is very cool that in this day and age, you can have an amazing connection with and work on an incredible project with someone you have never met. I am grateful to our mutual friend – Loretta Nauth – for introducing us and being the conduit to us being on *Our Gratitude Mission* together.

Kadia is the first Mom in the book, and it is excellent to see her insights regarding self-care. My niche as a Coach is "women who *finally* want to put *themselves* first" and nowhere have I found this more common than mothers. Ladies make excellent nurturers, which is a really great quality, unless one neglects oneself in the process. Hopefully her story will inspire you or someone you know!

Last but not least, I love and am quite impressed by how she instills gratitude in her three children. As I mentioned in the Introduction, I want my fourth Gratitude book to focus on kids, so who knows, maybe she isn't the only member of her family who will be in a book!

Russ Terry

Our Gratitude Mission

Chapter 4

Deidra Clark

I've Got a New Attitude!

Age: 29

Hometown: Brooklyn, NY

Current City: Brooklyn, NY

Our Gratitude Mission

Growing up, I just wanted to be happy. I wanted to be like the people I saw on television who smiled all the time and seemed to have great lives. Sure, their lives were scripted but that doesn't mean that a life like theirs is unattainable, right? But first, I had to figure out what happiness meant to me and what was missing in my life to make me feel like I lacked it. I never thought I deserved to feel unhappy. I grew up in a loving household. I have the most wonderful mother and an incredibly supportive family. My late maternal grandparents were truly one of a kind; I am so grateful I had the opportunity to know them. I have an amazing 8 year old daughter, a loving boyfriend and the same awesome friends that I've had for more than 15 years. I graduated from Syracuse University with a degree in Psychology and had a job offer in the fashion industry shortly before leaving campus. I've been working in fashion for 7+ years and have been promoted three times in the last two years. Why do I have the right to feel unhappy? I asked myself this over and over in my head. I also started to actually feel guilty for the unhappiness I felt...which made me feel even worse at times.

I knew something and/or several things in my life were not aligning with my spirit and causing this inner friction I had. I started taking notice of some of my feelings/actions. Getting out of bed was really hard. I became easily irritated with everyone and overreacted to simple things. I was often lost in my own thoughts. I had a sense of overwhelming sadness at times and would just cry in my solitude. Although I have never been diagnosed, I thought I was on the brink of depression. Then, there were days where I'd sometimes get an overwhelming feeling of anxiety that lasted for weeks at a time. As soon as I'd wake up, my stomach would be in knots for the entire day until I calmed myself to sleep. My appetite was usually affected and I couldn't think of anything else but the worries I carried in my heart.

One of the times I recall having this overwhelming feeling was at a former job I held. I began this new job excited about the opportunity to start anew, but my excitement quickly turned to being dispirited. I recall the very first day on the job; my new boss brought me into her office. After going through some of her expectations, she made it clear to me that she was going to be harder on me than the rest of the team because I was Black. The crazy thing is she was a woman of color as well. I remember thinking, "Who the heck does she think she is?" This set the tone for the rest of my time there. There was no way I was going to be able to get over what she told me. After weeks of what I felt was abuse at the office (being scolded like a child, name called, constantly picked on)...I went to HR to attempt to get out of this horrible situation I found myself in. This didn't help...they didn't help. I cried when I got home almost every night while I worked there until one day, I realized that I had started losing weight. The scale read seven lbs. lighter than it had two weeks prior. That was the last straw for me. The very next day, I quit. And the amazing part is, although I did not have another job lined up, the anxiety that I felt for weeks dissipated as soon as I walked out of the building for the last time.

Since then, I have had a few more of these bouts of anxiety. I've noticed most of the worries dealt with my career or my future. But I knew that I didn't like feeling this way at all. And I knew that not only was it unhealthy for me, but also for the people around me. I didn't want my worries to be a damper to anyone. I just wanted to be happy.

I did some research on things that I could do to minimize these ranges of emotion I felt. Because I never got diagnosed, I didn't know what it was. But I was willing to try anything. One of the suggestions was to keep a journal. Not too long after seeing this, I saw a post from Russ Terry on Facebook about his idea for his second book. His first book was his own Gratitude Journal and sharing the lessons he's learned on the way. His way of expanding this idea was inviting dozens of other people to document 365 days' worth of gratitude for different things, people, places and experiences. Russ and I went through the same Life Coaching Program together at The Institute for Professional Excellence in Coaching (iPEC). We connected almost instantly because we're both Syracuse alums and he has such an inviting spirit. I knew that his post was speaking to me and I decided to jump on board.

When I first started journaling, I did it because my soul needed it. My intent was to help myself continue on my self-awareness journey, ever conscious of the world around me and to have more "glass half full" approaches, and less half empty thoughts. I already had a taste of this during my training as a life coach but I found it difficult to keep it up not being around that energy every day. The "real world" can be an energy drainer. I loved that, even during those difficult, energy-draining days, there was always something to be grateful for. Take my entry below as an example:

Monday, May 12, 2014

Today was a hard day because I allowed every single little thing to irk me. To stay somewhat grounded, I listened to Marvin Sapp for most of the day. And then I decided to read my horoscope (which I haven't done in a while) because I wanted to see if I could find any relief there...and my relief came. #God

Today's horoscope:

The last thing you need to do is to drain the positive energy that is coursing through you now to address petty conflicts and minor aggravations. You do like things to be perfect, so naturally when you see something that needs to be fixed you jump right on it. But you need to let go of the "small stuff" now and concentrate on the big picture. You can accomplish quite a lot right now if you maintain an optimistic outlook and you don't get swept up with irritations that just aren't worthy of your time.

Between the music and the message, I remember being taken aback after reading my horoscope; it was just so spot-on. I still have a lot of learning to do spiritually but I do believe in God and I am learning first-hand about the mysterious ways He works. This has been another tremendous element to my journaling because I have consciously built a relationship with God through prayer, reading scriptures and allowing myself to experience gratitude the way He wants me to experience it.

A few weeks prior to this, He spoke to me through a homeless man on the street. On Tuesday, April 22, 2014, I wrote:

> On my commute to work, I got off of the train at my normal stop. Every day there seem to be people outside of local fast food restaurants and other eateries hoping to get someone's attention with requests for help. "Can anyone spare some change or food?" I see people with these requests on a daily basis. If I have some spare snacks, which isn't very often, I would offer the food to them. However, today, I saw a young man perhaps around my age who sat on the chilled concrete ground with a sign that simply said "Hungry...food is appreciated." I don't know what it was about this sign or this man in particular, but my heart was called to action. I walked into the nearby Pax and along with the turkey bacon, egg white and croissant sandwich I bought for myself...I also purchased an apple, a toasted muffin, oatmeal and a bottle of water for the man. "I hope you're not allergic to anything...there are a few choices in there if you are," I said to him as I handed him the bag. I could tell that he was surprised and grateful all at the same time. He showered me with "thank you" and "God bless you" multiple times each before I walked away. I was happy to know that he was going to have a good breakfast and hopefully a snack for later. I only wish I could've done more.
>
> I've never been without food for an entire day. My family wasn't a part of the upper class growing up but I never had to worry about

food, shelter or love. To be honest, I get cranky if I don't eat after about 4-6 hours. So I can't even imagine what those who go days without eating are going through. I'd love to make some time to volunteer in soup kitchens and/or other feeding the homeless initiatives. I want to get my daughter involved too. She doesn't realize how good she has it and it's important to me that she is aware of her favor.

"Don't forget to say thank you!" I say this to my daughter Samaiya often because this is how I was taught to express gratitude. "You have to be grateful for what you have because not everyone is as fortunate," my mother would say to me, especially when I'd catch a 'tude for not getting my way. Now as a mother, I hear my mother's voice exit my lips as I explain to my daughter the importance of gratitude.

I think being a mom has emphasized the significance of gratitude in our household. I try to set a good example for my daughter. I've read that First Lady Michelle Obama and her family share their "thorns" and "roses" at the dinner table. Roses symbolize the good things that happened that day and the thorns are the challenges that were faced that day. I decided to adopt this into our home as a way to reflect on the good and the bad and talk about how we can help each other together. Now I can barely get my shoes off when I come in the house before Samaiya asks, "What's your rose and what's your thorn, Mommy?" I love that she is so excited to be involved in such a subtly powerful activity.

Here are some of the "roses" that I've shared with her over the last year:

Wednesday, May 14, 2014

I am so grateful for the man in my life. My boyfriend Jay currently works in the entertainment industry, in the wardrobe department for various movies and television projects. It's funny how we both work with apparel. So the costume designer needed a fit model for a last minute fitting, someone who could fit into a size 4 dress. Well I am so glad that I didn't eat that last piece of cake for dessert because he sent her my picture and I am confirmed to be at the fitting tomorrow! Not to mention, this is my FIRST PAID GIG as a model. Boom!

Thursday, May 15, 2014

It's a wrap! So I went to the fitting today and literally was there for about 20 minutes and could not believe that I got paid just to try on a dress. It was a bridesmaid dress that will be seen in a simulated screen (like a fake website) on the movie, *The Intern*, which stars Robert DeNiro. And the icing on the cake (the one that I didn't eat yesterday) is that DeNiro himself was there! I was trying not to seem bothered but he was staring at me in the dress. When I told my boyfriend about it, he reminded me that Mr. DeNiro has a thing for the Nubian sisters. ::shoulder shrug::

Wednesday, July 16, 2014

I came into work today and saw an email from the Director of HR in my inbox that read, "Hey Deidra, tried calling - wanted to touch base." I was so curious about the purpose of this phone call that I called her back as soon as I read it. I didn't even take a bite of my breakfast sandwich yet and you know I was hungry since I barely ate anything the day before. Her voicemail answered - I left a message and proceeded to tear up the bacon, egg and cheese on a roll. Shortly thereafter, she called me back: "There is an opening in ladies sportswear that we think would be a great fit; this would obviously be a big promotion - higher wages - higher bonuses, what do you think?"

Our Gratitude Mission

Me: "Ummmmmmm..." (I had no idea this was going to happen...I think my umm lasted about as long as the Buddhist chant...maybe she didn't notice)

Me: "That's amazing, when would I interview?" (That's right Dee, turn the focus around)

Her: "Today" (of course, why would I expect any different?)

Me: "How about Friday?" (Good counter!)

Her: "Ok, we'll see if that works for them and we'll get it on the calendar."

I'm grateful for having the faith to stick it out at my job, despite the countless frustrations. What an awesome opportunity this will be.

Saturday, July 19, 2014

I am so excited to be starting Scene Study classes today with Pam at T. Schreiber. I have really missed being around fellow actors and working on my craft.

Tuesday, July 22, 2014

I got the JOB! I am so friggin' grateful for this raise that I am about to get.

Sunday, August 31, 2014

What a joyous day it was. I woke up early, a little anxious but very excited. I gathered my clothes and everything that I packed the night before, showered, got into the car and headed to my future sister-in-law's house. Today is the day she is marrying my brother. The day is finally here and what an amazing day it was. I smiled so much (not just because I was a bridesmaid and I basically am expected to smile the entire time or else my brother would kill me for ruining the wedding photos) but because I was genuinely so happy that he has found love. I am so privileged to have been a part of their special day.

Monday, September 8, 2014

Today was Samaiya's first day back at school! I know when this time comes around there is always an adjustment period. Well, after I got home from work, all she wanted to do was lie with me and I naturally obliged. I'm so happy she still enjoys cuddling with her mom. My heart is smiling.

Thursday, November 11, 2014

Today was my photo shoot with Sam Khan and I am exhausted. I am so grateful for his patience. We spent approximately six hours trying to get the perfect shot. Since it was taking so long, I started to feel a bit discouraged halfway through and I started questioning my ability to do this, but he was so comforting and gave great direction. I am also so grateful that my honey stayed there with me the ENTIRE time. I am so lucky to have someone in my life who is as supportive as he is.

Friday, January 30, 2015

What a day! What a week!

My mind, body and soul have been filled with so many different emotions and today I was just about ready to explode. Things continue to be somewhat challenging at work and I am trying so hard not to let it bother me, but that is something I still struggle with. I just couldn't wait to get home and get back to the book I've been reading, *A Challenge for the Actor* by Uta Hagen. When I got to my building, I checked the mail as normal and saw a bill (of course) and a small envelope addressed from Erica, a good friend of mine who I met during an internship one summer in college. I recalled that she texted me asking for my address earlier this week but certainly wasn't sure why. I sent it to her without question. After I took off my coat and kicked off my shoes, I sat at the kitchen table and proceeded to open the envelope. A handwritten note was inside. As I read it, all of the day's stress, anxiety, anger, sadness and any other emotion that I felt dispersed. "You are an amazing woman with one of the purest souls I know." I was taken aback as I started reading. She thanked me for my "encouraging words" and having a "beautiful spirit." I sure didn't feel very beautiful on my way home but wow, the power of gratitude! Erica's special note reminded me of why I started this journey in the first place. Thank you for your beauty, your transparency and your thoughts Erica. You have helped me in ways that you couldn't imagine. I am so grateful.

Why do I have the right to feel unhappy when so many fantastic things happened this past year? Well to be honest, after having the opportunity to go back and look at my year, it was an awesome year and I have the written proof. Without the journal, my mind would only allow me to remember a fraction of the good while the bad days at work, the crime in my neighborhood, the jerks driving on the highway and the Debbie Downers would all be prevalent in my memory. By writing it all down, I was able to make a choice to acknowledge that yes, there were some rough patches but there were so many more "roses."

The journal also allowed me to be very conscious of my thoughts, my emotions and my actions. There was a period toward the second half of my gratitude year when I felt my emotions becoming uneasy again and I decided to create a challenge for myself. This journal in itself was a challenge but I needed something more.

Monday, March 16, 2015

I've struggled with consistency and discipline for quite some time. I'll start something and won't always follow through. Keeping this journal has been a struggle. Some days I was just too tired to write. Other days, I just didn't feel inspired enough. I read an article once about Jerry Seinfeld and his method of success. It was very simple. He worked on his material consistently. On the days when he was too tired to write, he did it anyway. For him, it wasn't about quality as much...it was about consistency. Denzel Washington said something very similar in a video I came across on YouTube. "Consistency + discipline = success." I decided to start a new challenge today. Something that I will consciously be doing and it will allow me to shift some of the negative energy that I've been hoarding. I've started smiling through the day. I decided that I don't just want to get through the day...I want to smile through it. The ironic thing is, I just finished getting through Chapter 2 of *How to Win Friends and Influence Others* and the second principle is simply to smile more. No one is interested in being around mean muggers for too long. I don't even want to be around myself when I am in a bad mood. It can be so draining. My daughter is going to think I'm crazy - I don't know if she's seen me smile as much as I plan on smiling. I think it'll be a pleasant adjustment. I'm so happy that I was able to recruit one of my coworkers to do this challenge with me. #smilethroughit

And then, just a few days later:

Thursday, March 19, 2015

I have to say, so far I've been keeping up this smile pretty well and am super proud of myself. So today I headed into the elevator to leave work and noticed someone was in it already. When getting into the elevator, I'd sometimes smirk and attempt to appear somewhat pleasant (or if I've had a bad day, you might not even get that). Well today, I consciously walked in with an intentional smile on my face. This sparked an awesome conversation with the beautiful stranger in the elevator who spoke with me as if we were childhood friends. The energy was euphoric. She even came with me to the liquor store on the way to the same train station (I needed a bottle of wine to go with tonight's episode of *Scandal*!) I'm so happy to have been able to connect with this woman and am so grateful for my smile.

This was a simple experiment for me and it proved to be so effective. I made a new friend and added a beautiful new spirit to my life. Who knew a smile could be such a gift? Sometimes, a smile is all it takes. I've started to wear my smile more and it forces me to feel the inner peace that I've longed for.

Lately, my face is not the only thing wearing a smile. I often think about how my heart smiles when I think about the people in my life:

Sunday, May 11, 2014 (Mother's Day)

"Mothers and their children are in a category all their own. There's no bond so strong in the entire world. No love so instantaneous and forgiving." —**Gail Tsukiyama**

Ever since my Aunt Jackie had my little cousin just seven years ago, my mom, Aunt Jackie and I all get together for our annual Mother's Day brunch in Philadelphia. It's become our own little tradition. I am proud and so grateful to come from a family of awesome women. I know many people rightfully believe that their moms are the best in the world. I am no different. I can't fathom where I would be without my mother. She has been so many things to me over the years: my cheerleader during recitals and performances, my disciplinarian when I made a bad choice, my shoulder to cry on when I was sad, my motivator when I didn't have the confidence to take another step, and my advocate and supporter when no one else would stand with me. I got through college a semester early with a newborn baby because of her. I performed at Carnegie Hall as a teen because she wouldn't allow me to stay in bed on Saturdays like I wanted to. She knows me better than anyone and pushes me toward excellence. Through her example (and some trial and error), I've learned (and am still learning) how to be a mom.

Saturday, May 17, 2014

Today I am celebrating my best friend Ryan's birthday! We have known each other for more than 15 years and I have told him so many times how grateful I am to have him in my life. Ever since Junior High, we have continuously challenged each other to be better versions of ourselves. Although we haven't been in the same school since Elementary, we have always competed with one another to be the best in our class. I remember being upset that I didn't score as well as he did when I first took the SAT and decided to retake it so that I could beat him. Didn't happen. But I did get my driver's license before him :-). I am certain that it was this healthy competition that instilled the drive that I have today. My other best friend Neilia was there too. She has been such a staple in my life. A true friend who has always been a voice of reason and keeps me grounded. I have been blessed with great friends and for that, I am so incredibly grateful.

Saturday, November 8, 2014

Today, I am grateful for the fresh air, the trees and the quiet that surround us. Last night, my honey, the munchkin and I ventured off to the Poconos, where we'll be staying until tomorrow. Jay's aunt & uncle have a cottage out here and they were gracious enough to allow us to stay here for the weekend. Jay's cousin and his girlfriend, along with their adorable dog, are here also and it's such a refreshing trip. We're all really appreciating the break from the city. Who knew I'd love the sound of the leaves rustling in the wind so much? I couldn't ask for a better weekend with a better group of people. #soblessed

I'm even grateful for the people who weren't always in my life. As a child, my father wasn't around. I think his absence has affected me in more ways than I acknowledge. Although I knew he was in the military, I also knew that he and my mother were no longer together. That didn't bother me. But what did bother me is that I would only hear from him a couple of times a year. I remember opening cards from him seeing the German words *"alles Gute zum Geburtstag"* or Happy Birthday. "My dad is so cool," I thought as I continued reading his card. He lived in another country, knew other languages, worked with airplanes...he had to be cool, right? Despite his absence, I still admired him. But I couldn't help to think as I got older, why didn't he try to have a better relationship with me? He had two other children after me and he was present in their lives. What was it about me? Why did other children have their dads around but mine wasn't? I didn't know it at the time but now I realize that in every situation we go through, there is always a lesson to be learned. Despite the self-detrimental thoughts I had, I realized that there wasn't anything wrong with me. That was just something I needed to experience to better deal with another situation that was coming down the line. There was a lesson that I needed to take from his absence. Whether it was forgiveness or something greater, it was God's way of building and defining my character.

What would life have been like without consciously being thankful for the gifts we are given every day? It's a dark, scary place. It's a hole that gets bigger and bigger to the point where you feel like you have no choice but to succumb to it. I have felt it. How have I been able to come out of it? I know that I have a little girl who depends on me to be the best me I can be. That is my God-given responsibility. I refuse to let her down.

My favorite part about being involved with this gratitude project: knowing that there are so many other people who have committed themselves to taking this journey along with me. We have all been on this path together. When I became involved with *Our Gratitude Mission*, my goal was to come out of it with spiritual growth, a fresh look on life and a year's worth of accomplishments. As I look back on my year, it's unbelievable how fast the time has gone by. I remember starting this gratitude journey thinking, "What have I gotten myself into?" Not because I didn't think it would be helpful but because I have the tendency to sign up for things or get started with something and not follow through. I was scared that I would let myself down. Saying yes to this journey has probably been one of the best things I could've done. I have found my happy place in gratitude.

Now it's your turn! Here are the four biggest lessons that I've learned over the past year that I hope will be guidance for anyone who wants to start living a happier life filled with gratitude.

1. **Living with a gratitude mindset is much easier than I originally thought.**
When I first got started, I thought I would struggle to find something different each day to be grateful for. I mean, when you think about it, what normally comes up is God, family, shelter, food, health, etc. Doing this exercise forces you to become very specific and intentional about your gratitude. It also forces you to not only think about what you are grateful for, but why you are grateful for that item, person or experience, which allowed me to have an entirely new level of awareness.

2. **I am better, and stronger, than I give myself credit for. You are too.**
I have been my own biggest critic. I would see the balls that I've dropped and the weight that I've gained, or the times I lost my cool and the money that I spent on something other than what it was intended for. This

exercise helped me to not only look at my life differently, but it has also allowed me to have documentation of all of the things that I've done right. After going back and reading some of my entries, I was able to reflect on some of those wonderful moments I documented. Even the not so wonderful moments were more reason for me to be grateful for the former. This exercise will be especially helpful for those who struggle with self-esteem or self-worth.

3. Thoughts are more than just mere thoughts

Just like anyone else, my happiness and overall mental state is determined by the thoughts that I allow myself to have. Like the Henry Ford quote goes, "Whether you think you can or you think you can't, you're right." When I constantly think about everything that has, can or will go wrong, I'm engulfed with feelings of stress, worry, doubt and fear. Those are heavy burdens to carry around. However, when I come from a place of gratitude, finding the gems in every situation, I don't feel the same weight either in my head or in my heart. I feel lighter and I'm able to focus on the things that really matter. Once you change your thoughts, you can change your life.

4. "Keep eating fear until it tastes good." - Jai Stone

The fear of failure has been a part of me as far back as I can remember. I wouldn't even want to try something if I thought there was a chance that I wouldn't come out on top. I remember quitting karate as soon as I was able to start competing because I just didn't want to get beat up. I didn't even give it a try. How silly, huh? Going through the process of writing this chapter was incredibly nerve-wracking because I knew that once completed, people would be reading it. Duh! People are going to be reading it…it's a book! I've learned that being nervous doesn't mean that I lack the talent or ability to do what I want to do. I just haven't had the experience yet. It can be scary to go through something new but once that experience is gained, we'll realize it wasn't that bad after all. But the only way to get to that point is to give yourself permission to go through the process. Are you scared of that upcoming speech you have to give? Or maybe the thought of starting that new business keeps you up at night? What about the presentation that you're working on for that new client? That's great! Congratulations, you're human! The trick is not to allow the fear to stop you. Push forward. Do it anyway. You'll be happy that you did.

Our Gratitude Mission

Terry's Take

Syracuse in the house! It is so awesome to know and be friends with Deidra, especially since we met AFTER our time at "Cuse." I don't know about you, but I feel a connection with people from my alma maters. My friendship with Deidra is even more special though. Maybe it's because her birthday is five days before my sister's, or because her job is near my old job (which I am at often because I now have clients there) and we have randomly run into each other on NUMEROUS occasions, which always immensely brightens my day. Or maybe it's because she is so freakin' funny, as she demonstrates in this chapter! Regardless, I am glad she's in my life, and I am grateful I get to see one of the other members of this mission somewhat often.

I haven't said this yet in the other chapters, but Deidra mentions it and it's time for me to also. This book is clearly about gratitude, but it's also about journaling! As she says, there is SO much power when we write something down (or type it). The process of writing gives words to our thoughts, helps us heal and reminds us of the good. I recently passed 1,000 straight days documenting a different expression of gratitude. Pausing for a moment every day to share this happy thought ensures that I am tapping into my positivity, and hopefully inspiring others to do the same.

Russ Terry

Chapter 5

Diane Liewehr

Living Life Consciously

Age: 50

Hometown: Chicago, IL

Current City: Jacksonville, FL

Our Gratitude Mission

Baseline -- Where it All Began, March 2014:

As I embark on this coming year of gratitude, I am taking a moment to journal where I am at right now. One of my intentions for this project is to see how I grow, evolve, understand myself and my world (perhaps differently) in a year's time compared to today – and share that with you. So that said, in terms of where I'm at now, I am happy overall (I like to think I'm an upbeat person), yet in an unfamiliar space filled with an all new life and an unknown future. I am in a stage of my life and career that is shifting, and that is scary. My story...

I got married in June 2013, and went on a two week honeymoon to Hawaii. Such a PARADISE - I now know what the word really means! I returned to my job in early July and two weeks later was laid off after nine years at the company. I was in an executive position at a large global financial institution and there was a "global restructuring" and my role was eliminated. I had seen it before, and unfortunately had to lay people off myself, too many times. This time it was me. I was shocked, hurt, felt "less than." It is a natural feeling when that occurs even though my leader told me outright, and I knew for myself deep down, that it wasn't a performance issue. So, as everyone does when they are losing their health insurance, I got busy making all of my doctor and dentist appointments. Sure enough, I had my annual mammogram and they suggested I come back for one more screening. I did. I didn't think anything of it at that point. I was still picking myself up off the floor from being laid off. After that screening, they wanted me to go for a biopsy. Hmmm, nothing like this had ever happened to me before. I was in a daze, I couldn't believe this was happening at a time when I just lost my job – and what about the fabulous high I was supposed to be on since I just got married to the love of my life?!! Crash! I had that biopsy done (which was a terrible experience I never want to repeat) and the process still wasn't over. I was encouraged to go for a surgical biopsy. They told me to get a breast surgeon. Just hearing those words freaked me out! Not the Big C! I had never been in a hospital operating room. The thought of that alone was terrifying for me. I had the surgery. By this time, I had been out of work just a couple weeks. It took me a few days to recuperate at home and then I was feeling ok. The results came back benign – thank God! But, I had nowhere to go. I wasn't "needed" in my job anymore.

Meanwhile, several years back while I was still working, I got certified as a professional coach on my own time at night and on weekends. I have always had a passion for personal development. I want people to achieve as much success and happiness as they possibly can. When people are aligned with themselves and their goals, the ease with which they flow through life is beautiful and amazing. So when the news came that my role was being eliminated, I said to myself (and my husband said to me on that first call I made to share the news with him that fateful morning), "This is a gift and now is your chance to start your own coaching business." Sounds fabulous, liberating and exciting, right? But the reality is that I was terrified, insecure and wasn't sure I was "good enough." That voice inside of me kept saying, "What will everyone in my corporate business career think of me?" The voice said they will think "I jumped ship" or "she couldn't hack it, so therefore she's going to be a coach." I was concerned with what others would think of my choice to make a career and lifestyle change. Of course, this is a clear sign I have work to do with my own limiting beliefs. However, I know that this is a "normal" feeling and response to my situation. I trust that this is where I am supposed to be. I believe change happens for a reason and when one door closes, another opens. But it doesn't make it any less scary, intimidating or difficult.

The past six months have felt like the rug was pulled out from under me, when I was supposed to be riding high on my new flying carpet of love. It has been unsettling for sure – and renewing at the same time. Being able to take some time for me, get some rest, read a book for fun and watch TV in the middle of a weekday if I want, is novel to me! Not much time for that as a full time, high stress corporate employee these days. I have begun to appreciate that time, and I know it soon will also be gone. I need to start earning money and paying the bills like everyone else! That said, as I have learned more about gratitude and gratitude journals, I have considered writing down every day what or who I am grateful for. Hence, when Russ invited folks to participate in his second book on gratitude, I was very intrigued. I won't lie and say I wasn't hesitant – it took me a few weeks to translate the immediate "yes, I'm in!" reply into a commitment to him. Writing an expression of gratitude daily wasn't what was holding me back from committing. Sharing my personal journey publicly was! That part makes me feel vulnerable, but I took the leap anyway. I am excited to not only learn from my daily reflection, but to also share what I learn with others. This comes at a time when I am able to appreciate the events of my life in a new way. I can't wait to explore this journey over the next year!

"Life is what happens to you while you're busy making other plans."
-- John Lennon

Reflection on Where I am Now – March 2015:

One year later, what a year! So much has happened in my life. What a joy to witness it through this project. I am excited to share it all with you. This gratitude journey has been life altering! Don't get me wrong, I am not going to tell you each day was nirvana and I am now living on cloud nine in a "la la" land of gratitude. However, a purposeful focus on gratitude and creating it as a habit makes a big difference in how I choose to see, live and participate in my life. That is the point. It is that simple. And it can be yours, if you choose to make it that way. We all have the power to choose how we want to live our life.

Through this chapter, I won't share every daily entry, but I will sprinkle in some that demonstrate the themes of what my past year of gratitude held for me. Overall, I am in a much better place now than I was then – literally and figuratively. We moved from New York City to Jacksonville, FL. We relocated with my husband's company for him to pursue his career and the things he is passionate about. We have an entirely new lifestyle of driving cars and living in a real single-family home (an actual house, not an apartment!) I have built up my business nicely with several clients, have given in-person presentations, attended more than one hundred networking events, and I am more confident in my own abilities as an Executive Coach with a focus on Leadership, Career Advancement and Transition. I am incredibly grateful for all of those things and the journey through each stage in the process of getting here. What a ride!

I am grateful to not be in a full time corporate job. This gave me, and to some extent my husband Phil, a new flexibility we didn't have before.

> **Monday, March 31, 2014:** I am grateful for not having to wake up at the crack of dawn on Mondays anymore. I wake up at what I call a "normal" time. I always hated waking up Monday mornings to get to work. All the pressure is on suddenly. Why, I don't know. We have the same jobs we left at 5pm (or was it 7pm?) Friday, but somehow it comes with a much heavier energy by Monday morning. I am grateful I don't have that feeling anymore on my Monday mornings. ***

I am grateful for being able to support Phil's desire and passion for his work and life goals. I am grateful for the courage it took to move to Florida. We always said "never" to Florida, and now look at us! Like many folks do, we had preconceived ideas (and in this case, that trended negative) of what Florida was like. Those were based on various single data points (e.g., occasional vacations, short business trips, friends' stories, stereotypes, etc.), none of which are reliable sources of input for having your own experience living somewhere. Heck, we had never even been to Jacksonville before! Now, how can we make an educated decision without any real experiential data? So, with a couple of extended week-long visits for my husband to conduct business, we got a sense of life in Jacksonville. We explored the area to see what it was like. It is much more green and lush than we were familiar with in Florida. It is just 29 miles to the border of Georgia. There is the beach right here – 10 minutes away! There are a ton of things to do nearby: theater, the symphony, cultural museums, and the area is rooted in history. In fact, St. Augustine (a city 30 minutes from Jacksonville that is famous for being the home of the World Golf Hall of Fame) is the oldest city in the US. Settlement was in 1565! Who knew? We were each surprised how much we liked it and felt comfortable here. This is a big lesson to remain open-minded and accepting of new ways!

> **Tuesday, June 24, 2014:** Tonight Phil and I went to dinner with a guy who works for him here in Jacksonville. We drove about 25 minutes and had dinner at a restaurant on the water. It was amazing to be outside for dinner on a work night at what is nearly equivalent to the beach! It was something we would do on vacation. Not a weekday evening! As I have said earlier, it is such a great opportunity to experience a different way of life. I have spent a long time living in Manhattan and tonight was refreshing to see how others live.   ***

I am super excited about the potential and the adventures that lie ahead in our new locale. The people we have met so far are incredible. Folks might still be saying, "You left NYC for Jacksonville?!???" Let me be clear – it may not be for everyone, but it is a wonderful place for us right now. It has a slower pace than NYC and for where I am at in my life personally right now, that's just fine with me. It is an up and coming place and to be a part of that feel and vibe in the community is awesome! And by the way, it is the business capital of Florida. So many major corporations are here (e.g., Deutsche Bank, Merrill Lynch, Bank of America, JPMorgan Chase, CSX, Allstate, Florida Blue, Mayo Clinic, etc.) In fact, the cover story in the June 2015 issue of American Banker Magazine is about the Sunshine State outpacing the country again (it is bouncing back), and which community banks are in line to be the state's next homegrown success. Two of them are headquartered right in Jacksonville. There is much more to come, of that we are sure. Oh, and did I mention the weather?! (Sorry, I couldn't help it! That was specifically for my family and friends in the Northeast and Midwest this year – wink, wink!) As my husband has come to say over and over here, "Sometimes, life don't suck!"

I am grateful for my boldness to be an entrepreneur and start my own business. I am grateful for believing in myself. The safe route would have been to go back and take a full time position. My life would have been very different at this one year point. We/my husband might not have chosen to take advantage of the Florida opportunity. What an entirely different chapter of life I would be writing!

> **Monday, April 28, 2014:** I got my first paying client today! What a FABULOUS feeling! I have done a lot of bartering as I am getting going, but today, the situation turned into a paying client. I now know that my services are valued! Her continuing with me after the original agreement ended because she feels she is making such great progress is validation for me that I am good at this. I was so touched by what she said in a written recommendation, I share it with you here:
>
> *From the moment I met Diane, I knew that she was a smart, trustworthy, compassionate person, and has incredible integrity and a great sense of humor. I like to think of her like a trusted girlfriend with so many proven benefits! Her non-judgmental approach with wonderful intuition and insight encourage and empower me to walk away with a renewed energy and confidence in myself. She helps me cultivate the growth and change I want in my life. She is a great coach...creative, thoughtful, and knowledgeable. She has assisted me in pinpointing areas of struggle and focused me on the most important steps to move forward. She encouraged me to trust my own intuition in making choices for my new business. She has sincere interest in my*

achievements, believes in me and truly cares. Coaching comes naturally to her. She helps look at situations from different angles while providing a unique perspective. After a few sessions with Diane, I have seen major changes in ways I approach my goals and plan my business projects. She is the one that will help you make the necessary discoveries and changes in your life, if you are ready and willing to take her as a guide on this journey. I cannot recommend her enough.

I have a lot to offer, and I've known that in my heart. That is why I am making this shift in my career. However, the first paying client validation in just a short period of time makes it all that much sweeter! It makes me proud and inspires me to keep going on this path of coaching. Most of all, I look forward to our continued partnership and helping her grow her business even further. Seeing that is what is exciting for me. ***

Wednesday, November 5, 2014: I am grateful for my boldness today in putting into the Universe a new energy and declaration of myself and my business. I did it at a networking meeting by experimenting with some new thinking, positioning and formulating of my business proposition. It felt good. It was me getting even more authentic, which is the key to any successful adventure. I say boldness, because I actually brought to the surface some hidden "demons" and found the courage to continue beyond them to new space – and declare that space publicly – despite what my "demon" thought (which was that people will judge me). It felt so freeing! I am grateful for my own development! People in fact were asking me questions and a few offered some help. Maybe a few silently judged me, but so what? They kept it to themselves and I don't need to worry about what they think. This is who I am and what I have to offer – and it is GOOD! ***

I am grateful for all the new adventures, explorations and events in my life! Really, without them, my life would be boring. For my family and friends who have been with me through the thick and the thin, muffle your laughter please. ;-) Somehow, my life never seems boring – there is always something happening. Ha! Really, as I look back and acknowledge where I am now, going through all the fears, unknowns and nerves of life that have allowed me to experience, grow, learn and live each day and be better for it. The excitement of new happy things is amazing. The growth and personal development that happens through negative events, unknowns and fears is amazing. It's all amazing! The key is to keep that "attitude of gratitude" and by being grateful every day, it sure helps!

> **Friday, March 13, 2015:** I got my wallet stolen today. ☹ Yes, ironic it happened today. We are back in NYC for a visit over a long weekend. I am grateful for a wonderful Restaurant Week lunch with my friend and drinks with more friends before the hassle began. I am grateful that neither I, nor my friend, was hurt. I am grateful to my friend and my husband, who both helped me contact the banks and cancel my banking cards. I am grateful for them caring for me so much and helping me through it, even when I was a royal *@&%! to them at times due to the stress. ***

> **Sunday, March 15, 2015:** I filed my police report today and I am grateful to have a record of this crime. I am grateful for the Police Officer who was helping me. He was very kind and tolerated my attitude at times. I have been so frustrated, I feel violated and I am feeling vulnerable. At times I clearly am not channeling myself well. That said, as he began to understand me and my situation, he adapted quite well to meet me where I was at and help me. ***

I am grateful for the bumps in the road along the way. Of course, I say this in hindsight and not during the rough times (see above)! I'm only human, like everyone else! Upon reflection, it is amazing how we move through the tough times and come out more resilient on the other side. I met folks along the way who either didn't see things the same way as I did, or did not match my personality, style, professional approach, or were not as collaborative as I had hoped. But that is ok. The world is big – in fact, it is huge – and there is more than enough for all of us and I appreciate that. I appreciate all the differences. It is what makes the world go 'round. I learned how to navigate the seemingly threatened and competitive people, and I saw that it wasn't about me, it was about them. I didn't stop being me and giving and sharing as I thought appropriate. If I didn't get something of value back in the experience or exchange, I made a note and learned from it. Sometimes I learned more about me. Sometimes I learned more about others. Either way, as I have spent my entire career studying human attitudes, motivations and behaviors to affect positive change, I added it to my knowledge base and "research" files. I continue to learn – what to do, and what not to do. I won't stop being me, giving as I want and loving the impact I might just make on someone.

> **Monday, May 19, 2014:** Today was one of those days where nothing was excellent or noteworthy and in fact a few things were in the not so good category – nothing terribly bad, just annoying. However, I realize that, in part, it is how I am viewing things today. I feel like I am not making any progress on things in my life today. It may be because I don't feel well, I'm tired, and am a bit overwhelmed from all the 'to do' items and the ideas I have. I can't decide how to start. I met with someone who is supposed to be a resource for me but I feel like she is not working with me. I am grateful for a glass of good wine at the end of today. Days like today are more frustrating than they are good or bad. I like to think it is the rotation of the planets and chalk it up to the Universe. I also am grateful that days like these are few and far between for me. They are here to remind me that life (and all the good things it offers) is not to be taken for granted. ***

Tuesday, August 5, 2014: Today I am grateful for the Universe. Sometimes we understand it and other times we do not, but nevertheless, I am grateful it works as it does. I have been shown over and over again that I cannot control it, nor predict it. I must have faith that it is on my side - no matter what. I am grateful that when I am down, or feeling defeated, there is often a reason - sometimes it is subconscious and other times it is obvious. When I trust the Universe to take me where I need to go, I can trust all will work itself out and I am safe. That lesson is a hard one to master. Today I progress on my learning. ***

Monday, September 8, 2014: For the past week I have felt quite clogged, blocked, and stuck. I know it has to do with the stress I was feeling deep down and not able to name exactly why. We have decided to move to Jacksonville and we are excited. At the same time, clearly, I have a lot of stress and anxiety about the decision. It is paralyzing on a deep level and that gets in the way of my productivity. I am grateful today for being back on track! I was productive and balanced today with my tasks – which is a perfect day for me. I am so glad that I feel like myself again. A good weekend away with good friends and a different environment -- some fun and relaxation have been a great healer! ***

I am grateful for my clients, for many reasons. As an entrepreneur, having income is important. I'd be lying if I didn't acknowledge that. But I am also grateful to my clients for their honesty, vulnerability, enthusiasm and ongoing willingness to keep at it for themselves, even when they might be passing through a darker, harder, lower energy period. Their commitment to themselves and their desire to be the best they can be is exactly where my passion lies. I am grateful to be a part of their journey and helping them achieve their highest potential! I love the saying "Each person you meet is your teacher and your student."

Thursday, June 12, 2014: Grateful that I was able to help my client today. She was frazzled from her day, trying to get out of work on time to make her appointment, she hadn't eaten since breakfast and then on her way to meet me, the subway had several delays. She texted me in the subway she was running late. Then a few moments later she texted, "I know I will have to pay for the session but let's just cancel." She was exasperated. I asked if she was in a place to take the session by phone. She replied she wouldn't be, now that she was in the subway, for half an hour. I suggested we could speak for the remaining 30 minutes of the session if she wanted when she came out – after all, I dedicated this time to her. Let's see how we can make it happen. She said to me, "Thank you for helping me see it doesn't always have to be all or nothing." Separately, I am grateful for her respect of my time. She acknowledged to me that she knows she made a commitment to me (and herself!) and knew she would have to pay for the appointment since it was such late notice for a cancellation. So, in the end, with a few deep breaths, we were able to spend some good time regrouping and keeping her on track for her goals for the coming week. Yeah to my client!!! ***

Thursday, February 12, 2015: Today I was able to help shift a client's energy and produce excellent results from it. To hear and feel that shift, and then witness the productivity and enthusiasm from doing so, is incredibly rewarding. I am proud of myself for being so in tune with another person that I can help make the transformation happen. And, I am proud of my client for working through his difficult situation and choosing to go in a forward, positive direction with his own drive. ***

I am grateful for my friends, family, supporters and mentors, and in some cases, complete strangers! Many folks have shared everything from tears to joys and many words of wisdom through the ups and downs and inspirations of life. I am grateful for each of them sharing themselves and their encouragement or advice with me. I drew on all of it and it helped me navigate where I wanted to go and who I wanted to be through the past year. You all know who you are (well, I guess except for the complete strangers)! I thank you with my full appreciation and love, personally and professionally.

Tuesday, June 3, 2014: Today I received several compliments from people. A woman on the bus liked my blouse, someone in a meeting today also liked my blouse (note to self, nice blouse!), and a person I met for the first time today told me I have a terrific disposition. Last but not least, I presented some material today at a meeting and folks thought it was spot on. They'd seen some of it before and it needed some work. Today I presented my reworked material and they thought it was great. I am grateful for positive feedback – it really feels so good. And the neat part is most of it came from folks I don't know. Now, don't get me wrong, feedback of any sort is good – it's just that today I got a bunch of positive feedback in various ways and it was really nice. ***

Saturday, July 5, 2014: I am grateful to be with my friends enjoying a holiday weekend sharing good fun, good food (I'm with GREAT cooks!), good energy in Edgewater, NJ - which is just across the river from NYC but feels like a little country house! These are the kind of friends you can share everything with - good, embarrassing, anything - and they still love you! ***

Saturday, August 9, 2014: We spent today with Phil's kids and visiting his stepdad. I am grateful to have them in my life! We had so much fun!!!! Fred, his stepdad, is such a sweet soul. The man is 88 years old and pure love. All of Phil's kids have graduated college, have jobs out in the real world and are pursuing their passions. They are young adults each starting out full of energy, party, intelligence, warmth, kindness and humor. I am grateful to have such a wonderful relationship with each one of them since meeting Phil. I love them all! ***

Thursday, November 6, 2014: Today I dug deep in a meeting with my mentor coach. He was pushing me on something that was uncomfortable yet the exact thing I needed to be working through. Also in our session, he asked if I could help him with some internship connections for some college students whom he mentors. I reached out to two contacts to help make introductions for him. So today I am grateful for being pushed outside my comfort zone on an issue that was making me feel "less than" and yet at the same time sharing a valuable contribution to him via my own network connections. ***

Wednesday, December 24, 2014: Merry Christmas (Eve)!! We are at my sister and brother-in-law's house in Wisconsin for the holidays. Today is when my family celebrates Christmas with a full traditional dinner (all of my mom's recipes!) and opening presents. Both of my nieces are here – one with her husband and one with her boyfriend. This year that makes eight of us! My nieces are all grown up – wow. I'm so glad they still consider me the "cool" aunt! I am grateful for the wonderful meal that my sister prepares (with help from all of us each year doing the tasks she assigns!) and the thoughtfulness that everyone put into the gifts that they got for me and others. We work from lists, but not all are things we ask for – it takes knowing each other to find gifts that are just perfect. It is nice to see everyone and to feel the love! Thank you! ***

I am grateful for the time and circumstances of this year to learn new habits. More importantly, to not feel guilty for abandoning old habits and developing new ones that serve me better at this point in my life. For example, stopping the guilt I felt every day I didn't work 9:00am to 5:00pm (or, more likely, working 9:00am – 9:00pm) on tasks I thought I *should* be doing. That said it's still a work in progress to adapt. Learning to live in my new day requires me to find new structure and purpose and yet allows me to have much more fun. Right there is the rub. I felt guilty if I wasn't in windowless conference rooms attending meetings talking about the same topic for the hundredth time and ending the meeting with a next step to get together again in two days to pick up with the same topic so that we might make a decision. Ridiculous! I see that now, which made it much easier to finally let go and move into a more flexible schedule doing the tasks I wanted to do. People have flexibility in all sorts of industries – construction, healthcare, retail, etc. They just aren't on the schedule I had and became accustomed to in Corporate America. It was a hard path in the beginning for me, but when I realized that the new habits and tasks were the ones I really wanted to be doing, the ones that provided me a purpose, made me feel the most valued, contributed the most back to the world, AND provided me an income, I got new clarity. The guilt began melting away…slowly. I felt guilty for having fun. That's true. I didn't see it that way at first, but that is what it was. It was important to drop the guilt and accept the change. Be grateful for what I had been given. Find a way to make the most of it. Move on from the past. All of our limiting beliefs are rooted in the past. I have decided to embrace the future and seize its potential! I love going out for a midday walk, or taking an exercise class at 2:45 in the afternoon! I serve my clients and make all of my meetings; I can do what I want with my time in between. I am not working 9-5 anymore. Should I be? Who says? I needed to learn how to stop living within arbitrary limits and learn new habits. It is as much a mental as a physical timing issue. I see progress and that is the point every day.

Monday, April 21, 2014: I am grateful for a meeting in Central Park with a colleague. It's so much more fun than a hot apartment! Our juices were flowing with ideas and plans. We were both getting so excited with the potential. The energy of the spring air is energizing me this year! I'm thrilled to be soaking it in. After our meeting, I took a walk along the bridal path next to the reservoir and the trees were in bloom. People were luxuriating and sunbathing in the grass. The warmth of the sun and the smell of the blossoms – yes, spring is here! ***

Wednesday, December 10, 2014: I am grateful for the ability to take a day to play with my girlfriends and not feel guilty about it. I didn't feel bad about not being in meetings or networking, or not cleaning the apartment. I was able to enjoy the choice I made to meet two old friends for lunch today and wander around the Grand Central Terminal Holiday Bazaar. I will be moving soon and so it was lovely to hang out with them. We had a very nice time!   ***

I am grateful through this year to learn that what "flexible" and "productive" look like can change. How they are defined can be re-defined. What "smart" and "intelligent" look like can change. I wrestled with this throughout the year (and to some extent still do). How great is it that I can have fun and be productive and earn a living at the same time? I am not jamming everything in anymore. I have time to breathe. Maybe in the beginning, and on certain days, still, I may go a bit too far the other way. I burn the midnight oil when I need to. I am grateful I can work at my own pace.

Wednesday, August 20, 2014: I had the morning free today, so I went to the beach. It was lovely and nice to explore by myself. I was putting my feet in the water when a woman said something to me and pointed – there were dolphins jumping! So beautiful! Immediately, I knew what my entry was for today. How beautiful to see this bit of sea-world nature right out in the open. AND THEN, the woman and I kept talking and through it we shared what we each do for work and before you know it, she was asking me for business cards and saying that she'd like to work with me as she currently has some big changes happening and she wants to achieve her goals. WOW. I put it out there and I trust in the Universe. ***

Largely because of my new chosen pace, this year has allowed my body to heal. Beyond the scare with breast cancer last year (by the way, I'm happy to report that my mammogram this time around was good), I manifest stress physically in my body. I have had many injuries over the years exacerbated by the stress I hold in my body (e.g., bulging discs in my back, neck problems, shoulder issues, etc.) I am grateful for being kinder and gentler to myself. I am grateful to be ME – now, more than ever! Embracing ourselves with gratitude and love is the only medicine any one of us needs in life. Let your light shine, be you – warts, blemishes, super powers and all – nothing else matters. A year of gratitude helps you see something so obvious. At least it did for me. I am not perfect at it all. But I do consider myself a work in progress.

Wednesday, December 31, 2014: I am grateful for my health, strength and stamina! I am exhausted from the past two days, and today we rented a moving truck and helped Phil's son move apartments in Toronto. It is a very physical thing to move by yourself – not to mention he moved from a basement apartment to another basement apartment – the word is STAIRS!! I was completely spent afterward. From there we drove about an hour to Phil's friends' place to go out with them to a black tie affair for New Year's Eve. We went from the back of a moving truck to black tie is less than two hours! I got a second wind and rallied. I am grateful that I am healthy enough to do such physical work and just get stronger. And, all of it without any back, hip or other pains (which is especially exciting given my history of all of those!) ***

Our Gratitude Mission

My Journey:

Now, let me tell you about my journey. Before I signed up for this project with Russ, I will tell you that I felt I was an appreciative person overall, a positive person, a happy person. I believed I showed gratitude and appreciation. But interestingly, while I wouldn't say I took life for granted, I wasn't overt about my appreciations all the time, or conscious about it on a regular basis. Was I appreciative of others? Yes, always. Well, almost always. ;-) I just didn't think about it. I said please and thank you, of course. My mom taught me strict manners! OK, maybe what I am saying is that at times I took parts of life for granted. I didn't take a moment to think that others didn't have to say that nice thing to me or help me out. Sometimes, people did something for me and I said thank you automatically. There is some level of general expectation in life that you find yourself in a bit of a routine with your friends, family, colleagues, your values (learned or created), etc. That is what makes life go. However, when I did start to observe these acts one by one and make note of them mentally to myself, things changed for me. Specifically, I (like everyone on the planet) have become so habituated to actions and behaviors in my own life that I now subconsciously come to take many of them for granted. I just expect that is how it is. Doesn't everyone do it that way or feel that way in that situation? I know better about what to expect from people, but it still happens to me sometimes. Sometimes I have an image or perception in my head and everything I do is based on it because "That is the way it is *supposed* to be." Some old rule or family or social value taught me that is the way it is. Let me say this, gratitude helps open up your mind from its closed off quarters, its own limited parameters. I began appreciating things about myself and accepting them and honoring them. This is me! I am unique. I am different from others. I am perfect just the way I am. I have ME to offer the world! Despite all my personal "fears" I am great! I love when I am able to help others do the same and step into their own acceptance. Be grateful for WHO you are – there is nobody exactly like YOU! You can soar! I found a couple of quotes that seem to sum it up...

> "Acknowledging the good that you already have in your life is the foundation for all abundance." -- Eckhart Tolle

> "In ordinary life, we hardly realize that we receive a great deal more than we give, and that it is only with gratitude that life becomes rich."
> -- Dietrich Bonhoeffer

Also, as I began *Our Gratitude Mission*, I did think there was a bit of mystery to what everyone talked about with "living a life of gratitude." It felt like it may be too rah-rah, flowery and woo-woo, a way of life that is a constant loving, happy state of being in an almost sappy sort of way. That didn't feel comfortable to me. As I said, I am a happy positive person overall. I can be very rah-rah. I like to motivate people and showcase the opportunity, inspire and take bold steps toward new adventures. But somehow, I perceived the phrase "living a life of gratitude" as excessively "happy" energy about every little thing in life. It didn't feel real, authentic, or genuine to me. Sometimes I get mad! I get angry, stubborn, sad, hurt. I experience all those negative emotions. I wasn't sure how to find gratitude through those. When I am angry, sure I could say a positive thing to be thankful for, but it wasn't going to feel genuine. Instead, I am talking about real, meaningful gratitude as it should be if you are going to honor it. I have come to recognize that gratitude can be as big or as small as you feel it. It can be spiritually based, energetically based, practically/pragmatically based, etc. But at the end of the day, to me, it is attitudinally based. It can go where you go – physically, emotionally, and geographically – so bring it with you! Bring it with you through the bad and the ugly just as much as you bring it through the wonderful and happy. It will ground you one step at a time and help balance your overall attitude and journey in life. That will bring more happiness. And that is the power of gratitude.

> "If a fellow isn't thankful for what he's got, he isn't likely to be thankful for what he's going to get." -- Frank A. Clark

Our Gratitude Mission

Can daily recordings of even just one expression of gratitude change your life? It can. It does. My journey has been fun! First, did the entries really all happen for me DAILY? Yes, in practice at least mentally or verbally. Sometimes though, I won't lie, I didn't write them in the journal on that day. In fact, sometimes I got a bit behind in the journal per se. I used my iPhone to help me stay on track and recorded them in the calendar each day so I could come back to write more about it when I had proper time. That worked for me. I wanted to practice the concept of gratitude and not get caught up in the rules of "how." I knew if I did set rules, then I might not stay engaged or stick with it. Another trick I used in the beginning was to incorporate a moment for my husband and me to say what we each were grateful for that day just as we sat down for dinner together. We clinked our glasses (of tea, water or wine, whatever) each night at dinner to symbolize our new daily habit. It is a ritual we still practice daily, whether we are eating at home or out at a restaurant. In fact, even my husband will give me "the look" if I accidentally start eating before we have done our gratitude cheers. ;-) And, for that I am grateful!

It took some conscious effort to keep the journal. When times were particularly busy, my act of writing in the journal got behind. Like I said earlier, sometimes it was hard to make the effort. I tried through those times to just be there in concept and, again, not have to be restricted by some arbitrary rules I felt guilty about. Doesn't that counteract the pure act of gratitude? It was a wonderful thing to be part of the Facebook group we (Russ and the other chapter authors) shared. It was motivating to stay focused on the journey when you saw other posts. I found that to be a very helpful element to the program. And, how wonderful to share in such a precious topic with folks I do not know, but I knew there was only one degree of separation from Russ! I'm not sure how many degrees of separation from Kevin Bacon. My point is, if it helps you to stay with it, join a group. Although I haven't met anyone yet in person (I am scheduled to meet a new member of Russ' Gratitude Group Coaching Program who lives in Jacksonville too), I enjoyed offering my encouragement or congratulations throughout to all. And I truly appreciated seeing folks "like" a post of mine, or relate to my emotion or circumstance and share a kind word or cheer me on!

In keeping this journal all year, I noticed there is joy you get from consciously noting the moments in life when you are grateful. It is an incredible reminder that life is not so bad, no matter how bad it can feel at the time. An exercise in acknowledging something you are grateful for is a first step in taking control of your mind and situation and making lemonade from lemons. To know that it's within your own choice is powerful. For instance, simple gratitude for the warmth of the sunshine when you are having a bad day can bring a smile to your face (one of my entries), if even for just a minute, and that brings you one step closer to a better day. Taken together every day for a year – it brings a better year! And, trust me, it can bring a better YOU. I reflect back on the year and know that however difficult or seemingly inconvenient it might have felt at any particular moment, I knew I wanted to keep with it in whatever way I could. I love the outcome. And I know any outcome requires the work.

This was a wonderful exercise. I can better control my own mindset now. When I am angry or sad or frustrated, I can ask myself, "What am I grateful for in this situation?" Sometimes, it may not even be "in this situation," but something near me to help me take my mind away from my problem and understand my life in a wider scope – giving me more context to my life than just living from one situation at hand to the next. Remember to look up and see the forest, not just the trees, as they say. Doing that helped me know that I have a lot in my life to be grateful for and I am fortunate my hard work has paid off. It helps me to see that life isn't all about me. Living with a self–centered view and only from one situation to the next doesn't allow you to look up, smell the roses and be grateful for the amazing world we live in and the life that we have.

Our Gratitude Mission

How this Mission Transformed my Life:

There are a handful of things in my life that have had a profound effect on me with regard to gratitude. Just one that I want to share with you was a vacation to East Africa in February 2001. It was before 9/11. I went on that excursion with one of my dearest friends and it was a "dream trip" we both wanted to do. I went there thinking I was going to be awed by the animals, the landscape and the people. When I returned, in telling people about my trip, I actually reversed those. I was incredibly awed by the people, the landscape and the animals. I think that had a lot to do with my expectations. I knew a lot more about the African animals but did not know what to expect from the landscape or the people before I left the US. I look back on that trip and realize that I lived each moment present to what I was observing, and I fully engaged in it. I didn't think about work or anything else while I was there. I was so engaged in my vacation and what we were doing each day. I felt a sense of freedom and fun living life that I had never experienced before. The people that I met were so full of life and gratitude. I was so moved by how little they might have had, yet how much they seemed to give or how much life they lived. This changed me forever. I had such a sense of freedom that I too could be happy with what I have. I have skills that can be put to work. In fact, it helped me to see that I could do many things, not just the job I had back home, from which I was taking vacation time. There was no judgment among these folks, just appreciation for the moment. I was so grateful to meet those people and have that experience of a lifetime.

I tell you that story because there are some similarities for me with this project, in terms of its effect on me. Keeping my gratitude journal positively impacted me throughout this past year in three major ways. The first one is living life consciously. I have made note before of small things in my life. For example, walking by the flowers planted outside the NY Public Library on Fifth Ave. on my way to work in the mornings was always one of my favorites. It is glorious to see the birds and the colors of the flowers in the early morning, and even the greenery in colder months. But making an ongoing effort every day, where possible, to live in that state of consciousness is what I am referencing now. I was learning to take time to note things as they were occurring in my life on a regular basis – a new way of living my life. There is an abundance of joy in life when you take it to that level. It is a process to learn how to do this, but it pays off. An added benefit to keeping the journal is that I see my life. I was writing about my days and what was happening or important to me that day. For many years, at the end of the year when New Year's is upon us, I have looked back and said (maybe you have too), "Where did this year go?" The fun in writing a gratitude journal is that I have been a participant in my life this year, very consciously. I have been through many new adventures and am witness to them all! It is novel to have a recording of your year, sort of like keeping a diary, just with a twist of appreciation!

This leads me to the second key impact on my life with respect to gratitude. In the past year, keeping a mindset of gratitude for this project helped me stay present, "in the now," if you will. Oh, Eckhart Tolle's *The Power of Now*! (A great book if you haven't read it. Taking part in *Our Gratitude Mission* was the path I needed to follow his advice.) Gratitude helped me focus and concentrate on today, right now, this minute. Sometimes it was a tight and narrow focus that helped me power through many things. Fewer distractions, less worry and a lower frequency of getting caught up in fears and unknowns. And, you might guess, that kept me more productive. It enabled me to stay focused on my actions. Thinking time is important to strategize and make a plan, but too much of it begins to throw our minds into all sorts of "what if" scenarios and then at some point too far down that road with the inner "demons" that rear their heads. That, for sure, is when the immobilization (also fondly known as 'paralysis by analysis') comes in hard. So, coming back to the present is a gift beyond words in times like those. I have a greater ability to bring myself back to action now by taking a perspective of "What shall I do right now?"

These first two impacts certainly have led me to a third key outcome, which is that I am less stressed on an ongoing basis now since focusing on gratitude and by staying aware and being present. When I am stressed about something, I try hard to ask myself, "What is a more empowering way to look at this?" Using that question, I can move through situations more productively by noticing my own mindset and becoming aware that I am stressed. Then I can encourage myself to stay present in the moment instead of avoiding the situation by thinking of something else. Sound familiar? Are you laughing? When I give myself the gift of sticking with it, I often find an answer or at least a next step and the stress minimizes, because I now have a plan! We all like to have a plan – that is why vision and goals are so important. No matter what level of minutia or what higher strategic level you are working in, knowing where you are going is the best way to get there. Also, empowering myself in the moment to think bigger, think in a more detached way, think higher level, helps me gain perspective and understand that there is more to the issue (or life!) than it may at first seem.

> "Gratitude turns what we have into enough, and more. It turns denial into acceptance, chaos into order, confusion into clarity...it makes sense of our past, brings peace for today, and creates a vision for tomorrow."
> -- Melody Beattie

I look back on my year and I recognize that I am at my happiest when I am productive, when I am doing, not when I'm being lazy or immobilized by my own fears. Those things hold me back. When I reflect on my past (more than this one year), I see that I was very often, too often, motivated by external sources. If I look back on why and how that happened, personally, I am clear. Let's chalk it up to "my formative years when I was young." (Who knows, maybe I'll write a book on that someday!) In a nutshell, it germinated at an early age, like everyone, with the stories I told myself, and how I personalized all the things that happened in my life. Those stories stuck and I didn't know that I was "allowed" to change the rules I lived by as I got older. I lived by external sources as the truth. Today, I am happy to report that I have changed many of these old rules. I am an adult, I am me and I know me best. I have made my own rules. Who cares if someone else doesn't like it? That is OK. Their opinion is NOT a reflection of me. I have learned that I can detach from that idea and accept the different opinion and be OK with it. I am proud that I have made good progress in that regard. I am more aligned with ME than I have ever been. The power I get from that is extraordinary. Learning to accept myself and be grateful for what I am good at, what I am not good at, and honoring what I want rather than what I think I *should* be doing (according to someone else's rules or expectations) is liberating. This year of transition has allowed me to grow in this way.

I am grateful for this project and the many ways expressing gratitude helped me see all the good that happened this year:

- I am now more aware of my progress
- I'm present to my progress at each stage of development
- I embrace everything I'm doing and feel more at ease with life
- It has made me a better me
- I have started my own business
- I developed confidence in myself and my business
- I leveraged my natural ability
- I tapped into my passion for helping people
- It brought me some great early success, various opportunities and new connections
- I received high accolades from colleagues and clients
- I was supported and encouraged by my friends and family.

How I Choose to Go Forward – How Will I Practice?

This year was a year of transition and change for me. To have had the opportunity to record it, share my gratitude, chronicle my year and consciously see how it has transformed me is irreplaceable. How do I choose to go forward with this in my life? Will I continue to write in a journal? I am not sure I will commit to that. However, I will commit to continue to - every day - seek out and acknowledge with awareness the things in life that bring me joy, promise, love, opportunity and potential. And, when I am in a sad or angry or particularly ungrateful mood, I will ask myself the question "How can I see this differently?" Looking from a wider perspective at the situation, and putting my emotions at hand into context, almost immediately helps bring balance to my mindset. Gratitude won't turn bad into good but it does help bring perspective to a broader world. It helps to see that while you might think the world is falling apart, if you look for opportunity, love, and joy, you will find it. It has brought me a more conscious way of living my life, helped keep me present, which minimizes the worry of my unknown future, and has helped me live more calmly and stress-free. After all, the Chinese symbol for risk and opportunity are the same!

Last but certainly not least, I will continue to repeat my mantra, "It's all going to be ok." I truly believe that. You've heard the saying from Alexander Graham Bell that begins, "When one door closes, another one opens..." I have experienced it, so I am a believer. I do, however, acknowledge that at times it takes more patience and faith than at other times. As you read in the beginning of my chapter, I thought when I started this project that maybe the "reason" I was laid off was because I was supposed to start my coaching business. I see now that my circumstances played out this way to help me gain new perspective on life and take my next step to live my life to the fullest as gracefully as I am able, whatever comes my way. In the end I am grateful for all my life has brought the past year – the trials, tribulations, and roller coaster rides. I am in a great place mentally, emotionally, physically – and geographically! In some regards, my future is as unknown as it was a year ago (I haven't mastered reading the magic crystal ball just yet), but I am in a great place and looking forward to all of the opportunities that are ahead. Fear, worry and stress squash feelings of gratitude. And then there is no room left for happiness. I will continue letting go of the fear, worry and stress, and enjoy the present. In the end, isn't THAT what life is about?!

> "Yesterday is history, tomorrow is a mystery, today is a gift, that is why they call it the present." -- Bill Keane

If this story inspires even one of you who is reading this to take on and live in a more conscious mindset of gratitude, I will be happy. Keep a journal or practice it any way you like. I know change begets change. Change for positive effect is what I am all about. I want to live a life of happiness and fulfillment. I believe most of us here on Earth do. I want this for you. One small way that doesn't take much effort at all is to adopt a journey of gratitude. Start out very consciously. Writing things down daily will help. But, as you've read, even if you do it only mentally with yourself at first, please do grow to share it verbally with another. Create the habit – you will see (and more importantly feel) the change in your life! I wish you the best! I am grateful to you for reading my story. I leave you with these last quotes and a few lines from a song you might recognize...

> "If you want to turn your life around, try thankfulness. It will change your life mightily." -- Gerald Good

> "Gratitude and attitude are not challenges; they are choices."
> -- Robert Braathe

> "Gratitude is the best attitude." -- Unknown

> "If you want to make the world a better place, take a look at yourself and then make a change..." -- Michael Jackson

Thank You.

Terry's Take

I love Diane's chapter, especially her side comments in parenthesis throughout it. She often made me smile or chuckle. Diane is the first of a number of Coaches you will hear from. As a very social Coach, I know more than a few! Her story is a great example of the things to do – and think – to help grow a business.

Another excellent lesson here is how she ended up as the book's editor. She *volunteered* to help me proofread all the other chapters. I happily took Diane up on her offer. She provided such immense value I insisted on paying her. This is not the only example of people I know who volunteered to do something and ended up getting a job or at least some side income out of it. I am a firm believer in giving back, because it is a win/win situation for you and the others involved.

Russ Terry

Our Gratitude Mission

Chapter 6

Marian Ruiz-Diaz

Don't Worry, Be Thankful

Age: 35

Hometown: Brooklyn, NY

Current City: Los Angeles, CA

Our Gratitude Mission

Everyone has a story both intricate and unique. It makes us who we are. My story began in a negative, volatile environment with my father being abusive to my mother. Early on I was exposed to verbal abuse and violence at home, something no child should ever have to endure. When my mother divorced my father, she found strength in her independence and sustenance in her faith. She would remind us constantly to reflect on our blessings and give thanks for them daily. However, deep down, I struggled with this because I would always get distracted by negativity, since that is what I knew most as a child.

When I turned 18, I met my first love, but what seemed innocent at first would later turn into a nightmare. I found myself in an emotionally and verbally abusive relationship. I couldn't believe that history was repeating itself. For almost six years I was with my now ex-boyfriend until I found the courage to completely break away from the chaos. Later, I focused all my attention on my goals: I graduated college, met my best friend Jocelyn, dated, and traveled with my friends. Although I had great things going for myself, I couldn't help but feel like my luck would change and something negative would interfere and ruin everything. I couldn't savor happy moments completely because I was too caught up thinking something bad would occur.

After a few years of working in Non Profit as a case manager, I decided to take a break from my career and help my sister Lauri take care of my nephew Landon. She had been there during my most vulnerable moments, so this was my way of repaying her. It was an incredibly rewarding experience being with my nephew for his formative years. At the same time though, I was ready to re-enter the workforce. I had a lot of time to reflect on the past and present and knew I was ready to make changes. That same year my best friend Jocelyn got married in Florida and I met her cousin, Mike. We exchanged contact information, dated, and gradually in a few months, we fell in love. Yes, I learned to love again and give someone a chance, thanks to my better half.

With things starting to align in my life, I had a conversation with Mike about being focused on making positive changes and finding a job. For once I felt I was in control and wanted to make a conscious effort to silence the negative and work on the positive. Mike said he had a friend – Russell Terry – who is a life coach and might be able to help. I first met Russell at one of his group life coaching events. Soon after, I was inspired to start one on one life coaching with him, and saw my life slowly change. It was the best decision and investment I made. In less than a year, I moved with my boyfriend to Los Angeles and found a great job. When Russell mentioned he was working on his next book, *Our Gratitude Mission*, I was immediately interested in participating. (Editor's note: Some people call me Russ. Others call me Russell. I love both names!)

Though it is easy to focus on the negative, and I will admit it still surfaces from time to time, I decided to join the Gratitude Mission so I could solely concentrate on the positive. I am on a mission to unlock the beauty life holds that many take for granted. I want to be able to document and find awareness through my thoughts, feelings and surrounding environment. I hope to show that no matter what your story is or what you've been through, good or bad, there is magnificence in everything around us and within us if we just stop, breathe and take a moment to be appreciative. I am excited about this journey and I hope to inspire others along the way.

LIVING THE LIFE I'VE ALWAYS IMAGINED…

During Thanksgiving it is natural to reflect and have thoughts of gratitude for all the things we appreciate. But why wait for that one day out of the year to express thanks? Why not be grateful every day? This is something I asked myself when I learned about Russell Terry's Gratitude Mission. On April 20, 2014 I decided to embark on *Our Gratitude Mission* in hopes of finding more meaning and purpose in life, to live with intent. I began practicing daily gratitude by journaling for 365 days, and since then I've had an enlightening and transformational year. Doing this has taken me to heights I couldn't imagine before. I've experienced countless wonderful moments and some challenging ones as well. I could write an entire novel and then some on the people, places and things I was grateful for all year round and it still wouldn't be enough. Instead, I will share three pivotal moments I've experienced during this year, what I've learned, and how gratitude helped me have an optimal experience and ultimately change my perspective on life.

"*Palm trees, Ocean breeze, California Dreamin*"

When I was thirteen years old I remember being drawn to California. I loved the beach and wanted to live anywhere there were palm trees and sunshine. Or maybe it had something to do with being a fan of *Beverly Hills, 90210*? Who didn't have a crush on Luke Perry as a teenager? I was Team Dylan all the way! But I digress. There was something about the cold winter days in New York that had me California dreamin.

I was watching *The Sandlot*, as I recall, and I remember it inspired my mission to come out to California. Okay, so I had a crush on Benny "The Jet" Rodriguez also, don't judge me! The baseball movie is set in the San Fernando Valley part of Los Angeles, so I was on a quest to find Benny "The Jet." My grade school friend indulged in my silly idea and wanted to visit Hollywood too. We were two determined teeny boppers.

Those prepubescent pin-ups from Bop and Teen Beat magazines became my vision board on the wall of the Brooklyn studio apartment my mom was renting. I have no idea how she allowed all the posters of Luke Perry and Mike Vitar to cover our wall by the hallway near our bathroom. God Bless her patience for letting me be a teenager in the 90s and dream big.

Before my twentieth birthday in the year 2000 my plan of coming to California finally came to fruition. My grade school friend invited me to stay with her at her uncle's beach house in San Diego. I did not hesitate and jumped at the opportunity. We were both ecstatic as our plans were actually happening. We spent two weeks in San Diego and I instantly fell in love with California. Since then I knew one day I would move out West. I didn't know how or when it would happen but I had faith that it would.

Fast forward to thirteen years later, in November 2013, Mike received an offer from his company to relocate to the Los Angeles office. I was so happy and proud of him for the opportunity he had to advance in his career. He asked me to come with him, and of course I said yes. I was not going to let a good man move by himself across the country.

Mike asked for my mom's permission (which was important to me) with the promise that it would lead to marriage. I knew he was the one when he showed respect for my family, especially my mother. With her blessing, I felt I was making the right decision. I trust and value her opinion and know she would never give me bad advice.

At the same time, I was planning to re-enter the workforce. Life coaching sessions with Russell were a tremendous help in guiding me through this process. I took the information Russell provided me and focused on career building. With my sister being two months away from giving birth to my niece Mya, she had plans to leave her job to be a stay at home mom. This meant I no longer had to babysit my nephew Landon. The timing worked out for all of us. The first week of January 2014, my niece Mya was born. What a great way to start off the new year! With only a few weeks left in New York, I was glad I got to spend some time with my new niece Mya and her big brother Landon.

Soon thereafter, in mid-February, we left our beloved New York and California became our residence. I could not believe I was fulfilling my teenage dream! It only took about twenty years to happen but it goes to show you, you should never give up on your dreams. No matter how silly they may seem, thoughts eventually do become reality.

Our Gratitude Mission

When we moved into our apartment in Los Angeles it felt surreal but we were ready to start the next chapter in our lives in the golden state. Moving into our first apartment together was special. We were cementing the foundation for our little family and creating a home for me, Mike and our English bulldog Coco. Being the product of a broken marriage, this family environment we're creating was something I longed for as a child. This was my chance, our chance, to start fresh.

While I was excited, it was also a daunting experience. On the one hand, I was presented with this amazing opportunity to live in a city I've always wanted to live in. On the other hand, I was entering the unknown, not knowing how things would work out, leaving my friends and family behind. I have never been separated from them. Though I missed my family terribly, I embraced these positive changes and was determined to achieve my life goals.

Mike started work almost immediately, but I had yet to find a job. The first few days were fun. I was able to unpack and take care of our home, doing job search stuff in between. But as days went by I was getting antsy. I didn't know how to relax, and too much free time was exactly that – too much! I couldn't fully enjoy myself or take advantage of the pool in our apartment complex or the awesome neighborhood.

I actually felt guilty having all that free time. I was used to working and earning my money. Two weeks passed by and not one call back for an interview. I frantically applied to jobs everywhere and anywhere in LA County. I'm sure there was an email circulating to send my resume to spam mail. I felt desperate.

As we were approaching the third week I began to enter panic mode. Then one night I broke down in tears. Remember those negative thoughts I mentioned that would surface from to time to time? That little gremlin voice (the negative thoughts Russell referred to in his workshop) would tell me how much of a failure I was. I thought to myself, I am educated; I have experience why was I not getting a call back?

I would vent to Mike, my mother, and my sister. They all reassured me it would be ok, just be patient. That Sunday morning I woke up and went to church to find some peace. It was as if the sermon was speaking directly to me. The Pastor read Matthew 6:25, a scripture verse saying "do not worry" or be anxious. With tears welling up in my eyes, I felt touched and reassured. Everything was going to be alright. It was exactly what I needed to hear.

I took that as a sign that God was trying to tell me to relax and have faith. When he talks to me through others, I listen and feel deeply reassured. Literally, that Tuesday I got a call from an agency saying they needed someone with my background to work at a non-profit. I went for the interview that Thursday and was hired immediately. Was this really happening? I was overjoyed! On March 24th, almost a month after moving out to California, I found a job -- actually they found me on CareerBuilder.com! This was such a blessing and I know in my heart I had God to thank for that.

I was thrilled to start work and focus on my career. The timing could not have been better. I am a true believer that things happen when they are supposed to. My supervisor at the time, Kelli, was so welcoming and supportive. It was refreshing to work for someone who demonstrated great leadership skills yet was so kind. I didn't think bosses like that existed! Right around this time, Russell was seeking participants to join his year-long gratitude project documenting what they were grateful for.

With things falling into place, I was more than happy to amplify my new life by starting the gratitude journey. It was a new beginning for me – new job, new city, and I figured the best was yet to come. This was a great way to document my thoughts and feelings and also explore a different approach. I wanted to learn how to make the most of this process and not concentrate on the negative things as I'd done before. I was ready for personal growth and the challenges that would come with it.

I recognized that silencing my negative thoughts would be a difficult task for me. Therefore I made a conscious effort to shut that gremlin up! Any time that voice would creep in I would repeat "trust in the process" and attempt to silence the doubt. I found this worked for me and used it as a reminder to stay focused. I kept an open mind and let the day inspire me. Even from the beginning stage, I was already seeing some changes. The following are journal entries of the pivotal moment I found employment and moved to California and what I learned from this blessing:

> **5/19/14 -** *I can't believe it's been two months since I started work and one month of gratitude. I have to say I feel so fortunate to have a job. I can't stress this enough! It might not be the position I would have accepted BG (Before Gratitude) but I am not worried about that now. I am just happy to have a job at all. Today, on social media so many people complained about it being Monday and how much they detest their boss or job. A few years back I was in a volatile work environment as well. I remember being that person too, so I can completely empathize. However, as I think about my previous job, I see there is a purpose to every experience. It makes me appreciate even more that I get to come to a positive work environment. The culture here is peaceful and based on teamwork. I have an awesome supervisor, Kelli, who is kind yet demonstrates all qualities of a great leader. I'm so thankful to her for hiring me and I even thanked her for the opportunity. I feel I'm in a good place right now. Speaking of that I find it so funny that my job is located in San Fernando Valley, where* The Sandlot *took place! LOL, who*

would've thought I'd really end up here?! My inner child is content. I am grateful for my job, my amazing supervisor, the move to California and trusting in the process. Thank you God for listening to my prayers!

Reflection: As I look back on this post, what I learned from it is that this is the point when I was beginning to shift the focus to what I have rather than what I didn't have. Focusing on the positive is amazing! Many of us, especially pre-Gratitude, have a tendency to focus our energy on scarcity. In society today, emphasis is often on what's lacking. In the end, what we do is take things for granted and let everyday miracles go unnoticed. I recognized that the position I was hired for might not have been my dream job, still, that didn't matter to me. Aside from my job providing financial security, I learned I was happy. I was grateful to have a job to go to. I don't ever recall saying that about work. I was gratified for the opportunity given to me: a job with colleagues who are inclusive. I learned there is strength in unity and this builds team morale. Be grateful to be part of a team, especially when the team members are kind, and don't be shy about thanking them for supporting you and/or making you feel included. I am glad I was able to express thanks to my supervisor. Also, what I learned is to stop waiting for Friday to come and to be happy now! Make the most out of the moment TODAY.

8/23/14 - We drove out and took a scenic route to sunny Santa Barbara. While in the car I couldn't help but be in awe of the beauty of this town. The incredible climate, the tall swaying palm trees along the beachfront, the mountains, the perfect blue sky. Just wow. I felt peaceful and relaxed. I was basking in this glorious moment. I'm thankful for the natural beauty I'm surrounded by.

Reflection: Sometimes you just have to take a minute and detach yourself from your phone, social media, overthinking, and be present in the moment. This is especially hard for me. My mind races at the speed of light. I've always been distracted – thinking about the future, work, people, things that haven't happened yet, etc. When we do this we get caught up and ignore what's in front of us. I found that it's important to take a moment and be mindful of the present. It helps reduce stress and promotes well-being. When I think about this entry I find that journaling about gratitude has been a great tool in redirecting my focus to the present. I can remember how I felt that day and the connection I felt with my environment. Again, previously it had been a struggle for me to press pause and focus on today, however, being present has been beneficial in helping me savor moments and bring happiness.

> **11/18/14** - *Today at the end of our collaborative meeting I was ambushed by my two bosses and offered a job promotion! Ahhhh this is such great news! With funding issues and the uncertainty of our program continuing, I didn't know whether I'd have a job or not. To hear at this meeting that we got the contract AND I got promoted felt like a grand slam! I'm so happy to work in an environment where I can grow, where my opinions matter, and where I feel I am an asset in the workplace. All my hard work was acknowledged and this feels incredible. I am taking it all in, and I'm so appreciative of this blessing and journey.*

Reflection: I feel this is a testament to how developing an attitude of sincere gratitude and counting your blessings opens the floodgates of abundance and you receive more. When I first was hired I wasn't concerned about the job position as much as I valued having a job itself. This was the first job opportunity I had since taking time off from my career to watch my nephew. I wanted to show my boss Kelli gratitude for the chance I was given. I made sure that I did the best I could at work. Eventually, Kelli left the agency and my new supervisor Melissa took over. I was fortunate enough to end up having another amazing boss. We work well together, and Melissa empowers and enables me to grow professionally. Receiving acknowledgment for my work performance made me feel like I am a valuable employee. It gave me incentive to want to be a better worker. In all, gratitude attracts abundance -- it serves as the catalyst for extraordinary moments and changes in life.

The move to California and finding a job shortly after were major steps in my life. I am lucky and grateful to have been documenting gratitude as these crucial events happened. When I look at the course of my path from teenager to present day I see it was all part of the process. I am grateful for everything it took to bring me where I am today. Thanks to Mike being relocated from his job, I came along with him and was able to live my dream of moving to beautiful California. I met Russell through Mike, and the life coaching sessions with Russell eventually led me to join the gratitude mission and thus transform my life even more. Russell knew how important it was for me to focus on my career, so to find a job while starting fresh in California was truly one of the most important moments for me. Through the gratitude mission I became appreciative of what I have and learned to live in the moment and be present. These are all blessings and lessons from God that I am grateful for in my year of gratitude!

"*Every love story is beautiful but ours is my favorite*"

Love is more than a feeling. It's not only uttering the three little words to each other. Love is an action. It's how we treat another human being; love essentially is about showing our love, so that those we love can *feel* the love coming from us to them. When we find that person who we fall in love with, they become important to our existence. We learn to express love by acts of kindness, patience, affection, selflessness, and showing gratitude for them. A relationship without gratitude cannot thrive. John, a blogger on Love, Gratitude and Perspective, writes "Know gratitude, know love; no gratitude, no love." This is a great and interesting concept, and I couldn't agree more.

Our Gratitude Mission

I've always had hopes for finding true love. I like to consider myself a hopeless romantic despite everything I've gone through. Growing up I didn't have a good example of that at home. My father was physically and verbally abusive to my mother. What I witnessed were not acts of love, but of hate and anger. Being exposed to violence and living in an unstable home made me anxious and sad.

Countless nights I suffered from insomnia, afraid my mother's life was at risk. Many times I would shield her so she would not get hurt. Eventually when it was all over I would cry at night in my bunk bed or by my mother's side to protect her until I feel asleep. This was my experience of childhood up to the age of nine. In due course my parents divorced but I was left with all the memories and trauma.

Despite adversity, God was our sustenance and gave us strength to move forward. After the separation, for a month we were homeless and took shelter in my Aunt (Tia in Spanish) Edie's apartment. My mother became the breadwinner, so she would work many long hours until we could afford our own studio apartment. My Aunt (Tia) Oti would help and alternate with my Aunt Edie to pick up my sister and me from our elementary school. We had beach days with my Aunt Oti and movie and popcorn Fridays with my Aunt Edie. It is so important to have support and genuine love from family, especially when a child is that young. I'm so grateful to them for helping my family during this difficult time.

My mom did an exceptional job providing a stable new home for my sister and me. She is a pillar of strength and persevered through adversity. I have a deep love and admiration for all that she's done for us. I am not sure where we would be without her guidance. She would always remind us that, although we had a tough upbringing with my father, he was still our blood and that we must find peace in forgiveness. Not all men are the same. She would give us examples by telling us stories of my grandparents and how wonderful a man my grandfather Luis was. As a result, I held onto hope that good men are out there.

Years later, when I turned 18, I fell deeply in love for the first time. As I mentioned earlier, things with my first boyfriend got bad very quickly. In this relationship, I was uncomfortable to express my opinions. I was belittled and disrespected, which drained the energy out of me. I found myself in a toxic relationship and did not have the courage to leave. This was the only "love" I knew. I was fixated on the idea that I would not be able to find love again. It was an emotionally abusive relationship that thankfully ended.

After the breakup, I bonded and made friends with my co-workers, and am grateful that we instantly became close. This group of girls meant so much to me. They were encouraging, supportive, and we had fun! One in particular, who was a star among stars, is Jocelyn. My co-worker became my best friend. I am grateful to have her alongside my sister Lauri, who I love dearly and has always been my confidant. Jocelyn and I are so different yet we understand each other. She is a friend I can count on rain or shine. Back then, we shared our ups and downs and hopes for the future, particularly finding love someday. We always believed, maybe, one day it will happen.

I had hopes for love but I was skeptical at times. I decided to give myself time to enjoy being single. I dated for many years but somehow the timing or person was never right, and/or I wasn't ready. I knew deep down I didn't find "him" yet. On October 5, 2012, Jocelyn got married in Disney World! I couldn't be happier for her since I knew of the countless conversations we had that led to that moment. The day of her wedding, after the reception, I met Mike (who is Jocelyn's cousin). Ironically he and I crossed paths at a few family gatherings but never really talked to each other … until now!

Once we started dating we knew things would get serious between us. The timing felt right, but even more than that, we felt right for each other.

Our Gratitude Mission

I would not have made the move to California if we were not committed to each other. We would always have conversations about getting married. I remember telling Mike, "Wouldn't it be sweet if you proposed to me in Disney World where we met?" He automatically replied, "Absolutely not, that's corny." I didn't take this to heart though ... all I cared about was planning our future together.

On November 22, 2014 I got engaged! I was completely caught off-guard! Funny thing is Mike actually proposed to me in Disneyland. The entire time he had me thinking he would never propose in Disneyland. He got me good! He even tricked me into thinking he won two tickets to Disneyland. He put so much thought and effort into planning our engagement. It was incredibly sweet of him to make my dream come true even if it may have seemed "corny" to do it there. All in all it was an incredibly sentimental and heartwarming moment that I lived and will pass this story down to our children. Below is my journal entry of this special moment in 2014:

> **11/22/14** - *Earlier today the love of my life asked me to marry him in Disneyland!!! I am in shock ... still on cloud 9! This moment means everything to me. The outpouring of love we have received is incredible. I'm so happy. I'm toooo excited to write more. I am just so grateful I found my true love when I did. The wait was all worth it.*

Reflection: Without love, life can be lonely and cruel. But if you're lucky enough to find true love, cherish it. As I read this post, it takes me back to the emotions of that day – pure joy and excitement! Sometimes we have to go through things to appreciate what we have right in front of us. All along it was him. Even before the proposal, through our good and bad times I always knew in my heart I couldn't live without Mike. He was the man God put in my life, the man who would challenge me and make me a better person. I am grateful I get to spend the rest of my life with him.

If you asked me three years ago, if I would get engaged in 2014, my answer would most likely have been "impossible," especially with my skepticism and bad experience of love and relationships. Before gratitude I would question why I went through the negative experience with my father and the heartache of my past relationship. I did not see the purpose of the pain and heartache. Today, I realize it was all a learning experience. What I discovered is the lessons I gleaned from my past actually gave me strength.

I learned resilience and kept going forward. I held on to the hope that maybe it would happen to me. I finally gave love a second chance. In learning this I now realize no relationship is a waste of time. The past experience didn't give me what I wanted, but it taught me what I didn't want. It reminded me that, yes, I am capable and worthy of love.

Without that experience I wouldn't be so incredibly appreciative of my current relationship and what I have with Mike. It made me see how far I've come and how blessed I am to be learning to love again. I thank God for always listening to my prayers and manifesting in various forms. We don't have to dwell on the past or cycles of mistakes, even though they may seem insurmountable. You can move on and know the past does not define you. You have the ability to break the cycle!

The time I took to be single was crucial. Don't rush anything if you are not ready. Don't cave into the pressures of society because you "have" to be married. Take your time until you know you found the right person for YOU. Side note: it is also noteworthy to mention it's important to recognize the difference between the right and "wrong" types of love. Learn to differentiate between a healthy relationship and a toxic one. It is important to seek professional help if you are in an unsafe situation. Take the necessary, appropriate steps for YOU to move on from it.

Our Gratitude Mission

Relationships, like most things in life worth having, require effort. A healthy relationship is based on the understanding of two individuals, which leads to compromise in certain areas. The secret to a happy couple is compromise. It is the hallmark of healthy relationships. Equally, when we find ourselves in a healthy relationship, we grow together and show gratitude for each other. When we have a genuine appreciation for one another we display love and respect. When we are ungrateful for our significant others, we lose perspective and take them for granted, which can lead to a couple's demise.

Gratitude has made me understand and make sense of my past. It has helped me find the positive in the negative. When my last relationship ended I bonded with my friends and met Jocelyn. If it weren't for Jocelyn I would not have met Mike. Everything was set up to lead me to my one true love. In the broader context of love it made me trust in the process. I appreciate everyone and everything I had to go through to make me enjoy this moment.

Being vulnerable to love for a second time is a scary thing. I took that chance and have no regrets. I am so grateful for Mike, and the unforgettable day he proposed to me. Everything became clear from that moment on – the ups, the downs, the twists and turns, the love that kept us together through it all. He reassures me our life together will be different from my past and I appreciate him for it. I look forward to the next chapter in our lives as husband and wife. He means the world to me and has certainly made this journey worthwhile.

"Life is not about waiting for the storm to pass, it's about learning to dance in the rain"

All my life I have been physically healthy. Luckily I've never had any life-threatening health issues (knock on wood). In my twenties I thought I was invincible. I didn't really take care of my body, and thought I was immune to everything. I rarely went to the doctor because I didn't feel like I "needed" a checkup, though my mom would always encourage me to go for an annual physical.

It wasn't until March 25, 2015 (almost a year into my gratitude journey) that I started feeling sharp pains and had a health concern. Suddenly, I found myself feeling anxious as I knew my body was telling me that something wasn't right. The first thing I did was go online and ask Dr. Google. Though using the internet to self-diagnose was not a prudent choice, it was the fastest way to find an answer. Days went by and my symptoms were unchanged. Then that Sunday I felt the most excruciating pain. It was unbearable. It was so intense I almost passed out.

I didn't want to go to the emergency room because I wanted to avoid medical bills. In hindsight, I should have gone anyway. Our health comes first! Instead, I lay on the couch with a heating pad and took ibuprofen in hopes the pain would go away. I tolerated the pain and continued my research on WebMD: "See your doctor immediately if..." "Symptoms you shouldn't ignore..." "5 signs you might be dying..." ugh, just torturing myself. This was a terrible mistake, I know. I just didn't understand what this mysterious pain was and why was this happening now?

The next morning I went straight to the clinic. Never before did I feel a sense of urgency to go to the doctor. I had just received my new insurance the first week of March. Although I felt physical discomfort, and I wasn't in high spirits, I was grateful and relieved I had insurance at all. Once again timing was everything. Though I wanted to feel happy and grateful I honestly couldn't help but feel anxious and scared.

When I met with the physician she could not provide an accurate diagnosis without having lab work done. In addition to ordering lab work I was then referred to another specialist. Making an appointment for that doctor was frustrating because the next opening was two weeks away. All the waiting, not knowing what was going on, and the discomfort from the sharp pains was taking a toll on me emotionally. It was such a nerve-wracking time.

Gradually, I was being sucked into a negative vortex. Then I felt guilt for allowing fear to overwhelm my thoughts, followed by reprimanding myself for not being positive and grateful enough. I cried a good cry. I allowed myself to release these emotions and realized they could not be suppressed. After a month of several appointments and lab work, I received my final diagnosis. I will keep that part private as it is deeply personal, however, the important thing is I'm ok, I'm alive and I was able to bounce back from this experience. The following shows a glimpse of this critical moment in my year:

> **4/4/15** - *I am trying to compose myself, to keep it together. I've always considered myself a warrior. I'm trying to maintain and stay optimistic, but having a difficult time. The truth is I'm scared. It's hard to keep a straight face now but I do it anyway. I wouldn't be able to get through my day if it weren't for Mike taking care of me or my loving mom and amazing sister constantly texting to check on me. I'm so grateful for my mom who has always been a beacon of light and hope. She calls me every day! My sister is ALWAYS so supportive and encouraging. As much as I wish they weren't in NY, I keep them close to my heart and thoughts. Distance has nothing on us! My sister's messages get me through the day. I appreciate our bond and technology for facilitating that. I'm also grateful for my sweet nephew Landon. My sister always sends me videos of the kids. The other day she sent a video of Landon saying that he is praying for me to feel better and that he loves me. It was pure water works every time I watched it. So touching and sweet, I love him so! The videos of the kids put a smile on my face. I'm grateful for my sister sending them, she has no idea how they help me. Mike*

and my family are my strength now. In these times I realize how loved I am.

Reflection: Sometimes we fall and our emotions can get the best of us. In trying times when we don't feel strong enough, it is ok to rely on our loved ones for strength. Reaching out for help is not a weakness, it's a strength. Be grateful for those people who help you along the way, not everyone has that support. Humans are interdependent, we need one another. No man is an island. It is a blessing to have people who are not only there for you during good times but in bad times as well. My mom and my sister Lauri inspire me with their unwavering love and support. They have been there for me through it all! I remember it was my sister's words of encouragement that provided comfort during this time (along with the video of the kids). Though she is my younger sister, I look up to her because she has always been wise beyond her years. She knows what to say and shows that she cares. I am incredibly fortunate to have a sister I can count on. It is a wonderful feeling to be loved and a blessing to have a strong support system.

> **4/11/15** - *It's a waiting game at this point. In ten days I go back for another appointment. It's incredibly frustrating not knowing. I realize that some things are just out of my control. The only thing I can control is my approach to the situation -- my attitude. I've played out every possible scenario in my head (because I'm a planner and I like to prepare myself). And then I took a step back. Breathe. No matter what the outcome is I want to live my life now and continue on this path I've been on. Keep going ... keep moving forward ... you are strong. Time tells all.*

Reflection: In my undergrad studies, when taking a Social Work Practice course, I recall my professor teaching us about resilience to better understand our clients. Resilience is "the process of adapting well in the face of adversity, trauma, tragedy, threats or significant sources of stress." It develops over time. When I came to terms with my situation I accepted my circumstance and found inner strength. You see, we all have a choice, and no matter what happens, you can choose to either sink or swim. I am appreciative of the strength I found to swim and the people who helped me find my stroke.

In the midst of chaos I found that there is always something to be grateful for. I can empathize with anyone going through a health issue or loss. It can be crippling. However, the changes you experience affect everyone differently. Not everyone reacts the same to stressful and traumatic events. My hope is that by me sharing this experience it resonates with you and can motivate you through tough times.

I realized that, for the most part, things were going well for me since moving to California. Then suddenly, toward the end of my gratitude year, I was challenged with a difficult situation. It is natural to go through a whirlwind of emotions, like I did, yet I am grateful for the tears as they were part of the healing process. The feelings of sadness, and being scared and upset, needed to be released. I was fortunate enough to find strength to effectively adapt to my situation and be resilient. The choice was mine.

At any minute life can pull the rug from underneath you. In the end I realized how precious life truly is. We should make the best of it. Gratitude has taught me to appreciate every second I am alive. I have a deep respect for my health more than ever now. As I said before, it was something I took for granted years ago. I was careless as a young adult, but now, I feel motivated to take better care of my body so that I can live a healthy, long life and have children someday.

This temporary circumstance has taught me that gratitude teaches you to appreciate the rainbow and the storm. This did not derail all the good that I've experienced throughout my year. It made me stronger. I would not have gotten through it if it wasn't for my faith in God, Mike, my Mom, my sister and my colleagues who provided encouragement during this time. Every day we are given a chance to live life, which is a miracle in and of itself. I have my health, amazing family and friends, and so much to live for. My heart flows with gratitude and I feel like the richest person alive!

Train your mind to see the good in every situation and be inspired:

When stress levels are high, it is easy to let those emotions get to you. When we get caught up in the day to day activities, we get easily distracted. When we are surrounded by negative people and other external factors, we are left with difficult challenges to conquer. It is easy to focus on the negative. I had to figure out how I could redirect my brain to see the positive in every situation. I've been focusing on the negative for so long. It was not easy but consistency is the key. During my year of gratitude, I used the following techniques to help me reframe my brain and find the good:

- <u>Prayer</u> - My relationship with God is essential. Praying has been instrumental in finding peace and stillness. It has helped me count my blessings and focus on the things I have. "Pray not because you need something but because you have a lot to be thankful for."
- <u>Journaling</u> - The gratitude mission has been a great tool to find the positive and good every day. Writing has been cathartic. The more I wrote, the more I found something to be grateful for. Positive things just flowed like a bountiful river.
- <u>Meditation</u> - I learned to take a few minutes in the day to stay centered. I learned deep breathing helped to de-stress and I became mindful of the moment. I actually was sent to a work training that taught us Mindfulness techniques. I was so grateful for the opportunity and found that meditation does help to increase happiness. The happier we are the more optimistic we become.

- <u>Yoga</u> - I found this to help my body release tension. It created harmony between my mind and body. I've always been inconsistent with exercise but this worked for me. I would do it in the comfort of my own home, which was great.
- <u>Repeat</u> - Repetition and consistency is what keeps us on the right track. It doesn't work if you don't! At times I would get distracted, but I would find a way to bring myself back to my routine.

<u>Inspiration:</u>

"The King and the Shirt"

My Mom instilled lasting wisdom in my life. She has a heart of gold and loves my sister and me unconditionally. I am beyond blessed to have her as my Mom. I'm amazed at how optimistic she has been through hard times. She has always been so grateful. I distinctly remember a story she passed down from my grandfather Luis. He was a humble, good man who was a devoted husband and father. And the best grandfather in the Universe! The story my grandfather would tell my mother is "The King and the Shirt," a fable by Leo Tolstoy. In the story, the king was ill, and everything the doctors tried could not cure him. The young advisors suggested they find a happy man, take his shirt and put it on the king, and then he would be cured. The advisors traveled throughout the kingdom but only found people that complained about their life. Then one day the king's son came upon a hut and overheard a man say, "I am truly blessed. I have completed my work. I have nourished my body. Now I can enjoy the quiet at the end of the day. What more could anyone ever require?" The son was excited to find the happy man. When he knocked on the door to retrieve the shirt and offer him a gift in return he was shocked to learn that the only happy man in the kingdom had almost nothing to call his own – not even a shirt. Moral of the story: Some people have it all yet still are unhappy and ungrateful. Be grateful for what you have now rather than what you lack. I am so proud to come from a family that instilled valuable lessons. I treat them as treasures I hope to pass down to my children. I definitely see where my mother gets it from. The apple does not fall too far from the tree.

"Be good to those that are good to you. And to those that aren't, be good to them anyway."

Be thankful to those that have shown kindness and/or helped you in any way. Reciprocate it. Don't let pride get in the way and always say thank you to them for being good to you, be it the person who always holds the door for you, the friend who stays up late to hear you vent, a family member who has helped you or anyone that has been genuine. I am a firm believer that the good you put out attracts more good things. The bad you put out comes right back to you. For those that are not kind, don't let their bad attitude affect your day. Be kind to them anyway, they need love most.

"Fall seven times, stand up eight"

Even people who are strong fall sometimes. It's ok if you get knocked down, fall down, or feel down. The important thing is that you get up! When things are going well and life is good, it's easy to be happy. The true test comes in times of hardship -- this is when we show character. You have a choice every day. Make it count!

"Never give up on your hopes and dreams no matter how silly they seem"

Don't let anyone discourage you from your dreams. If you have a vision or a plan, begin to implement it by setting realistic goals. Stick to them and never give up. Keep trying until you accomplish your dreams. I remember being told as an adolescent that I was too much of a dreamer for wanting to move to California. I was told I lived in a fantasy world because I had hopes to find love and wanted to experience true love and get engaged and have a happy marriage. They would say the divorce rate is too high, all men are dogs, anything discouraging. I learned that some people don't want to see you happy. They are not content in their own lives and their defense mechanism is to bring you down with them. Misery loves company. Don't let it get to you. Dream big!

"Matthew 6: 25-34 – Do not worry"

25 "Therefore I tell you, do not worry about your life, what you will eat or drink; or about your body, what you will wear. Is not life more than food and the body more than clothes? **26** Look at the birds of the air; they do not sow or reap or store away in barns, and yet your heavenly Father feeds them. Are you not much more valuable than they? **27** Can any one of you by worrying add a single hour to your life? **28** And why do you worry about clothes? See how the flowers of the field grow. They do not labor or spin. **29** Yet I tell you that not even Solomon in all his splendor was dressed like one of these. **30** If that is how God clothes the grass of the field, which is here today and tomorrow is thrown into the fire, will he not much more clothe you—you of little faith? **31** So do not worry, saying, 'What shall we eat?' or 'What shall we drink?' or 'What shall we wear?' **32** For the pagans run after all these things, and your heavenly Father knows that you need them. **33** But seek first his kingdom and his righteousness, and all these things will be given to you as well. **34** Therefore do not worry about tomorrow, for tomorrow will worry about itself. Each day has enough trouble of its own."

Final thoughts: Know only one direction… Forward

This mission has given me a different perspective on life. I find that now I give myself more time to appreciate what I see and what's around me, be it the flowers, the birds chirping, or my friends and loved ones. As I do this, I find myself loving life more and feeling happy. In the beginning stage I was off to a good start with plenty of positive moments, then toward the end things spiraled downward and I hit a fork in the road. I had to make a choice, do I let it destroy me or strengthen me? I chose the latter. A friend of mine once jokingly said, "When life knocks me down I do a burpee!" Along with being hilarious, she has the right attitude.

As I worked to find deeper meaning, gratitude has been the vehicle helping me make sense of the past, present, and future. When I look at it from this point of view, I see the big picture. If gratitude were the vehicle, looking through my rear view mirror would be a reflection of the past. My past did not defeat me. All obstacles and trials served a purpose. They were all lessons that made me stronger. Learn from it just don't live in it. If gratitude were the present it would represent the steering wheel. I have the ability to control the moment. Being grateful has allowed me to focus on the present and be mindful of my feelings, surroundings, people, things and experiences. I have the ability to make choices for today. I am appreciative of it all. If gratitude were the future it would symbolize the windshield, creating a vision for what lies ahead and a vision for tomorrow. I know I can't project the future but I am hopeful for it. Being on this gratitude journey has helped me develop an optimistic attitude for the future. In turn, what I hope for is that in some way, shape, or form YOU have found my story inspiring and can take from it what I have learned. Remember, never let a stumble in the road be the end of your journey. Stay focused and keep moving forward. Enjoy the ride!

Our Gratitude Mission

Terry's Take

Mi amiga es muy bien! OK pardon my broken Spanish, but it is has been excellent to be on this journey with Marian. I am proud and happy to say I am equally great friends with both her and Mike. I am so excited for their wedding in 2016! When Mike brought Marian to my workshop (which by the way was the first one I had ever given on my own), he realized it could be an excellent win/win situation, which I am a huge fan of. I am so glad Coaching helped Marian win, which of course also helped Mike win, and I won too because as a new entrepreneur, every client is a big win.

It is sad to see what Marian experienced in the past with her father and her ex-boyfriend. However, she is spot-on in her assessment that going through those abusive relationships have helped her immensely today. She inspires me! One of the cool parts about this project for me is learning so much about all of the authors, whether we were friends before we embarked on this journey or not. I wonder how many people out there have a story similar to hers, yet we walk around not knowing it. Hopefully her chapter will inspire others to share their story – AND change their life.

Our Gratitude Mission

Chapter 7

Peter Franklin

And For This, I am Grateful

Age: 63

Hometown: Manhattan Beach, CA

Current City: Marblehead, MA

Our Gratitude Mission

June 1, 2014. The day I begin my Gratitude Mission. It's an auspicious day, as it marks the formal beginning of Taking Notice. Of Being Aware. Of Maintaining the Center. Of Being Fully Present.

Each day presents us with the choice of living in the past, the present, or the future. All too often we get caught up in what has already occurred, and/or what could have been done differently. Sometimes these thoughts are fraught with guilt, remorse, or self-doubt. We find ourselves haunted by the "what if...?" While intellectually we know that the past is over...water under the proverbial bridge...we still cling to shadows and ghosts, which only take us farther from the present moment. Rather than being grateful for what we have right now, we fall into the abyss of second-guessing. I'll raise my hand and admit that I am guilty of this!

At the other end of the spectrum, all too often we get caught up in what hasn't yet occurred, what looms over the horizon. We worry, fret, wonder what will be...and devote needless cycles trying to control that which is out of our control. We rehearse the other side of "what if?" that is the anxiety of trying to control the outcome of things, events, possibilities that are still far away on the horizon. We channel our energy into what often is the worst case scenario, and ruminate on all the possible outcomes. This is not planning...this is fretting. And, like fixating on the past, doing so takes our focus and energy far away from the present moment. I'm now raising my other hand...guilty of this one as well!

Patsy Rodenburg, in her book *The Second Circle*, further develops the idea that when we are in Second Circle, we are in the moment. We are present. We are aware. We are all in. While we all have First Circle (the past) thoughts, and Third Circle (the future) thoughts, we do have a choice. It is at this point, Second Circle, that we have the boundless opportunity of Gratitude.

We can choose to lament what has happened, or what hasn't. Worry over something said...or not said. But it's in the past...behind us...totally out of our control. The milk has already spilled. We can worry about it, feel guilty about it. Or we can clean it up, and move on with our lives.

We can choose to worry about the future. To rehearse, pre-choreograph, fret. Worry about what will be...or perhaps not be. But this is in the future, not yet fulfilled...and as with the past, not within our control. We get stuck in auto-pilot of worrying...getting anxious and worked up...about what may or may not ever come to fruition. The "what if" ties our insides in knots.

Or we can choose to be present. Here. Now. Present Moment. Wonderful Moment.

What we often miss - and I've already included myself in this club - is embracing the present. All we have is this moment, and we alone have the choice to be mindful of the present moment, or to be mindless.

I began my Gratitude Mission with the singular goal of being more mindful...and more grateful...of the present moment, and the gifts that it bears. Of not being mindless anymore! And by being grateful for this moment - large or small - I am thus being more mindful. Mindfulness = Gratitude.

Mindfulness, for me, is not only being present in this moment, but also using my breath to remain in the moment. I am grateful for my breath, for being aware of my breath. I cannot help but be full of gratitude when I'm with my breath. Cannot help being grateful when I'm present.

Auto-pilot. How many times do we get stuck on auto-pilot...not taking notice or being grateful for the present moment...the little things that make up the rich tapestry of our lives? We do this all the time! We default to the destructive...either second-guessing what has already transpired or being wrapped up in trying to guess the future. We worry. We stress. We let anxiety control us. We know well and good when that happens we are truly unable to be grateful for the small and large pieces of our lives. We are simply on cruise control, and rarely realize that we are missing the journey.

A confession of sorts:

On paper, it seems as though I have accomplished many of my goals: travel, career, friendships, love, family, and both physical and spiritual accomplishments. While I am grateful for all of them, I confess that I am often also guilty of leaping from the present moment into the next moment...what will be. I am prone to rehearsing an event or scenario in the future. As a result, I miss this moment entirely...and once it's gone, there is no retrieving it. I've then spent a lot of time "planning " for something (generally how to avoid or deal with a "situation") that begins to stress me out...and while that situation may likely never occur, I've missed the moment. Kind of like driving down the road, talking on the phone, and being so absorbed in the conversation that the landscape is totally missed. How did I get here? Yes, we've all been there.

No more of that!

Actually, I have a second goal. It's very much related to my own personal Gratitude Mission. In my quest to be more mindful...more grateful, I also want to unlock the same practice in my students. With my students.

I am a high school English teacher, and I encounter my students' stress and anxiety every day. Tests. Relationships. College. Self-Identity. It's all there. Being a teenager (and I think that most of us can recall this) is fraught with emotional turmoil. Who am I? What do I want? What do I like? Who likes me? Who DOESN'T like me? How much of an individual am I? How different dare I be? Who are my friends? Where am I going?

The following is a classic example of First, Second, and Third Circle...and how gratitude can evade them:

In my classroom (I teach primarily seniors), every October I hang up sheets of paper with "College Hit Parade" printed on them. There are two columns: one for a student's name, the other for the college or university she/he has been accepted to. Early on, I know that this exercise can cause stress and anxiety. Rather than it being a source of celebration (I've been accepted!) it can be just the opposite. And with Early Action, Early Decision, and Rolling Decision, students are getting news of their acceptances earlier and earlier.

Toward the end of October last year, just as class was beginning, a student somewhat hesitantly approached the College Hit Parade. He grabbed the marker dangling from its string, and as he removed the cap, stole a couple of furtive glances around the room. I was observing this...and noted that he was hesitant, and that he was hoping that not many were watching him. He didn't want to be "that" guy flaunting that fact that it was only October, and he had already been accepted to the college of his choice.

Oh, how wrong he was! I was aware that most every student in the room was checking him out...and their nonverbals were striking.

I parlayed this into a discussion about Second Circle and Gratitude. Some students very much went to First Circle: "I wish I had worked on my application last weekend." "I promised my parents that I would finish my essay, and I did nothing." Even one said, "I wish I would have been a better student as a sophomore."

Still others went to Third Circle: "Will I even be accepted to any school?" "What if I don't get into the school I want to?" "What will my parents say?" "What will my friends think?" And so on...

Sound familiar?

Our Gratitude Mission

The gratitude discussion was a natural segue into being present, and how to be grateful for this moment, this particular time. I told them that I was grateful for this event...as it really illustrated everything we had been working with. We pressed the reset button, and moved on.

More mindful. More grateful. More present. Less distracted. I know that my own daily practice of mindfulness and gratefulness will be a good example for my students to follow.

Onward.

Being mindful is being grateful. And this is my journey. I am grateful that I am able to share that with you.

Most of what follows is my (selected) actual journal entries for the year. I very much want to be authentic, and to avoid editorializing too much! I also simply want to illustrate just how simple and clean being grateful is. I am convinced that every single day there is at least one thing (actually, I believe there are many!) for which we can be grateful. The majority of them are small, minor, inconsequential. A few of them are monumental. But by focusing on the little bits and pieces, the mundane if you will, I have grown to realize just how many opportunities for gratitude there are.

The Gratitude Journal begins.

June 1, 2014

Today is an auspicious...and busy...day.

I am grateful for all that I have today.

I am grateful for my son Davis, as he endeavors to conquer his first triathlon, at the age of 18. Davis and his friend Paul Elder, as part of their senior project at Marblehead High School, have been training for the Greendale (MA) triathlon, and raising money for The Jimmy Fund at the Dana Farber Cancer Institute in Boston. I think the easy part has been fundraising and training. Today comes the difficult part!

I am grateful for Davis...his drive, commitment, focus, and willingness to take on new challenges. I am grateful that he has taken this seriously, and that he has a good, healthy, balanced perspective about the race.

I am also grateful that I am the Faculty Speaker at today's Swampscott High School graduation. Each year, members of the senior class vote for the teacher they wish to speak at their graduation ceremony. This year, they have selected me! Actually, this is the third time in seven years that I have been chosen. It's quite an honor, and really quite humbling.

I am grateful that I, as a high school English teacher, continue to make a profound impact on my students...as they make a profound impact on me. I smile inwardly when they feel like it is I who am doing the teaching...when many times it is they who are actually teaching me. I learn just as much from them as they do from me. We have a nice relationship that way...and for that I am grateful.

And today is one of those days when that appreciation, both from students and parents, becomes apparent. Quite a high, and very rewarding. I never know who I will touch, or what impact I will have on them...and I really do like that surprise.

June 3, 2014

Today I am again grateful for being able to ride my bike to and from work. There is just something about the energy created by an hour-long ride early in the morning. Everything is new and fresh...full of potential and possibility. Truly energizing...

Our Gratitude Mission

One thing I am particularly grateful for today is my ongoing (and developing) Mindfulness and meditation. I meditate mindfully for about 45 minutes each morning...generally between 4:30 and 5:30 a.m. I know that's early, and many consider it to still be nighttime...however, it is a calm and centered time for me. All things are possible, and my mind is relatively quiet.

I also take a "breathing break" at least once each day. I find this to be a great way just to disconnect for a few minutes...breathing, being in the moment. Very valuable.

In the evening, I do my third meditation of the day, this one for about 15-20 minutes. The routine varies each evening, but I am learning to avoid the Body Scan (or any other lying down meditating/yoga) as I tend to fall asleep. Not the point! I think it's comical that I "burst" into consciousness, temporarily not knowing what I'm doing or where I am.

I am also grateful for the daily one-on-one time I get to spend with my lovely wife, Jacqueline.

June 5, 2014

I am grateful for my former students.

We teachers don't always know when we are connecting with our students [sometimes lots of "noise" (as in students not actively listening...someone planning a response...judging what the other person is saying) in between...] or when one of our many messages has hit the mark. Some days you feel good about really making connections, and other days not so much.

It is quite rewarding...perhaps the finest of all rewards...when a former student drops in with positive feedback on how the experience with me in the classroom has made his or her college experience all the easier. Many of the conversations (or emails...) start with, "If it weren't for you and your class..." And you can fill in the blanks from there.

There are times when I'm not totally surprised by this...as a particular student and I communicated and connected well. There was an easy flow of ideas and dialogue...and the student was engaged and participatory. There are occasions, though, when a former student who I never really connected with...or who was on the quiet side and didn't participate much in class...will come back and lavish praise upon me.

Those are the fun ones...as they get me thinking about how many others like him/her there are! I am grateful that I receive that feedback.

June 8, 2014

I am grateful for Davis. I am grateful for his love. I am grateful for his focus and drive. I am grateful that he is his own person. I am grateful that he is graduating from high school today.

June 17, 2014

I am grateful for each new day, with the new energy and new possibilities that each day brings. I am grateful that I look forward to each day...and am learning to be grateful for developing a sense of child-like wonderment at each new opportunity. Here's what I've learned: getting stuck in a routine...feeling that you have to stick to your routine or else everything falls apart...is just another means of avoiding the enjoyment of the present moment. Wonder lives in the present moment. Fear, Guilt, and Anger do not.

June 19, 2014

I am grateful for Jacqueline. That's all I really need to say! She is an inspiration, motivation, and my grounding force. She allows me to dream...and also allows herself to dream. What a great combination! I am grateful that she is in my life, for it is all the more full and rich...complete. I am grateful that being with her never gets old...and as we grow "older" (age-wise) together, we still retain our youthful exuberance and giggles. Who could ask for more?

June 27, 2014

I am grateful for the legacy of my mom. It's been two years since she passed away, and while I often think of something I want to say to her, or share with her, I realize that while I can't, she's still with me. That makes me chuckle ... smile ... and be grateful for all of the wonderful things/memories she's given to me. Yes, today would have been her 85th birthday, and I know that she is celebrating with her favorite foods. I think I'll just call her and tell her what I'm having for lunch!

And today it was fitting to write a poem for Mom.

Heavenly Food

I'm curious as to whether

The deceased, be they in heaven, some islet in the Caribbean,

or wherever it

Is that they congregate,

Get to choose what they eat.

Is there a menu?

An all-you-can-eat buffet?

Do meals just get provided...chef's surprise?

Or do they even eat at all?

Russ Terry

Perhaps there's a meal plan...or maybe,

Just maybe,

The light in the kitchen is always on...and the fridge

Is never empty.

Today is my mother's birthday, and wherever she is, I'm sure

There is something tasty stashed somewhere.

Guilty pleasure foods.

Foods that weren't often eaten here on

Earth...and when they were, there was always

Just a little justification.

Foods that made her swoon...and utter,

"Well, I think I deserve this little treat."

Bacon.

A chocolate croissant.

Cheese. And more cheese.

Comfort food any time of day or night...

Something that flipped a switch and made everything

All right.

Our Gratitude Mission

So when I call her...if that were possible

(and I don't see why it's not)...

we will talk, once again, about

what's for dinner, what's for lunch.

"I just picked this up at the store...looked

too good to pass up."

You deserve it, mom...pamper yourself.

"Have you tried this recipe yet?"

No, but I certainly will...

And the conversation goes on...we skim lightly

Over family events...personal anecdotes...our mutual ills and ailments.

But we always linger over the food.

Drill deep into the nuances of this twist over that...

How much of this gem to add. Or not.

Remember when you made us...and my voice trails off a bit as I am

Transported back to the kitchen, or dinner table, or beach basket

When a small morsel set me free.

Wilted lettuce with just the right amount of bacon/onion dressing.

Sun-warmed chunks of cantaloupe, eaten in the shade at the beach.

Cracked crab...the mess and giggles...and how each of us

Had our own strategy for stockpiling and devouring.

And of course the Chatham Sandwich, which stops me in my

Tracks every time.

Yes, I'll call her.

I am curious what we're doing for lunch.

© 2014 Peter Franklin

July 4, 2014

Independence Day. 4th of July. Grateful for my freedom, my constitutional rights, my independence. Sounds corny, but it's so very true.

July 18, 2014

I am grateful for the time I have during the summer to explore, relax, dream, and read. It really is a gift, and I want to achieve a state of mind of not taking it for granted. The Taoist phrase "remember the source" is important to note here: never forget the source of all things to remain grateful for all things.

July 25, 2014

The other day I received an unsolicited email from a former student of mine who graduated this past June. Often times I take for granted how lucky I am to be a high school teacher, how lucky I am to have a daily mindful opportunity to make an impact on a young adult, how lucky I am to be doing something that I derive so much energy from. The email ended with: "I would say that you are, hands down, the best and most influential teacher I have ever had because I learned more than just history and English in your classroom. The values that I learned in your class will stay with me for the rest of my life..." Wow. This really made me stop in my tracks and take stock of how totally GRATEFUL I am for what I do. I am grateful that I have the opportunity to work with wonderful students. I am grateful for the smile that it puts on my face. And I am grateful for students who are comfortable enough with themselves to express their inner thoughts and feelings. I am blessed.

August 10, 2014

I am grateful for learning to see things with a child's mind. Simple. Fresh. Curious. It is quite the challenge but one that is fun to take on. I am grateful for the shift in energy and peacefulness that it brings...and my intention is that it will get easier and easier to achieve this state of mind.

August 25, 2014

Plenty of gratitude to spread around today: First, I am grateful that today is the first day of school. Sounds odd, perhaps, when most of my colleagues seem to be moaning the end of summer (as gleaned from their Facebook posts!) but I am grateful to get back into the classroom. My students inspire me, and I can't wait to get more servings of their inspiration. I am also grateful for my son Davis...big "double" for him over the weekend: On Saturday we moved him into his dorm room at Tufts University, where he begins his freshman year. He is our youngest, and now we are officially "empty nesters." Not sure how that feels yet...but it's definitely quieter around here already! And Davis also celebrated his 19th birthday yesterday. I am grateful that he has grown into such a fine young man...poised, confident, comfortable in his own skin...and ready to take hold of the many opportunities that lie ahead of him.

August 31, 2014

I am grateful for Air Conditioning. It is hot and humid today (and this weekend). Summer is making one last stand as September looms. I'm grateful for the refuge that AC provides...both in terms of comfort during the day, but also for being able to sleep at night. A few days ago it was beautiful San Diego-type weather...gorgeous and easy to take for granted. As soon as the heat and humidity return, no more taking for granted.

September 10, 2014

I am grateful for the ocean. I am grateful that I have the opportunity to see the ocean every day...beginning with my early morning walk with our dog Zorro. There is nothing so refreshing and empowering as to see the ocean at sunrise...just as light's fingers are beginning to spread themselves over the earth. Rather poetic, I think! It is a special time of day, and I'm grateful that I live where I can capitalize on this opportunity. (We reside in Marblehead, MA, just north of Boston, right on the Atlantic Ocean. Our house, our little beach cottage - my wife's term! - offers us ocean peeks most of the year, and is about 150 yards from the beach.)

September 11, 2014

On this day of infamy, I am grateful for my family, for my friends, for my life. None of them shall be taken for granted; each of them shall be embraced and enjoyed. Simple.

Our Gratitude Mission

September 25, 2014

I am grateful that I have been able to bring Mindfulness into my classroom on a daily basis. We breathe, we have brief meditations and we learn to focus and to decompress -- all very necessary skills today, especially with teens. I am also grateful that my students, in general, are open and receptive to learning Mindfulness techniques, and gladly go along with our exercises. They at least tolerate things. Even the kids who aren't "into this whole meditation thing" are respectful of the space, and allow their peers their space. Quite cool. And I'm always impressed with the energy shift in the room after we have done our opening exercise.

November 25, 2014

I am grateful for the "collision" of two significant forces in my life: coaching and Mindfulness. Coaching has allowed me to become a better teacher...as my students now have a greater say in their education. They are empowered to become advocates (though not all take advantage of this!) for their own learning. Now my classroom is far less teacher-centric, and far more student-centric. And along comes my training in the .b Mindfulness In Schools project. Creating a mindful classroom is a wonderful thing...not only creating a much more calm and focused environment, but solidly supporting the student-centric platform. It's all about breathing! Each class, every day, begins with a brief breathing/meditation practice. Some days it is just a couple of minutes...while on others (and the students frequently request this) we take it a bit longer...up to 15 minutes. Does this get in the way of teaching in the curriculum? No. Rather, it enhances it. And for this I am grateful.

December 25, 2014

Christmas Day. Bittersweet day. Warm...55° & rainy. Not what Christmas is supposed to feel and look like in New England. It is gray. It is dreary. It is a good day for reflection, and mourning. It is on this day, I am grateful for many things...but most of all, I am grateful for the nearly 30 years that my mother-in-law, Betty Dorner Gaier, has been in my life. Betty passed away yesterday afternoon after a long and miserable battle with dementia. I am grateful that I (and the entire family) was able to spend last weekend with her in Grand Rapids...though I'll never be certain that she knew I was there. It was important to say proper goodbyes...and just to sit and spend time. I am most grateful for what Betty taught me...and brought to all of our lives. She was kind and generous, almost to a fault. She was supportive, curious about our lives and, for each of us, was our most fervent cheerleader. She was everyone's favorite grandmother...or aunt...or whatever. Betty took a focused, individual interest in each one of us. She was authentic. Betty was wonderfully irreverent as well...never mincing words or failing to express what was on her mind. She never failed to make me smile. I am grateful for all that she was...and is...and I am particularly grateful for the place she will always have in my heart.

December 30, 2014

Two things today: First, I am actually grateful for my first root canal. I've been putting it off for a couple of years (didn't bother me...thus no attention paid to it)...and about a week ago, it started aching. So, no time like the present to address this little thing. Actually, not bad at all! I think the procedure is far too blown out of proportion. What I found interesting was that I was able to meditate throughout the entire process. Once the endodontist began working, I simply started a breathing routine (5/7...counting to five on each in-breath, and to seven on each out-breath) and before I knew it, she was finished. Really easy. And for that I am grateful that my breathing can transcend such an interruption. Did I hear what was going on? Absolutely. But I was able to push it to the far recesses of my consciousness.

Our Gratitude Mission

January 1, 2015

I am grateful for the New Year...a new year of growth, possibilities, successes, and riches. Davis and I went to Owen and Eileen's annual Black Eyed Pea and Greens New Year's Day event. Always fun. Always good greens and peas. Jacqueline didn't go this year as she's still recovering from a virus bug, and the death of her mom. Not yet ready for small talk. I totally understand...and am grateful that she feels comfortable in opting out. 2015 is already a great year...and I am quite sure I will continue to have much to be grateful for. Oh, lest I forget...I am grateful for my annual New Year's Day bike ride. This year, 11 miles. 18 degrees. Breezy, but sunny, lasted 45 minutes, same as last year. Brrr. Chilly. But the hot tub was waiting for me! Lovely.

January 13, 2015

What I think I am most grateful for today is being able to bring .b Mindfulness into my classroom. Today with my two senior classes, we did .b Lesson #6 (about the traffic in our minds...and how to play traffic controller). But, I also ended the session with a 15 minute body scan for them...lying down. (Yes, I have yoga mats in the classroom! Swampscott Educational Foundation generously funded a grant I wrote so that I could continue to pursue Mindfulness in varied ways. Very cool! Am I grateful for this? Absolutely!) They needed a good stress release, and it was perfectly timed. I am grateful that they are "in" for these activities. And that they are open to exploring Mindfulness with me. It makes my day a lot more fun...to be sure.

January 24, 2015

I am grateful that today is day 200 of my Gratitude Journal. I am grateful for the opportunity (and drive) to be able to express my gratitude on a daily basis. 200 days. Quite fun. And I realize that most days, I am most grateful for the little things...the sometimes barely noticed things...that make up my life. There are certainly momentous events that occur...a wedding, a death, a discovery, an award...from time to time. But it's the little everyday things that are much more in focus. It's difficult to take things for granted when you notice them! And Gratefulness is certainly akin to Mindfulness. To be grateful, you need to be mindful...as without being awake and aware, the daily steps are not noticed. And to be Mindful, you need to be grateful, for it's the gratitude that keeps the focus on being awake, being Mindful. It's a lovely symbiotic relationship!

January 27 and 28, 2015

The Blizzard of 2015 is upon us...and I'm grateful that a) we did not lose power, and b) I had Jacqueline's help in moving all of the snow around. We received upwards of 24"...quite large drifts as a result of the howling winds that we had. So, we ended Monday with bare ground...and the barren winter look...and end the day on Wednesday with so much snow that it won't melt until spring. And yes, I am grateful for the two snow days we had. But enough already!

January 29, 2015

The Taylor Twins. Gulu Gulu Café in Salem, MA. Our first performance there. [I play in a band (a duo actually) called the Taylor Twins. Peter Franklin & Fred Shepard. Why the "Taylor Twins?" It's become kind of a joke actually, as we tell people we are twins, just to get their reaction. We are NOT twins! We are NOT related. And we don't even resemble one another. The "Twins" piece? We both play Taylor guitars when we are onstage.]

I am most grateful for this performance. We played from 9:00 pm until midnight. Yikes. Way past my bedtime. I would have preferred a 7:00 pm – 10:00 pm gig. But it doesn't work that way, does it? I think we did okay...and hope we get to play there again. Quite a few friends showed up...and even a handful of students. But they all thinned out around 10:45...and the room was somewhat empty after that. It blows me away that there are people out and about on a Thursday night after 11:00. Quite a different lifestyle than my own!

February 4, 2015

Oh, I am grateful to be back in school today...and to revel in the energy that is high school. I find that after a day or two of being away, I miss the place...miss the kids. I am grateful to be in a career that affects me that way. Even though our schedule is totally messed up because of the snow days... it's okay. It all works out in the end. Today was a good day...a long day, but a good day nonetheless. I am grateful for the energy that I had...and for a nice hot tub and meditation at the end of it all!

February 12, 2015

Gonna have to dig deep today for gratitude, as my day has been overshadowed by learning that my Mindfulness class will not be offered next year. Seems as though there is another class already in the course of studies that no one told me about... Surprised me today, actually, when I was reaching out to further codify the class. Right Hand? Left Hand? Do you know what you are doing? I'm grateful that this is not about me...as it's easy to go to the world of "I'm not good enough" and take this personally. But the decision was apparently made before my idea surfaced. Oh well, that's why I breathe! Hmmmm...I know this is here for a reason. And I'm grateful for that.

February 25, 2015

Of all the things I have to be grateful for today, the one that needs to be mentioned is that I am grateful for all of the snow we have had this winter in Marblehead. Oh, it's overwhelming...and seems to be never ending...and there's still a lot of it around. Roads are narrow. It seems like we've been shoveling non-stop. Snow banks are really more like mountains. And now it's getting all ugly and brown. So what's there to be grateful for? Well, because of the 100+ inches we've gotten this year, we've had to do a lot of shoveling. OUTDOORS. This means neighbors are outside working cooperatively ... and not hibernating inside where it's nice and warm. So, we've been talking, laughing, sharing our pain...and getting to know one another better. And for that I am grateful.

March 15, 2015

I am grateful for 29 wonderful years of marriage to Jacqueline. Wow. Hard to believe that not only did I find the love of my life, but that she's been my partner for three decades. I am one blessed and grateful man. I am who I am today thanks in large part to Jacqueline's support, encouragement, and unconditional love.

March 25, 2015

Grateful for the sunrise. Grateful for the sunrise from the seat of my bike! First day of the season cycling to school. It's been a long, long winter...and though it was a chilly 27 degrees at launch time, it had to be done! It's not a major feat, but the exhilaration and "afterglow" is wonderful...and sets up the day in a most wonderful way.

April 4, 2015

Hilary's 25th birthday! Wow. I am grateful for my daughter...the joy and laughter she brings to my life. What a fine young woman. I cannot be more proud of her, and all that she has accomplished in these short 25 years. Hilary has brought me more happiness than I can even come close to remembering. But I am grateful nonetheless. She laughs at my jokes. She runs errands with me. She gets my humor. She has the best hugs...and the best smile. And when she calls me Daddy-O, I just melt. Could I be any luckier with a daughter like Hilary? Nope. Could I be any happier? Absolutely not. All smiles, that's me today!

April 25, 2015

A spring poem:

>Perhaps the chill in the air would be
>
>Greater were it not
>
>For the daffodils
>
>That have finally decided to
>
>Cautiously emerge from winter's sleep.
>
>Yellow is more luminous than white
>
>On this particular day.
>
>Or perhaps the wind would be
>
>Even more biting were it
>
>Not for the pair of cardinals
>
>Who've come to feed outside
>
>The kitchen window...cautious and
>
>Nervously glancing about...
>
>Perhaps fearful that a late season squall will

Hearken them back to dreary days of

A seedless February.

Their scarlet downiness is the harbinger

Of warmer days.

I am grateful for chives and rhubarb...simple

Little things...that remind me that

All is possible, all is right,

Even after the darkest days of

Death.

© 2015 Peter Franklin

May 6, 2015

Ride Your Bike To School Day. Grateful to have ridden Pugsley today. Really needed to take a day off, but couldn't resist. Glad I rode! Grateful for spring, and all of the lovely blossoms. It's too easy to take the burgeoning aspects of spring for granted...as the "good things" are like Teflon...and we often overlook them. Riding home yesterday was full of noticing smells and sights of spring...and how wonderful they are. I am grateful for our first "sitting out" of the season (front porch, wine o'clock) with Jacqueline. A bit chilly once the sun began to go down, but again, the beauty of spring did not go unnoticed.

Our Gratitude Mission

May 25, 2015

Memorial Day. I am grateful for all the men and women, including my father, who stood up for freedom and liberty. Many made the ultimate sacrifice for our country and its Constitution...and for that I am grateful. The Bill of Rights, more than any other document in history, gives us freedoms and protections that others only dream of. And I am grateful on this day that we have many who are willing to protect those freedoms. They are not to be taken lightly.

June 3, 2015

The day of Natali Masarskaya's passing. I am grateful to have known her. Grateful to have had her as a student. Grateful for all that she taught me. There is much that can be said about Natali...her strength, her perseverance, her choosing to not be the victim. Natali was charming. Natali was brilliant. Natali was opinionated. Natali was compassionate. Natali was Natali...a unique, wonderful, gifted young woman.

Natali once told me, early on in her senior year, that she hated me. Oh, yes, Natali was honest! I had thrown down the gauntlet about how in our English class we would work on writing, then work some more on writing, then work even more on writing. I guess this is not what Natali wanted to hear! She crossed her arms, rolled her eyes, and dug in her heels.

However, Natali, as we all know, was not a quitter. She never did quit...and throughout the year, worked harder than any student I've ever had at "cracking the code" on her writing. And she succeeded.

At graduation last year, Natali thanked me for pushing her. And said she no longer hated me. She smiled. I smiled. And I know that she never really hated me. That was just Natali being Natali.

We are all sad...and shocked...at this turn of events for Natali. Natali taught all of us so much about life...about not giving up...about how to take challenges head on...and how to keep all things in perspective. Natali never had it easy. But you would never know that.

Natali came to visit a couple of weeks ago, and she looked marvelous. She was upbeat, dressed to the nines...yet revealed that the pain she constantly endured was as bad as it had ever been. Yet when we chatted via email earlier this week, there was no mention of that pain. Natali was never a whiner.

Natali is no longer in pain, and for that I am grateful. And I am grateful to have had Natali in my life...and that will be forever.

June 7, 2015

Graduation Day...a year later. My, how time flies. Time flies like an arrow. Fruit flies like a banana. Thanks, Groucho. Today I am grateful for my (now) former student, Luke O'Brien. After graduation yesterday, Luke said to me, "Thanks for everything, Mr. Franklin. It's because of you that I want to become a teacher." Wow. It's all about changing lives and touching souls. As a teacher, the greatest compliment I can receive is just that...that I have made an impact on a student, and he wants to follow in my footsteps. Will he? Who knows? But Luke's soul has been touched...and I have fulfilled the unwritten manifestation of why I teach. I teach for many reasons...all of them good. But I also teach to make a difference...and I guess I've just done that. Could I be more grateful? Absolutely not!

And the year is now behind me.
My, how time flies.

Our Gratitude Mission

While there were days that I was hard pressed to think of something for which I was grateful…simply because not every day contained a major event or milestone…upon reflection, I realize that I was present more than I wasn't. I was Mindful far more than I was mindless. Able to live more in the moment than I'd ever done before. Able to savor the little flavors and nuances of life that generally go unnoticed. I experienced life and love. Experienced success and victory. Experienced death and loss. Experienced sadness and happiness. But most of all, I experienced. And for that I am grateful.

My journey. Your journey. Everyone's journey. All are special. All are remarkable. And I now know that more than ever.

This was just a peek at a year's worth of gratitude. There is so much more! And the best part for me…and I hope for you, as you perhaps embark on your own gratitude journey…is that it continues every day!

To end, one of my favorite Loving Kindness exercises:

May you be safe from suffering.
May you be as happy and healthy as it is possible for you to be.
May you have ease of being.

Be well.
Be grateful.

Terry's Take

Note to self: Don't read the super eloquent musings of Peter Franklin on the train! Even though I've read his chapter at least five times, I nevertheless was moved to tears AGAIN this most recent time. I need to carry tissues more often! I am so lucky to have a high school English teacher as one of the authors. Never in my wildest dreams did I imagine publishing a book that had poetry in it.

I have a major soft spot for kids and education. Hearing from a teacher in here touches the deep part of my soul. Even in writing my take on him, my eyes are welling up with tears once more! I am inspired by what he does AND *how he does it.* Teachers are molding our future. Just like I am always energized when I speak with Schelo from Chapter 1, I am motivated to do even more good in the world when I hear from people like Peter. Gosh, if every one of us had a teacher as incredible and forward-thinking as him, imagine how much we could accomplish and how happy we would be!

Our Gratitude Mission

Chapter 8

Donna Newman-Robinson

I Have a T-Shirt For That Too!

Age: 59

Hometown: Washington, DC

Current City: Atlanta, GA

Our Gratitude Mission

When I think of gratitude, I think of one of my favorite quotes. I meditate on it often as I go throughout my day. "Life is an experience of living every moment with commitment, grace, gratitude and love. Make your life a mission." (Anil Sinha) When I look at the different roles I play in my life I have to say: I have a T-Shirt for that too! You know, been there and done that! Often when I speak to someone who seems to have done or experienced everything you share with them, I think, "Yeah right, she knows everything about everything." Sound familiar??

I often say, "Well yeah, been there and done that too!!" As a woman, wife, mother, sister, aunt, cousin, grandmother, military veteran, nurse, teacher, and coach.....need I go on? The experiences I've had are mostly good and some not so good. However, I am forever grateful for them all. I have grown and learned about me as a result of living those experiences.

My gratitude mission started on April 1, 2014. April 1 is a date that is very special for me, as my only granddaughter was born on this day. I spend a lot of time reflecting on lessons and blessings bestowed upon my life. However, it wasn't always that way. My professional life consisted of twenty years of military service, which molded me into the woman I am today. During my military service, I spent very little time on my thoughts and feelings about gratitude. "Mission first" is the mindset of a military service member. Once the uniform came off for the last time, I felt disconnected on so many levels. Most importantly, I felt disconnected from myself. Journaling, prayer, meditation, and affirmations have been soul searching tools for me to discover the true power of gratitude. Since transitioning from military service I have been on a journey of commitment to the next mission in my life and that mission is ME. I am so grateful for this journey because through life's ups and downs, joy and pain, I am so humbled by it all! As eloquently stated by the late, beloved Dr. Maya Angelou, "Wouldn't Take Nothing For My Journey Now."

This journey of gratitude has opened me to the joy and pain of vulnerability. When my children were younger, they never really saw me cry. They shared that with me when they became older. When their dad and I divorced, I was emotionally detached. I had to be this way to survive years of a tumultuous marriage. Of course, when you are going through hell, you don't have the time or energy to process your deepest thoughts and fear. I was in complete survival mode.

After years of counseling, coaching, praying and journaling, I felt strong enough to trust myself more. I began to share my emotions with my daughters and others whom I trusted and cared for. They expressed discomfort and awkwardness with this change in me. However, I was committed to teaching them how I wanted to be treated and, more importantly, to articulate what I needed from them.

What a transformation! This opened my heart to vulnerability. This opened my heart to intimacy. This opened my heart to expressing and showing gratitude on a deeper level. This level became very spiritual for me. In some ways, it was a spiritual awakening in my soul, where gratitude was seeping through my pores. "There is a lesson in everything that happens to us, wisdom to be gained and gratitude to be given." (Nishan Panwar)

If we are to grow and move forward, we must learn from and live through life's lessons. It's hard to have growth without challenges or lessons. I am proud to be a lifelong learner and I seek out ways to gain knowledge and wisdom, with goals of becoming the best person I can be. There are several lessons that come to mind when I think of gratitude:

1. Do the right thing with the right attitude consistently. For that to happen, I strive to practice positive and on-purpose thinking every day. Through the self-work of journaling, praying, meditating, and practicing daily positive affirmations, I discovered and understood my purpose in life. My purpose is to serve and share with others. I relate that to my "I have a T-Shirt

for that too!" To share my story and experience is to empower, inspire and encourage.

By nature I am a very private person, so trusting my faith to step out of my comfort zone continues to be a challenge I meet every day. This challenge fills me with gratitude because I know that, in order to live my life's purpose, I must be consistent with the right attitude of transparency and authenticity.

2. Self-love is not selfish. To be the best of who you are, you must take the time to invest in your physical, emotional and spiritual well-being. It is difficult to do that if you are not holistically balanced and open to receive all the positive energy from the Universe. Your life doesn't shift by chance, it shifts by choice. I was so compelled to live this affirmation that I completed my vision board. This may sound silly to some, but for me, I considered this an act of self-care. Upon completion of this project, I felt accomplished because I knew once I completed it, I had something I could look at every day to keep me focused on my vision and my purpose. I was so grateful for this experience because I created a description of what defined me as ME:

D: determined, **O**: open to all possibilities and opportunities, **N**: non-negotiable, **N**: never quitting, **A**: authentically awesome. I am inspired. I am enough. If it's to be, then it's up to me.

3. Don't regret what might have been. Accept what is and rejoice in what is yet to be. It's easy to think and reflect on certain experiences with regret. We tend to call those experiences mistakes. I beg to differ. Without those experiences there would not be a story to share to empower, inspire or encourage others.

On this journey as a new business owner and life coach, I've come to think God has a sense of humor. I find myself thinking this way and get so excited when women veterans reach out and say they want to work with me. I am grateful when one of my sister veterans compliments me on my style of connecting and engaging with others. However, when it's time to sign on the dotted line of the contract, they change their mind at the time of true commitment. There was a time when I would get so upset and mad at God, because in my mind, I did all the right things to secure a client contract. I would think God was saying, "PSYCHE! Not yet! I fooled you this time!" Talk about crazy thinking!!! I am so grateful that I was able to reframe my thinking, stop giving my inner critic so much credit and believe that there is something bigger and better waiting just for me! You know why? Because I believe God wants me to share my gifts with the right people at the right time!

The 2014 holiday season was a period of time when my faith was tested on so many levels. There is one experience I would like to share with you. I was dealing with a tough situation: I needed clarity on the motivation behind the actions of a potential business partner that left me feeling disrespected and devalued. I felt confused and didn't know how to shift my energy from victim to victor. After some time reflecting on the entire situation, I prayed about it, meditated on it and marinated in it until I felt my energy shift to a place of being in the "present" at that moment. I am so grateful for that experience because I am a stronger person for it. A day of being in the "present" full of renewed energy and renewed focus on my purpose is a day to give thanks. I am grateful for the discernment of awareness and clarity. It's important not to take either for granted. Can you imagine how lost and discouraged we would be if we did not understand how critical awareness is to our very being? I am so grateful for family, friends, and colleagues who hold me accountable to the person I strive to be every day.

4. Faith is more powerful than proof. Living and learning from life's lessons is something we don't think about much because we are too busy living, that is until a significant event happens that captures our attention. When our lives change due to divorce, loss, pain, health issues, etc., we hope

and pray that we will become stronger as a result of living through those events. I know about these from firsthand experience.

In October 2014 I had a medical scare. My doctor discovered a mass in my right breast. I can't even begin to tell you all the feelings and emotions that came up for me. In the beginning of this experience, I had several other issues going on at the same time, so it was understandable that this medical scare was keeping me off balance. During this same time period I was preparing for family to visit to attend a popular women's conference with me hosted by the spiritual leader, Bishop TD Jakes. All I can remember during all this was telling myself, "Hold on Donna, you will be fed with the word of the Holy Spirit. God knows what you are going through. Just hold on. Everything that you are going through right now will turn out okay, just hold on until you get to the conference." Trust and believe I was holding on. My youngest sister, a dear cousin and a close friend were joining me for the event. None of them knew about my medical scare at the time. The anticipation of spending time and worship with Bishop TD Jakes had been building for months even before the diagnosis. Once I entered that building on the first day of the conference, my heart poured out such gratitude for holding on as promised. My soul and spirit were purged through my tears and I felt lighter and comforted! I was so grateful to share all that I was going through with my family and friends. They had no idea what was going on. This was the first time they ever witnessed me feeling so distraught yet at the same time exhibiting such strength. Does that make sense?

On the day of the scheduled biopsy, my doctor repeated the exam and diagnostic tests. Good news! The breast mass had decreased in size. In the meantime, I had started on a medication that had extreme risks and side effects if the biopsy was performed while taking the drug. Because these risks outweighed the likelihood of a malignancy, my doctor canceled the biopsy! More good news! I was to return in 4-6 months for a follow up. I was so grateful that my nursing experience helped me ask the right questions regarding my health. I was grateful for the medical team's patient and compassionate explanations, including showing me the different images of my breast mass. With that being said, I trusted their recommendations and my decision to re-evaluate this condition in 4-6 months. I have since been re-evaluated, and the breast mass is unchanged. It has not increased in size nor have the images changed. Another follow up is scheduled in six months.

I felt so grateful for the opportunity to share my vulnerability and transparency with my loved ones. I was empowered, inspired and encouraged by all those who kept me in their prayers during this difficult time. I'm sure I would have dealt with the medical scare differently if I had not been transformed in dealing with my emotional pain. I was so grateful to be strong enough to ask for help, share my fears and allow my family to comfort me without feeling ashamed. This experience left me feeling empowered – empowered to be confident and clear about what I need spiritually, emotionally, and physically.

This may sound simple to some who read this, but I've always struggled with asking for help. This comes from a complicated childhood. At the time, I always felt alone and like I could not depend on anyone but myself. I have since realized that I was not nurtured enough. I was loved and protected with no real sense of being nurtured. That was painful to admit, but imagine how I felt when I realized that was it!!!!! My work with a life coach helped me and supported me during this personal breakthrough and spiritual transformation. I couldn't help but wonder if this was the reason my children felt uncomfortable with the change in me. Maybe I wasn't very nurturing to them during their formative years. Deep isn't it? Gratitude is a funny thing. I believe, at times, we take that word for granted. If we don't take the time to step back, get quiet, and reflect on our "present" we miss so much.

5. Making life less difficult for others is to be encouraged. Creating happiness for others is to be rewarded. One of the many roles I cherish and

am most grateful for is being a grandmother. In this capacity, I have been able to make life less difficult for my daughters. I did not always have an opportunity to live this way though. I was a very busy mom raising four girls while on active duty serving my country. There was very little time for fun and relaxation. My household was very structured with little opportunity to do impulsive things. Time flew by and before I knew it I became a first time grandmother at 43 years old. When he (my first grandson) was born, I knew nothing about having little boys around, although as you'll soon read I would learn all about it. Two years later, my second grandson was born. I was in complete awe of them. I was so grateful to see my two oldest daughters become mothers and tackle the joys and woes of motherhood. So many times, they would say, "Mom, I don't know how you did it with all of us." I would smile or chuckle and then say, "Please, don't remind me."

    At this present time, I am the proud grandmother of five: four boys and one girl. I do not get the chance to see my grandchildren every day because they are being raised by their parents in different parts of the country. However, this past year, I did get the opportunity to become more connected with my youngest grandchild. I cared for him 24/7 for approximately five months while his mother traveled extensively for work. He's seven years old and his name is Daniel. Daniel is a funny child who affectionately calls me "Meema." Daniel and my husband played a teasing game about their displays of affection for me. My husband would tease Daniel with words like, "What did I tell you about kissing and hugging my wife?" So Daniel would slyly wait until he knew my husband was watching and purposely snuggle on me and sometimes kissed my cheek just to get a rise out of my husband. They love playing that game together. I love it too! Daniel loves to play video games, and ride his bike and he even loves math. Boy, is he a wizard with numbers! Spending time with him was so precious. Memories were created during his time spent with us. Daniel rejoined his mother and now has relocated to California. I miss him very much but I am so grateful for the time we bonded together. I once saw a bumper sticker on a car that read, "I should have had grandchildren first." That would be me!!

I believe to live a life full of gratitude you must practice self-awareness. Self-awareness is about self-acceptance. Self-acceptance gives you the necessary energy and freedom to grow. I strive to have an attitude of gratitude every day. I use my favorite gratitude quotes as daily affirmation practices to live by. You may notice several of my gratitude quotes are from Buddhist philosophers. I have a strong connection to the teaching and thinking of Buddhism because the practices are a means to changing yourself in order to develop qualities of awareness, kindness and wisdom.

1. "A moment of gratitude makes a difference in my attitude." (Nishan Panwar) This quote brings to mind a day of gratitude when I had a great telephone conversation with a friend I adore. Her name is Regina Collins. Regina and I spent a lot of time talking and catching up over many things. I miss seeing her and spending time with her like before. Our time on the phone brought up feelings of gratitude and appreciation for our friendship. Since my relocation to Atlanta five years ago, building new relationships became a priority to me. These relationships have since developed into special friendships with a few amazing people. However, the special friendships with those I left behind keep me grounded, grateful and appreciative of their continued support and love.
2. "Feeling grateful and not expressing it is like wrapping a present and not giving it."(William Arthur Ward) This quote reminds me of how blessed and grateful I feel knowing that divine intervention connected my husband and me after a forty year history of knowing each other. Feeling loved and being in love is one of God's greatest gifts because God is love. Not expressing gratitude for this is like NOT saying "I love you" to my husband every day.

3. "An attitude of gratitude increases abundance and diminishes fear."(Unknown) This quote is one of my favorites because it helps me take action when I feel stuck and afraid. I joined a community of like-minded women called Happy Black Woman. That's right! Look it up on the Internet! I signed up and became a part of this community's intense mastermind group. This is an example of true abundance in sharing and supporting each other as we multiply our personal effectiveness in quantum leaps. I am grateful to know "fear means go" with this group. Yes, that phrase is one of many that we consider as an affirmation to help us stay focused and motivated.
4. "Look back only with gratitude. The happy moments created memories and the sad moments created character."(Unknown) I think of this quote when I think about my transformation and personal breakthrough. I am grateful for love, light and a spiritual relationship with my Lord and Savior. I am grateful this relationship gives me peace and comfort when I navigate through feelings of pain and disappointment. I am grateful for the understanding that "this too shall pass." I have a T-Shirt for that too. Tomorrow is a new day!
5. "There is no one as strong as a person whose heart is always filled with gratitude." (Senora Roy) Strength is both subjective and objective. In December 2014, one of my daughters suffered a life threatening illness. I felt completely helpless. She lives in another state, yet I had to be strong for her and my entire family. The clock was ticking on getting her condition stabilized while I coordinated plans and obligations to be at her side as soon as possible. I am a believer in positive self-talk. Talking to myself sounds a little crazy but that kept me together. It kept me from breaking down from worry and fear that my daughter would lose the fight as well as lose her life. I arrived at her side with a heart

of relief and gratitude because I knew she would get better having her mom, her nurse, taking care of her. I was so grateful for the strength it took to overcome the fear of a near fatal medical emergency. The words from friends and family sharing their thoughts on how "strong" I was during this time encouraged me. The inner strength and faith kept me calm and at peace through this crisis. It kept me strong enough to share and articulate what that experience did for my family and me. My sharing of such detail is meant to empower, inspire and encourage others as they meet life's challenges every day. I am happy to report she has healed from this medical emergency and has resumed her activities of daily living.

6. "Develop an attitude of gratitude and give thanks for everything that happens to you, knowing that every step forward is a step toward achieving something bigger and better than your current situation." (Brian Tracy) This quote helps me remember to stop waiting around for the world to change. Change it myself.

7. "Life is an experience of living every moment with commitment, grace, gratitude and love. Make your life a mission." (Anil Sinha) This quote brings up memories of my years as a military woman. Those experiences transformed me into the woman I am today. The lessons learned helped me appreciate all that life has to offer and then some. It takes courage to live your life on purpose, and courage is the most important of all the virtues.

8. "Gratitude is a quality similar to electricity. It must be produced and discharged and used in order to exist at all." (Unknown) This quote is about getting out of your comfort zone, expanding your borders and challenging yourself. There was a time when I was confused and conflicted about whether I wanted to move forward in branding myself and my new business. I am so grateful for this shift in my mindset and being vulnerable enough to trust the

process of sharing that with my "Sisters United" networking group. I was so grateful for the positive energy we all felt, which allowed me to feel empowered by my transparency and authenticity. During a presentation at this meeting I told them how I kept getting in my own way and felt confused and frustrated. I learned a valuable lesson and was grateful for the opportunity to empower, inspire and encourage others in my networking group. No more stinking thinking!

9. "Gratitude also opens your eyes to the limitless potential of the Universe, while dissatisfaction closes your eyes to it." (Stephen Richards)

10. "Do not let your past rob your future. Each new day is a chance to make a new beginning. Count your blessings, live with gratitude and love with all your heart." (Unknown) This quote keeps me focused on appreciating the journey of defining and sharing my mission and purpose with all those who share my space. I spoke so passionately today with a sister veteran colleague about what I feel "called to do" in this season of my life. Although I articulated it so clearly, I still find myself having feelings of doubt. "Am I moving in the right direction? Why are things moving so slowly?" I'm pushing through areas where I feel less qualified. What she said to me validated and confirmed to me ... am I ready to erase my doubts? The answer is a resounding YES!! The wait is over! I am so grateful for that, knowing as long as I stay focused, and don't give up, the "signs" will continue to show up!

There are no impossible dreams, just our limited perceptions of what is possible. Letting go of fear, doubt, unrealistic expectations, shame, loss and regret opens our heart to all the wonderful and exciting opportunities here for us. In my mind, the following are things to let go of to create space for more gratitude in our lives:

1. *What isn't helping your soul smile and grow.* Life is to be enjoyed, not endured. Follow a path that moves you.
2. *Believing the best is behind you.* Your life isn't behind you; your memories are behind you. Your life is always right here, right now. Seize it! Choose to let each of your experiences today be a gateway to an even better tomorrow.
3. *Emotions that often get the best of you.* Stay strong. Even when it feels like things are falling apart, they are not. Take control of your emotions before they take control of you.
4. *All your reasons to be unhappy.* Stop looking for reasons to be unhappy. Focus on the things you do have and the reasons you should be happy. Positivity changes everything.
5. *Your ungrateful thoughts.* Happiness never comes to those who don't appreciate what they have.

If you can see the beauty of your aspirations, it doesn't matter if you achieve it all. Simply to aspire is no easy achievement. Appreciate the grey area between the extremes of success and failure: the journey, the experiences, etc. If the future seems overwhelming, remember that it comes one moment at a time. Breathe, exhale, give thanks and take one step at a time. Remember, no matter how slow your progress, you are still way ahead of everyone who isn't trying. Create a life that feels good on the inside, not one that just looks good on the outside. You can't expect to feel good if you surround yourself with negativity. Be with those who bring out the best in you, not the stress in you.

As I prepare to close this chapter of my gratitude mission, I am so full of emotion that it's hard to describe. Living a life with purpose is important. It gives me the opportunities and possibilities to show and share gratitude with the world. I would like to first give thanks to my Lord and Savior Jesus Christ, whose love I cannot live without. My life has been blessed in so many ways it brings tears to my eyes when I sit back and reflect on how powerful faith is in my life. I thank my Leo brother and coach trainer and colleague, Russ Terry, for giving me the opportunity to share in this mission with him. Last, but never least, I want to express my heartfelt thanks and appreciation to my wonderful husband, Wesley, and my beautiful children, grandchildren and extended family. I am who I am because of YOU!

Terry's Take

I love my Leo sis! The bond we have – sharing a zodiac sign, a love for gratitude, and more – is amazing. I also want to recognize Donna for all her years serving our country. My #1 amigo Craig Washington is also a veteran. I cannot express how grateful I am to Donna, Craig, and all the other men and women who make so many sacrifices for us and for others around the world.

I very much enjoyed Donna's writing style in sharing her gratitude pearls of wisdom. She gives us a few lists in her chapter. Maybe it's because I used to be a C.P.A., but I like numbers. Because her story is presented this way, it is as if she's telling us, "Hey you, pay attention, I am about to share some important stuff with you!" Her quotes, the things we should let go of, etc. are all excellent ways for us to live a better – and of course more grateful – life.

Our Gratitude Mission

Chapter 9

Toqeer Kazmi

The Journey Begins

Age: 53 years young!

Hometown: London, England

Current City: Ramsey, NJ

Our Gratitude Mission

This chapter is dedicated to my family both near and far who have encouraged me and supported me throughout this journey and continue to take the steps alongside me.

Back in 2012, I turned fifty and convinced myself "This is not a big deal, after all fifty is the new thirty." I proudly told friends of the upcoming event and that I welcomed "The Big 5-0." I can't say this for sure, but I think reaching the milestone caused me to start reflecting and taking stock of my life for the first time. Here I was a wife, of 23 years, a proud parent of two children, with two cats and a successful business career.

In truth, I was unhappy at work. The environment was toxic and I felt as if I was suffocating. My first child had left home to go to college. It had been a difficult transition for me, and coupled with being miserable at work, contributed to me being irritable and angry at home, seemingly all the time.

I was introduced to the concept of "reframing" by a friend, who suggested that I look at other reasons for situations rather than feel a victim of someone or something. I tried it, and began to feel and see things differently. A year later, I found myself enrolling to become a certified career and life coach with a professional coaching school. While I was still miserable at work, I was now seeking solutions and taking back control.

Last year, I realized that, if the next phase of my life was to be an empty nester, I needed to rediscover who I was, other than daughter, sister, wife and mother. This proved challenging, because I felt I had no identity other than those labels thrust upon me.

I met Russ Terry at the coaching school, which led me to read his first book, *My Gratitude Journal*. I must admit that I was somewhat skeptical, never being one for journaling and not fully understanding what a profound impact such a simple endeavor of gratitude could have. I read Russ's book at the end of March in 2014 and was charmed by the truthful and simplistic approach and how life-changing it turned out. I contemplated keeping my own gratitude journal.

As April approached, I was still considering the process of keeping a journal, but had not committed to take action just yet.

April 4, 2014

The day started with the realization that our beloved pet of 13 years had suffered a saddle thrombus, which left him paralyzed. This was devastating news. I spoke to my husband and we came to the conclusion that the humane decision was to put him down. I called my son, who lived in Virginia, to ask him if he wanted to drive home; he felt that we should not wait.

I went to the high school and broke the news to my daughter and took her with me to the vet's office, where they explained the procedure to us. We walked into the room to be greeted by Smokey Joe, our beloved cat who immediately started purring when he saw us. It was so hard to see him paralyzed and to make the decision to let Smokey go. He unconditionally loved each of us for the 13 years he was a part of our family, which was the majority of my kids' childhood. He comforted them when they had nightmares, listened to their problems (I came to learn this later) and played with them when they were bored. He'd been a steady companion to my husband when he was recovering from cancer and enjoyed the meals I cooked (many a snack was slipped to him under the dining room table).

My daughter, clearly distressed, turned to me and started questioning why things like this had to happen to such a kind and gentle cat. Grief is a difficult emotion to handle and I wanted her to remember the good times with Smokey. I thought of My Gratitude Journal *and suggested to her that we had a lot to be grateful for and that perhaps we should list some of the things that came to mind. We started compiling a list of what Smokey had brought to our lives. I still remember my daughter saying I am grateful for having had a pet even if he has to pass because he has given me the capacity to love and care for others.*

The story about Smokey is a simple yet powerful demonstration of how you can change the way you look at life by reframing your thinking and finding something to be grateful for. It inspired me to start my own gratitude journal. This chapter is about my gratitude journey and how it helped reframe my life.

Many times we have heard the adage "older is wiser" but that's not always the case, as I discovered during this year-long gratitude journey. There are many lessons I have learned from my children and others younger than me. The first lesson is the concept of limited vs. limitless. As an adult, I have found myself imposing limitations on what I can, or cannot, achieve and I have begun to realize that these self-imposed boundaries have been like ropes that have created tethers to hopes, dreams, and ambitions.

I learned this lesson from what I would have previously called naiveté and now I call dreams. When my son wanted to buy a theater and run an ecotourism company I kept asking him, "What about finances? How will you live? What can you do with this career? Isn't there anything more practical for you to pursue?" While I asked him these questions, privately I yearned for the opportunities to be able to explore and see the world unencumbered by practicalities.

When my daughter was given the chance to go to Peru and hike the Andes, she didn't give it a second thought – she set out to raise the money to do so. She succeeded, and with money to spare!

I am grateful that my children have taught me this lesson. During this year of gratitude, I decided to turn purpose into a plan, to stop dreaming without taking action and finding excuses for why I couldn't do things, and find the path to make them happen. I decided that I wanted to see more of the world, so this year I combined business trip opportunities with time off and managed to visit England, Vienna, Prague and Alaska, all within the space of a year. The moment I stopped thinking of why I couldn't do something and lifted the self-imposed barriers, I found the creativity to make things happen instead.

During the latter half of 2014, the news was filled with fear. The fear of Congress not passing a budget and the country reaching a fiscal cliff, the fear of the price of milk, the fear of rising terrorism in our own backyard, the fear of losing our children to social media influenced cults and groups, the fear of disease. This has been a year when the fear of infectious diseases has become all too real with Ebola outbreaks in Africa and a few cases literally too close to home. The concept of immunization and parents' rights to choose are hotly debated after an almost obscure infectious disease such as Measles became a major source of concern. So how does one focus on gratitude when fear is so widespread? It can come from the smallest of things; the following is a tweet from my son in February 2015.

Happy Birthday to my mom! I love you, and thanks for vaccinating me #VaccinateYourKids

February 3, 2015

I am grateful to have raised children who are thoughtful, kind and have passion for what they believe in. Whatever side of the vaccination debate one chooses, it is better to have an opinion with passion around that belief. Both my son and daughter are passionate about helping others, caring for the environment, and donating to causes in which they are interested. They believe in the benefits of living a full life, and continue to do so. I am blessed that they have a strong sense of adventure and of self-identity.

Looking back, I think the signs of the type of adults my children were to become were always there. My son spent his childhood rescuing injured animals to rehabilitate them, exploring the woodlands and hiking trails in the search for new plants and animals, and collecting water samples to view under a microscope. My daughter, who tries constantly to bring people together, is uncomfortable with conflict and tries so hard to please others. I recall an instance when my daughter, who was away at college, called home frustrated and upset that she had observed a person in a wheelchair who needed assistance to navigate a particularly steep ramp. She became overwhelmed with the guilt of not having helped the individual. Her hesitancy had been because she was fearful that the person would reject her offer/feel insulted with the offer/be embarrassed by her offer of help. It was interesting that it was her fear that held her back and that this fear had created such an overwhelming sense of guilt that she called home. We talked about the situation and she admitted she felt guilty that she hesitated in leaving the building and waited for someone to help, only to realize that help was not immediately forthcoming.

A moment's hesitation can lead to a lifetime of regrets. So for me the lesson learned is that fear should not be the reason to hesitate and that action will lead to good things.

During my year of gratitude I have faced my fear directly. I am very afraid of heights; as a child I cried on the Ferris wheel, closed my eyes on sky rides and avoided roller coasters. This obviously limited options at the carnival. Prior to starting my gratitude mission, I often felt that there were things I wanted to do, but I didn't prioritize their importance in life and held back. I never expressed out loud what I yearned to do, waiting for just the right time. Life moves on and I realized that there will never be a right time unless you allow it to be the right time.

One barrier that I set out to break through is my fear of heights. For as long as I can remember, I have been afraid of heights. I asked my daughter to take pictures of the scene as we drove around a mountain in Montserrat in Spain so I could see what I missed as I turned away from the mountain edge. I was tired of missing out because of fear so I set a goal that during this year of gratitude, I would step out of my comfort zone and face this fear.

I started out by setting a goal which I stated out loud, wrote down, and told friends and family of what I intended to accomplish. I decided that I wanted to zip line. I am not a thrill seeker and much prefer more sedate hobbies, so for those who know me it was a surprise for them to hear this.

I set a timeline: during the family vacation to Alaska! My husband and children were committed to supporting me and joining me on the adventure.

During the time leading up to the "grand adventure" I did a number of things in preparation. I spoke to friends who had experienced zip lining, read about the constraints, challenges and experience. I decided I needed to be more physically fit, and to do that I had to lose weight. I began to exercise more, made better choices with the food I ate and set an interim goal and a challenge: to participate in a ropes course. I asked my daughter to join me on the course. She was going to be my accountability partner to ensure I remained committed to the goal.

June 27, 2014

I did it! Grateful for the support of my daughter and the guide at Palisades Park Mall – who encouraged, cajoled and supported me as I climbed the ropes course...

I met my interim goal and managed to climb two levels of the ropes course of an 85 ft. high ropes and ladder course in the middle of Palisades Park Mall in New York. Throughout the experience I did not look down, and I was sweating profusely and relied heavily on the guide to stabilize the beam. I did it! If you asked me, "Did you remember going through each level?" my answer would be no. Before my year of gratitude I would have spent an inordinate amount of time brooding on what I did not do rather than celebrating my accomplishment. My gratitude journal has helped me celebrate the "what is" as opposed to the "what could be" and helps me live in the moment.

July 7, 2014

Today we arrived in Juneau after traversing the Tracy Arms Fjord. We arose early and made our way to the deck to join fellow passengers who huddled in blankets and listened intently as the guide described the history, and the plants and animals native to the area. I am grateful for the serenity and peace as we cruised through some of the most beautiful terrain I have ever seen.

We sailed through water, which sparkled as the light hit the small crystals of ice. All four of us were marveling at the exquisite shade of blue as chunks of ice drifted serenely alongside our ship. This created the perfect mood to start the day.

I had arranged for the four of us to zip line while on shore. Not just once, but five consecutive opportunities to traverse the line between majestic trees.

Zip Line One – knees shaking, palms sweaty I held fast to the trunk of the tree and had to be coaxed into turning around to face outwards as I prepared to step off the ledge. I took the step, held on tight to the hand grips and held my breath until the trunk of the tree loomed close. I gasped with relief when pulled in by the guide.

Zip Line Two – I took several deep breaths, took a step and ventured to look right and left (not down) before seeing the next tree which meant safety.

Zip Line Three – It took some coaxing but I agreed to release my death grip from the hand grips – for one fleeting moment I was airborne and hands free!

Zip Line Four – Time to look down, I told myself. I did so even if just for a second – I saw a river, smaller trees and an abundance of foliage all around.

Russ Terry

Zip Line Five – Time for the victory dance. I jumped off the ledge, waved my hands, wiggled my feet and just yelled really loud. It felt good!

I am grateful for the support of family, friends and for weight loss – being able to zip up the raincoat provided by the zip line company ... a simple thing that shows how far I have come.

Looking back I realize that if you are able to face your fears, nothing seems unattainable or improbable. It's true what they say "the sky's the limit." In my case the sky above the treetops and the forest below defined my limits on my great adventure on July 7, 2014.

When I was a child growing up in London, my parents took my siblings and me on a trip to Black Pool, England. We visited a carnival and more than 40 years later I still remember vividly standing alongside a display booth that just emitted raucous laughter each time you walked by. There was nothing to see, just to hear the many variations in this canned laughter. As children we laughed and laughed, and our parents joined in. Passersby stopped to join in the fun. This was a moment of sheer unadulterated joy. As adults we so easily lose sight of the essence of pure joy.

Being on this journey has taught me that joy is infectious. Seeing a child laugh, a simple smile from the barista in the coffee shop or some light-hearted banter can lift the spirt and create a joyful day.

My children have introduced me to so many internet-based humorous vignettes, from "blueberries, blueberries," to humorous lip sync videos and political parodies to witty memes and "100 ways to love your cat." Many times we have been sitting together during the evening, pulled up a video and laughed until the tears flowed. Laughing from the belly clears the lungs, exercises the muscles and feels good! During this last year, seeing a child smile or the sound of laughter or happy chatter has helped lighten the mood, and made the dullest weather day seem not so bad. When you find opportunities to smile the day passes in a most pleasant way.

June 21, 2014

Today I am grateful that the entire family was together for dinner. It has been a challenge with my son travelling to Peru, plus college visits and business trips. We had a simple meal and settled in to relax for the evening. I sat back and watched the children in one moment tease one another and in the next have a thoughtful and intense discussion with their father. I am grateful for these moments together and realize that life can change as rapidly as the topics of conversation have today. The one thing that can remain constant though is our memories. My gratitude journal is one way to capture these memories before they dissipate. I hope that when I look back and read these lines I can recapture the joy and peace of this day.

This year, I had the opportunity to visit England to see my family, which is always a bittersweet time. Leaving England more than 26 years ago, I missed out on many of the family gatherings, was not there when my mother passed away and have missed out on seeing my nephews and nieces grow up to be such wonderful and accomplished young adults.

One night my sister and I were seated at the kitchen table reminiscing about the past. We talked about our mother. We laughed and we cried. During her life, my mother had such a joyous and optimistic outlook. Her favorite quote was, "If you worry you die, if you don't worry you die…so why worry?" We shared our favorite stories about growing up and about our mom's life and legacy. It was at that moment that I realized what it was that I truly wanted in my life….

I realized that the legacy I want to leave is not that I was a successful executive, or that I was a great mother, wife, daughter, friend (or whatever label the relationship gave me) but that I left the world a better place for having known me. We grieve for ourselves for what we are being deprived of when a loved one leaves us, and as time passes people will say that time heals all wounds. I say though that time gives us the opportunity to come to terms with what our initial grief did not, and that is: "What did we gain, learn and experience in that fleeting time we had with the departed?"

So as I reflect back I am thankful that I had a great role model in my mother. The following is the excerpt from my gratitude journal on Mother's Day:

May 11, 2014

I was attending a workshop once and was asked the question "Who do you admire and want to be like?" While many people name celebrities and famous people, I had a sudden realization that the person I most wanted to be like was not famous, rich nor on a reality show but had made a profound impact on my life. It is only after she passed that I realized that she had positively impacted not only me but many others in the community. That person was my mother, so on this Mother's Day let me share a few things about my mother that have served to shape my life.

My mother was a "universal mother" – my parents owned a business and my mother often had a pot of food cooking in the small kitchen at the back of the store. The store was in a college town and often students would drop in hungry and homesick. My mother opened her kitchen and heart to them and fed them. My mother never saw people for their differences and never seemed to be bothered by the heavily tattooed or pierced people that came to shop. I realized this when I came home from college on Mother's Day to find a very heavily tattooed and pierced young man towering over my mother, brandishing a huge bouquet of flowers which he presented to her for Mother's Day. It seems she had adopted him as well.

My first vacation after graduating college was a trip to Turkey with my mother. I was amazed at her sense of adventure and spirit (a side I had seldom seen in the day-to-day life we lived). On this journey I discovered her keen interest in the people, places and history and we immersed ourselves in the culture. She managed to convey her optimism, and language did not seem to be a barrier for her. In fact she "was adopted" as everyone's mother on our coach trip across Turkey. My mother received letters from her "Turkish children" after our return to England.

When I left Britain to live in the States, my mother was extremely concerned about being able to stay in contact with me. This was long before computers and Skype and other modern conveniences. She promptly enrolled in an evening class to further improve her written English so that she could write to me. I have the first letter she sent me as well as the essay she wrote in evening class. The lesson I learned from this was that you should always seek ways to grow and if you face an obstacle don't let it deter you. Find a way around it or over it, or simply overcome it.

My mother's work ethic was unparalleled. She worked full-time alongside my father, raised a family, and participated actively in the community. We never felt neglected or unloved. The community was her extended family, and when she died I truly got to see the person she was. Her service was attended by many people, a very diverse gathering of individuals who shared stories of their experience with my mom. It is interesting as I think back that very few people probably knew my mom's name because she was always called mom, sister, or aunty. My mother's legacy, upon which I strive to emulate, is best described by the people who say, "The world is a better place for having known her." I can safely say, blessed am I to have known you, to my Mother on Mother's day - may you find eternal peace in heaven.

The best thing you can do is make time for yourself, which will free you up to make time for others. When you don't take time for yourself, the quality of your interaction diminishes.

As I look back on my life, I spent many years in the pursuit of building my career. As a result, I felt guilty that I was not as involved in the school activities as some of the other mothers. The guilt that I was not "like the other mothers" was ever present. I felt that the other mothers were active in the PTO, baked for bake sales, volunteered as chaperones and were intimately familiar with the activities in town and at school. There are many working mothers who are probably in the same situation and face the same type of guilt. This is a question I have spent a lot of time thinking about. My mindset shifted though after I asked myself the question "Do you work to live? Or live to work?" When I started this journey, I was "working to live." I was not happy at work. I felt undervalued and frustrated to the point that I lost motivation. I was working solely for the income so that I could continue to help meet the financial needs of the family. I found that even when home, I was only half present, often preoccupied and distracted on work-related matters that created even more stress.

Prior to marriage, family and other commitments, I had "lived to work" – I thrived on learning, growing and building my career. I was undivided in my pursuit of being successful. Now, I am at an interesting crossroads – I could stop working and we could scale back on how we lived, or I could find another job where I could be happier.

I started a values exercise which forced me to identify what was most important to me. The following is what I came up with:

- Work in a place that treats people with dignity and respect, and has integrity
- Where I can bring value and be valued as a business partner
- Where I can make a difference

The values exercise helped me define my needs. Good news! I found a workplace that better aligned with my personal values, and am happy to say the company offered me a position, which I gladly accepted. The following is an excerpt from my journal describing something at my new job:

May 22, 2014

Today, I received an invitation to attend an informal get together with employees after work. I assumed I had received the invitation in error because there were names of people in various departments that I did not work with. Upon inquiry I discovered it is a common practice for employees to get together to socialize after work, and the invitation is open to anyone and any level in the company. I am grateful that I am now working with a group of people who value the folks they work with and are so warm and welcoming. What was even better is that the executives attended as well. A great leadership group to join!

This has been a year of reflection and I realize now that, up until this point, I spent a lot of time on needless guilt. My family has remarked how much happier I seem. I have had conversations with my children and husband about the guilt I had about being a working Mom. Needless to say, they never realized it, and never expected me to be any different than I am.

As much as I enjoy the work I do, at the end of the day it is a job that satisfies financial needs and some personal needs. Having spent so much time reflecting on the possibility of not working, I realized that if I didn't work I did not know what I would do.

May 15, 2014

I had a great conversation with Brynn, who has been considering a career in organization development (which is my area of expertise). I was glad to help someone. The coaching conversations sparked some great questions for her, which I realized I should also ask myself. I am grateful that this conversation took place.

My thought for the day... If you did not do what you do and could make a choice what would you choose to do?

The question was very timely – I had always "lived to work." What would I do if I didn't work?

As the prospect of becoming an empty nester loomed, I realized that work - while satisfying - was not something you elect to do "when you feel like it" and came with certain expectations and commitments. What would I do if I had the freedom of choice with no obligations and responsibilities? What was I interested in? Could I even specify my hobbies? Upon reflection, it seemed that most of my time had revolved around family and work and I had given no time to myself. As a working mother, I didn't carve out "ME" time. I was already guilty (in my eyes) of not being like the other mothers and for taking time away from my children. The reality is that we all need time for ourselves and I became quite creative at making the time for them, even though I was not conscious of what I was doing.

Looking back, I realize I made excuses for not doing things. I cannot go hiking because it is raining/my back hurts/I have other things to do. We shouldn't take vacation without the children, because vacations are meant to be family time. Or are they?

I realize that there is guilt associated with inaction as well as action. Each time I did not go hiking with the family or with my spouse, I was guilty of "not spending time with them, guilty for saying that I was not interested in the same things as them, guilty for secretly enjoying my few hours of solitude."

Is it better to accept things for what they are (it is what it is) or create the change you desire (where there's a will there's a way)?

Our Gratitude Mission

If I had acknowledged the need for personal time and prioritized it as a part of life, the guilt would have gone away and I would have enjoyed my time more purposefully.

One of the reasons we claimed for not planning a vacation was since this was the first year of college for our daughter and it was a transition year, how could we go away in case she "needed us"?

I am grateful that technology has given us the solution for some of these obstacles. The use of FaceTime, Skype, WhatsApp, Snapchat and quite simply texting has reduced the dependency factor.

During my year of gratitude, the topic of technology has come up many times: the ability to binge watch TV shows (a guilty pleasure), to instantly capture moments in time with Snapchat, to have engaging dialogue (Twitter, IM, text), to receive instant news, weather, traffic alerts, and to keep in contact across the miles (Skype with dad and family in England).

December 31, 2014

I am thrilled my children bought me the Amazon Fire – I can now binge watch Downton Abbey! I am amazed and so grateful for the technology that helps me speed watch programs and save time!

It was one of these moments of realizing accessibility is so easy that "allowed" us to vacation overseas without the children. This allowed me to renew my interest in travelling, explore local customs and culture and enjoy the history of the region and the unique architecture of the places visited. The guilt that prevented earlier action quickly dissipated as I realized that we were still accessible and in contact and no one was bothered about the decision except me -- yet another case of self-imposed guilt. So what was the lesson learned? Simply that we spend too much energy worrying and constraining ourselves with self-imposed limitations and if we simply changed the question from why we shouldn't do something to why we should, that may be the momentum to take the next step forward.

In other words, look at the possibilities and whatever you're considering is more likely to become a probability. Hearing my children, friends and others remark on how "happy and content" I seem is a validation that this is the right journey for me.

October 20, 2014

Today, I realized how awesome technology can be: we skyped with Mohsin (our son) in Peru, where he is getting ready to lead another group into the Amazon. I am happy to see that the accommodations in town are relatively good and the wireless reception is even better. It seems parrots are now a regular feature in our FaceTime conversations!

After the call with him, we called Masooma (our daughter) through FaceTime. I was most concerned about leaving the country since this is her first semester at college and she is all alone in the United States. She seemed happy, and has already identified the friends with whom she will dorm next year. She showed me how she had decorated her room and it looks warm and inviting, and the bed was made!

October 21, 2014

Today we went to Wienerqald Wunderling just outside Vienna and took a boat ride on the largest underground lake in Europe. The history of this region is fascinating. The castles are opulent, and the murders/deaths/suicides are big mysteries just waiting to be solved. I am so grateful to the historians, who have made so much effort to preserve and maintain the stories and antiquities for many generations to come.

We ended our day at the Opera house. Even though there was no show today, I have been inspired to add attending an opera to my bucket list

Our Gratitude Mission

October 22, 2014

Until today, Prague had been one of those destinations that I had only heard about and never would have imagined that I would be able to see it for myself. I am so grateful that travelling around the cities has been so easy, with great rail service and excellent bus tours. Today I spent a lot of time browsing the marketplace. It was so incredibly neat to see the many shades of crystal and glass and the exquisite detail to each piece of blown glass sculpture. I have always admired glass chandeliers, however was amazed at the craftsmanship and quality of those on display in one store in Prague.

My husband saw me admiring two chandeliers in particular and suggested we buy them. I looked at him and said, "We can't do that – how are we going to carry those back with us?"

He simply said, "Why not?" This reminded me again of my new philosophy – looking for reasons to make possibility a probability. We ordered the two chandeliers and arranged to have them shipped home.

Every time I look at these chandeliers, I am so grateful that my husband challenged my assumption. It is not so much the item but the memories it evokes that makes it so worthwhile.

Since making the decision to take time for myself, I am trying a variety of hobbies to see what I like/don't like.

In May I enrolled in a class to learn upholstery. I found I enjoyed looking for items that needed work and TLC, browsing antique markets and estate sales. I did not like the precision and slow pace needed for working on each project though! In June I pulled out my sewing machine (after all you have to sew the fabric for the upholstery projects). I discovered that while it is easy to sew, the challenge is in the straight lines and threading the needle. I continued with the projects, especially since I enjoyed meeting with my classmates and watching the progress of the various projects.

In October I started knitting – I had forgotten how much I enjoyed it! The various textures of yarn, the ability to play around and discover a "new pattern," the satisfying click clack of the needles. It's very rewarding to see the end product and get requests for college colored scarves for my daughter and her friends so that they could wear them to the college sports events. I was so surprised when my nieces, brother and sister asked for their own custom colored scarves. (What was even more gratifying was the sincere pleasure each person had in receipt of my humble gift.) There is no greater joy than the gift of giving and being appreciated. Take the time to acknowledge and appreciate those around you for the simple pleasures they bring to make the quality of your life better.

So what's next for me? This month I am going to learn how to crochet, and over the summer learn new recipes and make good use of the bounties from my planted vegetable garden. In fall, I plan to take up photography to make most use of the beauty of the colors of the fall foliage and the transition that seasonal change brings.

Much as each season changes, we too need to be ready and accepting to change. There is beauty and purpose for every segment of our life's journey.

The lessons learned cannot be taken away and can only be added to.

1. Lessons from the sandbox – as children we have a thirst to learn. We ask the question why and don't settle easily. Take a lesson from the child you were and continue to ask the question why. When we stop questioning, we stop learning.
2. Fear has its limits. If you face your fear, you will stop limiting yourself.
3. Joy is infectious – look for moments of joy until you no longer have to look and it becomes a part of the way you live.

4. Live your life for the legacy you wish to leave and ask yourself will it be a legacy worth leaving?
5. Guilt is self-imposed and can result from action as well as inaction. Sometimes we spend so much time thinking about reasons to be guilty that it takes away from the satisfaction of a decision being made.
6. Make time for yourself – because when you do, you free yourself up for more meaningful time spent with others.

Dear reader I hope you enjoyed taking this journey with me and encourage you to start your own journey.

Best of luck

Toqeer

Terry's Take

I met Toqeer at the Coach Training school in April 2013. Reading her chapter made me feel so much closer to her, and to her son, daughter and husband. This past summer, she hosted a lovely get-together at her home. I was so excited to meet her family and I am honored to say the feeling was mutual. Furthermore, many of her colleagues from her new job were there, and EVERY one of them said, "Oh wow YOU'RE the Russ Terry that we have heard so many great things about!" Life is so great when people say nice things about us, and I am grateful to Toqeer for doing so. Who can you say something nice about today?

I appreciate her sharing some of the struggles she has had over the years. Even though I'm a man, I was raised Catholic, and went to Catholic school from first grade through senior year of college, so I know a thing or two about guilt. Women in particular though seem to feel guilty more than men. Ladies, if you are reading this, I hope you are inspired to let go of that guilt. You are working hard and giving your all, and I would bet money you're doing a pretty darn awesome job.

Our Gratitude Mission

Chapter 10

Marguerite Pierce

My Gratitude Shift

Age: 32

Hometown: Brooklyn, NY

Current City: Queens, NY

Our Gratitude Mission

Interested in improving the way you think and feel? Becoming more grateful is the answer. I don't just mean the perfunctory type of gratitude, but a more mindful, directed and conscious expression of gratitude for any and everything that affects you. Did you wake up this morning? Be grateful. Did you have clean water to brush your teeth and shower? Be grateful. Did you tell someone you loved them? Be grateful. Did someone tell you "You are loved"? Be grateful. You see where I'm going? Express it as a complete thought - not just one that's fleeting never to be recovered - but as words aloud, as a journal entry, poem or even a song. There was a time though, that I didn't grasp this concept because I was too busy focusing on what was wrong and what I DIDN'T have and why I didn't have it – I had a limited mindset.

Before I discovered the wonders of gratitude, I had a lot of resentment. This self-directed resentment was shrouded in more than $50,000 of student-loan debt I collected to earn a degree in a field that barely held my interest from a school that was a last minute choice. I went to a really good high school and got good grades but choosing which colleges to apply to was an enigma. There was pressure from my parents not to go away like I initially wanted. In hindsight, that pressure wasn't overwhelming and I should have just done it. But as a goody two-shoes 17 year old, I assumed leaving for school was not an option. I was headstrong but not rebellious enough to break rules or go against my parents' suggestion. I don't say this to assign or even share the blame; I accept full responsibility for my decision or lack thereof which is why it haunted my mind. I had control over the situation and I just let it slip completely through my fingers.

I thought of the school choice and the student-loan debt as the heart – or "chest" – of my resentment that mutated and grew other parts, like a creature from a horror story. The head with its gnashing teeth represented my anger for being an adult who didn't know what I wanted to be when I grew up. It also had five misshapen appendages likened to arms to represent all of the industries I've worked in. Some were short and stunted nubs to represent opportunities that were short-lived. Others were muscular with calloused hands to demonstrate years of hard work dedicated to an unappreciative small-business owner.

The legs and feet were sinewy and gargantuan like tree trunks; always slimy with sweat from continuously running in one direction without a sense of any final destination. And later a second head formed. This one was more docile than the first. It was responsible for doing all of my jobs well despite a lack of fulfillment and passion. It never said no and took on more work without additional compensation.

Picture such a creature – covered in black and green scales, on your back, weighing you down for ten years, like the Acme Anvil did Wile E. Coyote. I was stuck in a past that remained unchanged no matter how often I visited it. I would play decisions over in my head but I could never have a different outcome. It was similar to the *Black Mirror* (on Netflix) episode called "The Entire History of You," which takes place in a futuristic society where we [humans] have a "grain" implanted in our brains that allows us to literally rewind moments in our personal history like a DVR. That's essentially what I was doing, constantly.

My perspective began to shift in 2011 after I read Don Miguel Ruiz's *The Four Agreements*. While they may each seem like common sense, when applied, they will alleviate most conflicts. However, when ignored, misery and suffering ensue, which is exactly what I experienced. The first agreement encompassed the resentment I felt: Be Impeccable with Your Word is what the Toltec wisdom advises. Speak with integrity; don't use your words against others or yourself. Did you get that? Don't use your words against yourself. Over the span of ten years I used a ton of words against myself: "You should have gone away to school." "Why didn't you transfer out?" "You really blew it," "Good luck paying off those loans," "You're a coward, for not asking for more money but taking on even more responsibility." This is interesting to recount because I can bet that none of my friends or loved ones thought I was unhappy or that I was plagued with such thoughts so often.

Not only were people unaware of how I felt, but I exacerbated the issue by choosing not to tell them, making it that much more intense. I wouldn't say I was depressed though; perhaps it was more like I was addicted to feeling sorry for myself. Reading that book was the start of my path to healing. The next thing I had to do was take some form of action.

There was no dramatic meltdown on a subway platform or any "I hate you, God" conversations in my head. I was just tired of brooding instead of living. The worst part: believing that everyone else had it all figured out and I was the only one with this plight. I thought no one else was carrying their own resentment burden. But, the more I thought consciously about it, the more I realized how untrue it was. I was slowly taking responsibility for my thoughts. I began to take a closer look at each aspect of the resentment I harbored. There was nothing wrong with any of it; the major, the university, the aimless jobs. The two heads, five arms, slimy legs and feet ... they were a product of a negative perspective. I wasn't angry, but rather ambitious to succeed and to find my way. The five arms were experience. The two legs were rooted in resilience; stopping and quitting weren't options. Once reframed it wasn't a hideous creature after all, but rather a skewed view of what makes me unique.

Instead of complaining about what I didn't have and why I didn't have it, in early 2012 I started to pin visual representations of the things and experiences I wanted to attain on a corkboard in my bedroom -- my first vision board. It sits on top of my oversized hard-cover makeup case, facing my bed. It is the first thing I see when I wake up and the last thing I see before going to sleep. It has more words than it does images. Each time I glance at my vision board I'm reminded of what qualities it takes to obtain these milestones or attain a certain mindset and I see the power in every single step I take forward. In the center are the words "DEBT FREE" in neon orange and blue, to signify my mission to abolish that student-loan debt that often feels like shackles on my feet.

Across the top are the four agreements, each in a distinct font and color. 1. Be Impeccable with Your Word. 2. Don't Take Anything Personally 3. Don't Make Assumptions 4. Always Do Your Best. When things go off track, I'm able to determine which one of the agreements is being challenged.

If I wanted to invite more into my life, I had to accept and be grateful for all I already had. This alleviated the strain felt by carrying that resentment burden for so long. My finances, health and love life suffered as a result of not letting go. I felt inadequate and I was settling for jobs that I never wanted and a boyfriend that treated me poorly. Luckily, though, I had an 'a-ha' moment to start being more grateful. I reframed my complaints into expressions of gratitude. I wanted to try the exact opposite of being resentful. Yes, my student loan debt was outrageous, but I was grateful I had a job that paid a decent salary for me to meet the monthly payments consistently. My job didn't necessarily provide fulfillment, so I was grateful to volunteer with TheFutureProject.org. Through it, I was paired with a high school senior to work on completing an end of year project of their choosing – be it a dance performance, art gallery exhibit or fundraising for a specific cause. In my experience complaining begets inaction, and when I became more aware of all the things to be grateful for, the more I wanted to DO something to improve my circumstances.

Now, I know that I am where I am because that's where I ought to be. The Universe hasn't conspired against me. There's no dark cloud above my head. Being grateful allows me to take ownership of everything I wasn't happiest about. During this process I started to watch *Super Soul Sunday* on the Oprah Winfrey Network. Deepak Chopra was Oprah's guest on the episode that aired on April 29th, 2012. He shared a mantra that has been with me ever since. "The past is gone. The future is not here. Now I am free from both." This too, sits on my vision board.

This gratitude mission complements my shift in perspective. Adding the daily focus on the things, experiences, ideas, and people I am grateful for allows me to tune in to everything around me at that very moment. I'm committed to being fully present in the present.

Fast forward a year and practicing gratitude daily has definitely provided an additional shift in mindset. The time it takes me to get out of a sour mood has decreased tremendously. It keeps me rooted in the present instead of ruminating on past events I cannot change.

This journey has made me even more resilient. It taught me to savor the positive and let go of everything else. That's not to say that I didn't experience any disappointments or challenges over the course of the year. There were times when I doubted myself over the big and small alike. I just chose not to wallow in those moments. Instead, I managed to provide a good example by moving forward despite my fears and doubts. I've grown familiar with discomfort and now correlate it with signs of growth.

Being able to dig deep and uncover the lessons hidden in my lowest moments was extremely valuable. This is where perseverance and resilience are born and I'm grateful to be able to claim those traits as my own. The thing about those disappointing and challenging moments, for me at least, is that I often painted them to be far worse than they actually were.

One of the themes that was present throughout my journal was "living in the now." Positive thinking and self-awareness have allowed me to be more conscious of those self-sabotaging moments and overcome them. Sometimes it was a quick fix like reciting my favorite affirmations aloud: "One of the hardest decisions you'll face in life is choosing whether to walk away or try harder," "Excessive worry will never change the outcome" or in times of complete exasperation my go-to is an over dramatized "Jesus, take the wheel" which always generates a chuckle and my entire mood is changed for the better. Other times it took sticking to a plan long-term. Overall, participating in this mission has kept me grounded and in the present. I'm grateful for ALL experiences because I get to learn and grow from each and every one. This journey has allowed me to savor the things I sometimes take for granted: a wonderful home, an amazing fiancé, a stable job, a budding business and phenomenal friendships. Gratitude can be SO unlimited when we think of all the things and people we have been taking for granted.

Writing this gratitude journal has also taught me patience. While I'm familiar with the concept, up until now it had been difficult for me to practice it. I may have been cool as a cucumber on the outside but the cacophony of thoughts in my head indicated otherwise. Luckily, I've been able to reflect on such moments with humor and when necessary, several glasses of wine.

I used to be in such a rush to experience the next accomplishment, goal or phase of life that I forgot to relish the present moment. When I was 13 I couldn't wait to be 16 so I could get a learner's permit. When 16 came, I couldn't wait for 18 for that college experience (that I never really had). When 18 came, I couldn't wait for 21 to be able to graduate, head out in the world and order my first legal Amaretto Sour. My palate sure has changed. I'm not so sure I could get one of those down now. I was always in constant need for the next thing without realizing where I was and what I had currently were once among the things I so excitedly wanted to obtain. I was so focused on climbing the mountains ahead of me that I forgot to look back at how far I had already climbed.

Writing these gratitude journal entries made this abundantly clear. Slowing down is not a detriment, it's a necessity.

Let's begin with a few pivotal entries from my year.

July 7th, 2014

Anyone's journey is as unique and valuable as anyone else's journey. This is a foundational principle taught during my year-long training to become a Certified Professional Coach. I put a lot of stock into this one, but I still have a habit of comparing my journey to the journeys of others. Comparing journeys hasn't served me well. It has left me with feelings of inadequacy. However, I am grateful for comparisons when comparing where I was in the past to where I am now, because focusing on the accomplishments I have made instead of the accomplishments of others provides me with so much motivation! I know I can make the changes I want because I draw strength from previous experiences. I started speaking up more frequently after a couple years of constantly being misunderstood or taken advantage of. I started working out more when I wasn't comfortable with the way I felt or looked. My energy is best served by looking at the steps I'm currently taking to get to where I am going instead of deconstructing the steps of others that got them where they are. Going natural with my hair really emphasized to me that journeys aren't one size fits all, what worked for some may not work for others. Keep reading, because this concept of comparison was emphasized again in February 2015 when I took a Capoeira [kap-oo-air-uh] class.

July 22nd, 2014

Sigh, today was tough for me. I felt completely overwhelmed by building my Life & Career Coaching business and by my current workload at my day job. It was the former that was most pressing and little things happened all morning that compounded my mood. First, part of my homemade lunch spilled through two plastic bags and stained the canvas bag I carried it in – beet juice leaked out from the plastic container I thought I sealed them in. Additionally, I left my bottle of mineral water on the Long Island Railroad as I was rushing to gather my things to get off the train.

During the subway ride I decided to use the time productively, brainstorming some additional business names, as I was no longer satisfied with the ten I came up with last week. Also, the advice I got from a Meetup on July 17th was really getting to me, so I felt determined to come up with a more powerful and creative business name. The Meetup organizer, Christine, had gone through the Institute for Professional Excellence in Coaching (iPEC) program a few years back and suggested I come up with a business name catchier than BLIS Coaching. BLIS stands for Believe. Love. Inspire. Succeed. Normally, I wouldn't become obsessed with someone else's opinion; however I wasn't entirely set on that business name myself. It was something I intended to change eventually, but now this has jumped to the top of my list.

I continued to come up blank during my ten minute subway ride and became frustrated with my efforts. I got to work and I could hardly focus and concentrate on any one of the dozens of tasks I'm responsible for – I worked through as much as possible and I asked my supervisor for permission to leave early that afternoon (1pm) as I needed a mental breather.

I left and went to do something nice for myself to lift my spirits. I visited my favorite nail salon near work and got my usual manicure, pedicure and 20 minute foot massage. I hadn't had the foot massage in a while and I sure needed it. That brightened my mood immensely, but there was still anxiety about having a strong business name, and being a successful business owner period. So I decided to spend the remainder of the afternoon in Brooklyn Bridge Park. I ate my lunch there and felt this was an opportune moment to meditate.

I managed to find a guided meditation album, via the Amazon Cloud App, on releasing anxiety and fear. Being out in the sun and feeling the breeze was an added bonus for my meditation experience. I felt a sense of calm and protection and I had faith that everything was going to work out as it should. My confidence was restored and I was able to breathe normally again. I'm thankful for today's experience as we can get so bogged down in our ambitions and our day-to-day responsibilities that sometimes we just have to take a break from it all, get some peace and simply go back to the basics!

February 13th, 2015

In the spirit of doing new things, I took my first ever Capoeira class at Capoeira Nago Academy in Midtown Manhattan. I am grateful that my friend Sara Manii invited me. Capoeira is a Brazilian martial art that combines dance, acrobatics and music. Since this was my first time, the instructor had me stick to the basics. The basics were no joke and this is coming from someone with a decent fitness foundation – albeit I haven't worked out in several weeks, but that's neither here nor there. I practiced a lot of defensive moves, lunges and kicks to the left and the right. I also practiced some intense leg hops. I have no idea what they are called, but you place your palms on the floor, butt in the air, lift one leg up, hop up on the standing leg and switch with the other leg. That works out your shoulders and core.

Throughout some of these moves my balance was horrible and I got frustrated. That frustration intensified when I glanced over at the other class participants who were executing moves with the grace of swans and the speed of a cheetah.

Lesson Emphasized: So what if I was off balance. It was my first time. To top it off, I was better at all the moves at the end of the class than I was at the very beginning. Be happy with and grateful for whatever progress you make no matter how small. You have to start somewhere.

And now let's take it from the top.

April 7th, 2014

I'm grateful to have been invited to the book-release party for Russ Terry's *My Gratitude Journal*. I met Russ during the spring session of my coach training at iPEC. His energy is contagious, which is why I wanted to keep in touch with him -- to constantly be inspired and to be able to learn from his success. He managed to write personal notes in everyone's books as well as signing it. What a tremendous undertaking! I was absolutely impressed by such a personal gesture. He actually took the time to remember an encounter with each person that showed up. How amazing is that? Within the first pages of the book Russ makes a suggestion for the readers to start their own gratitude journals and possibly be part of his second book which would be a collection of different entries from different participants. I want to be a part of this project; hence this first entry.

Lesson Learned: When you're inspired by something DO NOT let that moment pass, take some step toward whatever it is you were inspired to do. In this very instance I practiced what I preach and sent Russ an email the very next day, April 8th, expressing my interest in participating in this journey. Often we tell ourselves "later" when it really means "never." So, I didn't allow any doubt to kick in and, even if it did, I already made the commitment so I would have to follow through to remain impeccable with my word, which is the first of The Four Agreements (mentioned earlier).

April 16th, 2014

Today was a big day! I facilitated my first workshop ever on anything! I spoke about developing self-awareness and how that can lead to better decision making skills. I was worried about low turnout, but there were 16 people in attendance! I am completely grateful for and thrilled with my performance.

I was not one bit nervous and absolutely loved seeing everyone's interaction and energy. After the workshop ended I spoke with one of the attendees, Mayra. She was extremely receptive to the subject matter of the workshop. So much so that she invited me to a networking event she was hosting over the summer. I'm excited to learn more about her event and the people who will be in attendance. I am grateful for her participation in my workshop and her invite.

April 28th, 2014

I'm grateful for birthdays. I enjoy celebrating the birth of others. I use my own birthday as a reflection point. I consider all that I've accomplished as well as those things still remaining on my to-do list. Additionally, while waiting in the doctor's office I realized that this year I'll be celebrating my golden birthday! This is when the age you're turning matches the day you were born. In my case I will be 31 on the 31st of August! I'm so excited to celebrate this milestone in about four months. On top of that, not only was it my boyfriend Dexter Henry's birthday this past Saturday, the 26th, but I had the opportunity to celebrate the birthday of one of Dexter's colleagues this evening. It's an amazing feeling to be immersed in so much birthday love and energy.

May 13th, 2014

Chivalry is not dead ladies and gentlemen! On my way to work this morning I got on the number 3 train at the Atlantic Avenue stop in Brooklyn, and a man gave up his seat for me even after I refused because I didn't actually need it. Yes, I had a couple of bags - my lunch and my gym clothes for the week - but I was far from struggling with my packages. Additionally, he didn't even get off the train right away so his offering of the seat was truly genuine. I absolutely love to see kindness among strangers. I'm used to chivalrous behavior as my Dexter is a complete gentleman, but there is something about being on the receiving end when it's a stranger that's admirable. And no, it wasn't a ploy to hit on or flirt with me; as far as I can tell this man had no ulterior motives outside of being polite!

Lesson Learned: Extend kindness to strangers. You never know how much they'll appreciate it!

May 24th, 2014

I lost my phone, which I seem to do often. This time I left it at Woodland, a restaurant in downtown Brooklyn near the Barclays Center on Flatbush Avenue. Luckily enough the staff found it and I was able to retrieve it later that day. I am fortunate that, all SIX times I've lost my phone, it was returned by a Good Samaritan. People say New Yorkers are mean and rude; that has been far from my experience, thankfully!

Lesson Learned: First one: see previous lesson above. Second one: keep track of your belongings and stop rushing, doing too many things at once, or carrying too many packages. This was the set of circumstances for each and every time I've lost my phone!

July 13th, 2014

I had a great session with my coach, Lindsay Jackson, this morning. We discussed how much judgment I place on myself. This has caused a ton of paralysis by analysis on my end, so I have committed to beginning a judgment journal to make these judgments more tangible. I think this is the first step necessary to release this negative energy I have toward myself. Lindsay said something really poignant in response to my disappointment: "Clarity has no benchmarks." In other words, be happy with the one hour of clarity for now and it will continue to grow and expand especially as it pertains to the more stubborn areas of my life.

July 19th, 2014

I'm grateful that I was finally able to complete a meditation session! This is something I've been committed to doing since the beginning of the year, but have never actually done it. It came up in my most recent coaching session with Lindsay on the 13th. I committed to meditating for just five minutes over the course of the next week. Not only did I do it, but I did it for ten minutes and it was fantastic! I went with a guided meditation via Positive Magazine's YouTube Channel. I highly recommend this for folks just starting their meditation journey.

The one I chose was focused on getting rid of negative energy and thoughts and it was well paced. I couldn't believe how quickly the ten minutes passed. I'm grateful I kept my commitment and completed this goal I've had on my mind for many months.

This goal is of course tied to several others so I'm thankful for my progress. To top today off, I also had the pleasure of going to an apartment warming party in Harlem and it was on a rooftop. The weather was gorgeous and once night fell there was a pleasant surprise of fireworks off the rooftop of a nearby building!

Lesson Learned: There's a great quote by Arthur Ashe: "Start where you are. Use what you have. Do what you can." You don't need to overwhelm yourself by making unfeasible commitments as this will usually result in failure. This is what delayed me even attempting to meditate at all. I was under the insane impression that I had to meditate for an hour or more for it to be beneficial. Don't even ask me where I got that from! And if I remember correctly, during my coaching session with Lindsay, I committed to 10 or 15 minutes and she felt my hesitancy and suggested I start smaller and add on if necessary since small successes breed larger goals; it's all about progression. So start wherever you are, use what you got and give it your best shot.

July 25th, 2014

I'm grateful for my best friend, Michele Jarrett. We decided to have an impromptu picnic in Brooklyn Bridge Park. We grabbed some wine, snacks and a blanket and sat by the water and talked. Michele and I have been friends for more than 15 years! We met sophomore year at Brooklyn Technical High School and have been close ever since. I love spending time with and talking to her; she's a great sounding board and one of the best people to keep me grounded and to motivate and lift me up when I'm down. Best thing of all she is single-handedly responsible for my new business name: Follow Your BLIS (with one 'S' intentionally) – I was super grateful that my original acronym (*see July 22, 2014 entry*) worked perfectly. Michele was talking about an acquaintance that made a huge life decision and muttered "Follow your bliss, girl" at the end of her statement. It was all so serendipitous.

August 4th, 2014

Today was the last day of my trip to New Orleans. I toured two of Louisiana's many plantations. The first one was Oak Alley. The view of this plantation is absolutely stunning! The long walkway leading up to the "Big House" was flanked by these gargantuan oak trees in perfect symmetry. It's downright breathtaking. *(Being able to see the beauty in a place linked to historical horrors is complex.)*

As I made my way to the back of the house where the tour began I took a quick look at the replicated slave quarters on the property. I popped into one which was filled with many slavery era items such as scythes, shackles, chains etc. On one of the walls of the cabin was a list of names. These names presented the slaves that "belonged" to the Oak Alley plantation. Adjacent to that wall was a plaque that read "Between 1836 and the Civil War, 198 men, women and children were enslaved at Oak Alley. Dehumanized and quantified like any other commodity, they appear in sales records and inventories, yet as people they have been all but forgotten by history." At least there was some sort of recognition of the people on whose back this plantation was built. For most of them, a name is all that remains of their story. I snapped a picture of the plaque and of the names on the wall and hurried along to catch the start of the tour.

Once I made it to the house I had a couple minutes to spare, and in looking around I noticed the inventory of slaves for this plantation was listed outside one of the windows, so I took a couple pictures just in time before the tour started. It wasn't until I was back on the tour bus reviewing all of my photos that I noticed that my name "Marguerite" is not only listed on the wall but also listed on the slave inventory!

The dollar amount next to my name was a whopping $350. The tour guide said to multiply that number by 23 to get our current market's "value," which amounts to $6,900 today. That struck me so intensely that I shed some tears. It's not surprising to see my name listed, it is a French name and of all the places it would pop up no wonder it's in Louisiana! We made our way to the second plantation, Evergreen, and lo and behold a "Margueritte" (this time with two T's) is listed on this plantation's inventory as well. I recognize this is "only" a first name but I cannot help but imagine whether or not one of these women is a direct ancestor. I was extremely humbled by this experience and grateful that they toiled under unimaginable circumstances so I can be here today!

Commentary: A few more things about the plantation tour in general. First, there was some degree of reconciling both my feelings and thoughts for not only touring the plantations along the Mississippi River, but paying $80 to do so (this included lunch and roundtrip transportation). If you drove yourself the entry fee for each of the plantations was approximately $20 - $25. Why was this difficult? It wasn't simply a matter of spending the money. It was the knowledge that plantations profited off of the free and exploited labor of Black people during the slavery era. Fast forward only 150 years and income is still being generated via tours and gift shops, etc. I have no idea whether or not these admission fees just cover the maintenance cost of the property or if any additional profits are being produced. Additionally, in doing some research it appears that Oak Alley wasn't as forthcoming with the slave narrative as my entry may suggest.

The replica cabin with the slave names was only installed after complaints that the tour focuses solely on the narratives of the slave owners, their financial holdings and their lineage. Not much was said about the people that toiled there. I guess that's the part of the story that motivated me to take the tour in the first place: to be able to get an up close look at this part of history that I feel is constantly downplayed and hidden as America's dirty secret. Despite my vacillating between unease and interest, I am grateful I took the tour and got a small glimpse of what life was like for those who came before me.

August 23rd, 2014

Today, I led a workshop about intuition and it went well. Twenty people showed up, which was the most so far within this workshop series (Friends with Benefits Workshop). I'm most happy that each attendee participated to some degree. Everyone generated ideas, asked questions and shared perspectives. This was a huge improvement from the first workshop I led in April.

I am grateful for those attendees who challenged my own ideas and identified some things I hadn't acknowledged previously. One person stood out the most. His name is Eric and he shared that he never ignores his intuition. What a unique way of thinking! I am grateful he not only shared that but also that he added context as to how he got to that point. He learned to overcome fear at an extremely young age through the use of meditation. We're talking as young as 5 years old. How many people have that story?! I gained a lot of insight from his comments and am glad he came today.

Lesson Learned: I made a comparison in this entry. I didn't compare my journey to that of another person, but rather to a previous version of myself in a similar circumstance. This is about acknowledging progress and learning and growing from your experiences.

Our Gratitude Mission

August 29th, 2014

Dexter, my boyfriend of five and a half years, asked me to marry him! I'm beyond ecstatic. The event was executed flawlessly and the ring is pure perfection. We've been discussing marriage for a while but I had no idea what he was planning. He is the perfect mate for me. I am thrilled he will be my husband! Ha, I just said "husband" – pardon my cheesiness as I grin like the Cheshire Cat. I am beyond grateful for his proposal and beyond ecstatic for this next chapter of our lives.

Lesson Learned: Being vulnerable is one of the most freeing things a human being can experience. I think that this is one of the many facets that make our relationship successful. I don't have to hide who I am. I don't have to be someone I am not. We took our time to establish a foundation in friendship and built on that for more than five years. We've seen each other's highs and lows and know what it takes to build each other up during those low moments. This entry may appear to be short but there are truly no words that can express the magnitude of several emotions that culminated this night.

August 30th, 2014

I'm still on cloud 9 from last night. I could hardly sleep because of the excitement of the next phase of my life. Additionally, I've been overwhelmed with all of the well wishes of our family and friends. On top of it all we had to get up earlier than normal to head to Turks and Caicos for our week-long vacation. We had a woman pilot by the way; I have never been on a flight piloted by a woman before, so that was great to see and experience. The engagement timing couldn't have been more perfect!

We arrived in Providenciales safely this afternoon. It is absolutely gorgeous here. When we got to our villa, towels shaped in a heart adorned the table and a bottle of champagne was left on ice to celebrate. Even better, our host managed to get us a reservation to one of the most popular restaurants on the island, Coco Bistro. Dinner was amazing. I am overflowing with gratitude. I am beyond blessed. The night sky here is unimaginable. I have NEVER seen this many stars in the sky EVER. I've been to many of the Caribbean islands and this starlight sky cannot compete. Jamaica is a close second. They were shining so brightly and looked deceivingly close to make you think you could just jump and catch them.

August 31st, 2014

As the string of happy events continues, today I celebrate my 31st birthday, my golden birthday (my age matching the date I was born on). I am thankful my maker has had me live this long and pray that I have many, many, many more years ahead of me. These past few days have been extraordinary and I'm thankful to all of those who've made it possible. I thank my parents, Albert and Jacqueline Pierce, for bringing me into this world, for teaching me to be kind and to love others and especially to love myself. They taught me to be a leader and most importantly to keep trying no matter how many times I may fail.

I thank my sisters, Samantha and Alana, for being the epitome of joy in my life. No sense of humor can compare to ours collectively. We've shared thousands of laughs and most recently tears of joy. My life would not be the same if they weren't in it.

I thank my community of friends who continue to keep me grounded, encouraged and motivated. They each elevate me intellectually, creatively and emotionally. They are my rocks and each holds a permanent place in my heart.

Lastly, my beloved, these days have been amazing because of you. Your timing was impeccable and our vacation is spectacular and only just beginning. You allowed me to love you and to be loved in return. We've grown so much together these past five years and I'm ever so grateful to continue this journey called life with you by my side.

September 6th, 2014

Today is the last day of our Turks & Caicos vacation. I convinced Dex to wake up early so we could take pictures of the sunrise. We had done this once before on our trip to Jamaica. We ventured out to the beach and waited for the sun to show us its glory. Despite some clouds, it was spectacular. We took great photos and I stood in awe of God's creation. The reflection of the sunlight in the water was simply breathtaking. I stood basking in God's light with humble gratitude. So thankful for the past week and where I am in life. I said a thank-you prayer to God at that moment.

In addition, our flight home was onboard a brand new Airbus 321 JetBlue plane. It had all leather seats! The ride home was smooth, which is all I ever ask for considering I've been so nervous about air travel lately. So glad my nerves can finally rest!

Lesson Learned: This entry epitomizes my commitment to being present in the moment, to be still and let go. This was such an amazing week that all of my worries, doubts and fears were minimized and even nonexistent. Those moments during the sunrise were all that mattered. I loved and was loved in return.

November 3rd, 2014

I came across the same quote on two separate occasions today. It first appeared in a post I was reading on LifeHack.org. The post highlighted the habits of successful people. The quote was the opening to the post. The second time I saw it was about nine hours later as I worked through one of the Franklin Covey OnDemand courses for work. The quote was the closing to the course. It's from Aristotle: "We are what we repeatedly do. Excellence then is not an act, but a habit." The Universe, God, and Spirit are shouting at me with this one. I'm grateful for the guidance. This time I will listen.

Lesson Learned: This instance reminds me of that God-Will-Save-Me joke, are you familiar with it? I've included a condensed version below.

There was a huge flood in a village. One man said to everyone as they evacuated,

"I'll stay! God will save me!"

The flood got higher and a boat came, and the man in it said "Come on mate, get in!" "No" replied the man. "God will save me!"

The flood got very high now and the man had to stand on the roof of his house. A helicopter soon came and the man offered him help. "No, God will save me!" he said.

Eventually the man drowns. He got by the gates of heaven and he said to God, "Why didn't you save me?"

God replied, "For goodness sake! I sent a boat and a helicopter. What more do you want?"

With that said, if you're looking for a sign from God or the Universe, you have to be open to receiving it. Seeing this quote twice in one day let me know that I wasn't working as hard toward my goal as I could have been, so I had to step it up a notch.

December 17th, 2014

It feels awesome to do good things for others, especially if you know it will go a long way. One of my best friends, Jade Kearney, just moved into a new place a couple weeks ago and I know she doesn't have everything she needs yet, so for Christmas I decided to send her some stuff that would help get her kitchen in order: dishes, drinking glasses and flatware. She was so appreciative that she dedicated a Facebook post to me today out of gratitude.

February 8th, 2015

I came across a *Huffington Post* article titled "3 Ancient Parables to Challenge and Shift Your Perspective." I was only familiar with one of the three included, called the Two Wolves. However, the one that resonated with me the most was The Muddy Road. I have included it below.

The Muddy Road

Tanzan and Ekido were once traveling together down a muddy road. A heavy rain was still falling.

Coming around a bend, they met a lovely girl in a silk kimono and sash, unable to cross the intersection.

"Come on, girl," said Tanzan at once. Lifting her in his arms, he carried her over the mud.

Ekido did not speak again until that night when they reached a lodging temple. Then he no longer could restrain himself.

"We monks don't go near females," he told Tanzan, "especially not young and lovely ones. It is dangerous. Why did you do that?"

"I left the girl there," said Tanzan. "Are you still carrying her?"

Lesson Learned: I was meant to read this parable! This again has emphasized how disadvantageous it is to hold on to the past. The second monk was so obsessed with the first monk breaking the rules. Even though the first monk only carried her across the mud, the second monk "carried her" (figuratively) well into the night. It can be difficult to let things go when they don't fit into your box of expectations. I think that is why I was angry with myself over my college and job experience; it didn't fit into the expectations I had for myself. To top it off I didn't take any of the necessary actions to mold my reality to meet those expectations. I expected to have chosen a major to be enamored with, to have been challenged and pushed to new heights intellectually. None of that happened and it's ok. I just had to put "it" down and not pick it up again.

January 17th, 2015

OMG!!! I discovered the most adorable dog ever. I came across a picture of a Pomsky! A Pomsky is a crossbreed of a Husky (which was my favorite breed) and a Pomeranian. Take a second and Google Pomsky, I'll wait….Isn't that the cutest thing ever?! My fiancé promised to get me one as soon as we get our place. So grateful this dog exists!

January 27th, 2015

Tonight I'm grateful for all of the other contributing authors in *Our Gratitude Mission*. It's amazing how much gratitude is being shared and expressed on a daily basis. I cannot express how excited and grateful I am to be a part of this journey with so many phenomenal individuals. There is nothing like joining with like-minded people to accomplish greatness.

March 25th, 2015

This evening I went to my first event hosted by The Academi of Life. It featured Positive Psychologist and Life Coach Diane Lang, who was so inspiring and encouraging throughout the seminar. She described positive psychology as the study of happiness and resilience. I loved every second of it. To top the evening off Diane and I rode the subway together to Penn Station from

Columbus Circle. During our short time together, she gave me a lot of ideas on how to expand my coaching business and book speaking engagements.

March 26th, 2015

I'm so grateful for Facebook this evening. It can be a great source of information. Tonight, as I was scrolling through, one of my friends shared a lottery application to a brand new condominium that's slated to be completed by the end of the year in Brooklyn. Dexter and I live separately at the moment and our goal is to move in together first and then plan the wedding. This could be a great solution to our apartment hunt. Now if only we could command that our application is chosen! In the meantime we will continue our search and see what happens.

April 7th, 2015

Today's entry makes a full year of gratitude entries! I started this journey on April 7th, 2014, and in the snap of a finger it's a year later. It's only fitting that today was amazing!

A handful of great things happened today. The one woman whom I got to speak to the most at yesterday's Wix.com event contacted me saying she was interested in my coaching services and wants to schedule something as soon as next month. Great thing No. 2: I had a call with Sharon Beason, the founder of Womeneur.com, about me being a contributing writer to the website when it launches. I loved Sharon's energy, passion and thought process. Her mission is to empower entrepreneurs and small business owners who are women of color. Her platform is going to be dynamic and inspiring and we agreed that I will be on board to contribute self-improvement and career development content every month!

The Womeneur.com launch event is scheduled for April 28th and I simply cannot wait to meet Sharon in person as well as all the other fabulous ladies who will be part of this movement.

Third great thing, my May Career Nomad, Mukti Banerjee, confirmed her availability for the interview. Each month I feature a Career Nomad Profile on my blog. I compile a story based on an interview with someone that has successfully made a career transition or is currently undergoing one. I highlight this individual's thought process for making the change as well as any challenges or opportunities experienced as a result of the transition. So far, each person I have asked to participate has agreed. I'm "batting a thousand" as the saying goes. In the words of Ice Cube, "Today was a good day" and I am grateful for that!

Commentary: I actually got to meet Sharon sooner than expected. We were both at a networking event hosted by Passionistasinc.com. I spotted Sharon about halfway through the event and made my way over to introduce myself. What a wonderful spirit and energy. I'm glad I was able to speak with her for as long as I did and am excited for our collaboration in the coming months.

I'm grateful to have maintained the discipline necessary to complete this mission successfully. Lots of determination and discipline went into expressing gratitude for a unique person, thing or experience each and every day. It was tough remembering to add this exercise to my daily routine. There were moments where I slipped up and would have to write entries for the past three or even five days in one sitting! Five days was my absolute maximum number of entries I allowed myself to skip. It was easy enough for me to recount the past three days' worth of grateful moments, but five took several additional moments of stillness to be able to capture the very things I was grateful for on those particular days.

I was all about making this journal a habit. There were also days when it took me longer to find something to be grateful for than the previous day and not be tempted to just go the perfunctory route. It was important for me not to take the presence of discomfort or disappointment as a sign to quit or turn back. Instead, it was a sign to push through and move forward. I made this journal a priority. It was something I intended to see through from the very beginning. Abandoning this journey was never an option.

What was even more fascinating was reading those stressful moments a year later. They don't seem nearly as bad as they were at that moment in time. In fact, I doubt I would remember so vividly, had they not been written down. Expressing gratitude is the foundation of positive thinking and personal happiness; it feels good to not sweat the small stuff, it feels great to smile more often. It's also liberating to acknowledge when you may need assistance without shame and when to offer your assistance to others without hesitation. This mission was incredible, but I still have more progress to make. The journey doesn't end when a milestone is reached as it should always be replaced by a new one.

It wasn't until the end of March that I began reading through the entries from top to bottom, to determine which ones would make the cut. I combed through 365 entries to see which ones correlated with one another, which ones were contingent or were synchronous in any way. After this review, I was proud of myself, and of course grateful, that I expressed my vulnerability in admitting to a panic attack then ditching work as a result. I also noted my moments of manic obsession over what to some might be categorized as minutia. Perhaps something for me to work on going forward!

This daily journaling exercise has built up my positive thinking endurance. I take advantage of reframing my negative thoughts quickly, and coming up with alternate perspectives that create solutions. This way I avoid dismissing my challenges, in order to work through them more effectively.

Creativity and critical thinking are stifled when you're fuming with anger by solely focusing on the problem.

You get to choose how to see and experience the world! Henry Ford said it best: "Whether you think you can or whether you think you can't, you're right." Since I've already spent time believing I can't, I'm grateful to now believe that of course I can!

Terry's Take

Three things jump out at me about Marguerite's chapter. First, I am SO happy for her and Dexter on their engagement. What are the chances that not one but TWO of our authors (Marguerite and also Marian Ruiz-Diaz) would get engaged during *Our Gratitude Mission*? Considering about half the authors are already married, it gets even more amazing. Want to get married? Spend a year documenting your gratitude! No guarantees, but I like your chances.

Another major item I want to address is Marguerite's experience visiting the former slave homes in Louisiana. I was putting my hand over my mouth as I read this part of her chapter. I know slavery existed, but she's right. It has been kind of swept under the rug. I am glad she shared her detailed experience and the range of emotions she felt. That helps all of us understand what went on a little better. I'm grateful to Marguerite for educating us.

Last but not least, it's fascinating how we are often hard on ourselves. At my book launch party that Marguerite mentions, as I was writing the note to her in the book, the venue's manager interrupted us to tell me that I needed to move the party upstairs. I got stressed about it and felt bad that she had to wait until we moved all the books, people, etc. up to the mezzanine so we could continue. It's great that she recalls the good moments of that night. We would all be well-served to do the same in challenging situations, myself included!

Russ Terry

Chapter 11

Tracy K. Pierce

Fitting Life Puzzle Pieces Together Through Gratitude

Age: 38

Hometown: All over the United States!

Current City: Iowa City, IA

Our Gratitude Mission

Baseline (4/22/14)

I practice gratitude daily, but not always in the same way. About two years ago I made it a habit to write down at least five things I was grateful for every day in a dedicated Gratitude Journal, but I have fallen off from that practice in recent times. When I practice gratitude now, it's usually in small bursts throughout the day, sometimes just mentally, sometimes vocally, and occasionally in written form.

Gratitude for me includes things such as taking an extra few moments to send thanks to the Universe before eating, sending love and gratitude to my home for supporting me, or having a few moments of thankfulness for my bed and awesome bedroom before rolling out of the sack in the morning. Other examples are sending a "thank you" to the Universe when I find a parking stall that already has money in the meter and being grateful when my flight gets cancelled and I'm easily booked on another that takes off less than an hour later. This kind of stuff – it's really about the small things for me.

One other way I am very conscious in practicing gratitude is thanking the people who are helpful to me by making eye contact, if possible, and telling them out loud. Sometimes I'll take the time to write a "thank you" note to someone who went above and beyond.

I come from a long line of jobs where many times the people I was serving took for granted that I would serve them. It really meant a lot to me when someone would take a sincere moment to say "thank you" so I like to be aware of when I can do that for others.

How many times do we thank our waitresses, our cab drivers, our tow truck drivers, our carpenters, our plumbers, our emergency communications (911) dispatchers? I can tell you from experience that it's pretty rare, and that has made a big impression on me as I have gotten older.

Overall I feel I have a pretty happy life. My life certainly has not turned out the way I thought it would when I was younger. There have been a lot of twists and turns along the way, some positive and others not so much.

Doing a gratitude journal previously was one of the things that helped me put more focus on the positive things in my life instead of zeroing in on all the negative things like I used to. It helped me to realize how much I really DO have going well for me in my life instead of only being aware of the things that weren't working out.

I have found that when I get sucked into a downward spiral, it's almost always because I focus on what I DON'T have, when I yearn for something I see in my future that hasn't arrived or happened yet.

The reason I've decided to take part in *Our Gratitude Mission* is to help me stay grounded in the present. There were also many wonderful surprises that came into my life when I did gratitude journaling before, so I'm curious to see what other interesting things will pop up in my life during these next 365 days.

After My 365 Days of Gratitude, Looking Back on My Baseline

Having recently finished 365 days of logging my gratitude, it's interesting to look back on what I wrote about gratitude before I started this project. As I reflect, I realize that although I did a gratitude journal before, I was never challenged to acknowledge different things every day. I would often end up writing similar things from day to day.

I have to laugh looking back because at the beginning of this project I found myself "rationing" my "everyday gratitudes." What I mean by "everyday gratitudes" are things like I mentioned in my baseline: waking up in a nice warm bed with a roof over my head, having nutritious food to eat, having a reliable vehicle to drive, etc.

Our Gratitude Mission

I figured if I couldn't think of anything I was thankful for on a particular day, I could always revert back to one of my everyday gratitudes to fill the gap. Funny thing is, I was always able to find something new and beyond these everyday gratitudes. Once I started writing daily, it was almost simple to find something new every single day to be thankful for!

Another thing that made this challenge different for me was instead of just writing what I was grateful for, I usually included a "because" statement after it. For example: I am grateful for _____ because _____ (it did "this" for me).

It's one thing to make a list of the things you're grateful for. It was a different, and better, experience for me to acknowledge and write down the why behind it. Looking back at my previous gratitude journal, it would often look something like this:

Today I am thankful for:

- my nice warm bed
- access to healthy food
- the 45 free minutes of parking right by where I was going
- my awesome husband
- my reliable car.

These are all well and good, but notice how different it feels when the gratitude statement includes a "why":

5/18/14

Today I am thankful for down time, because I am definitely the type of person who needs time away from others and obligations to rejuvenate. Today was perfect for that.

Or

5/24/14

I am so thankful for a new air conditioner in my office because this one runs quietly and does not rattle the window like the old one did. I am actually looking forward to working in my office this summer!

What Did It Take for Me to Do This For a Year?

Remembering to write down my gratitudes was actually a bit of a challenge for me at first. As a clutter coach, time management is one of the areas I work on with people. So I dug into my toolbox and realized that putting up a sticky note or just making it part of my morning routine wasn't going to work for me.

In my previous gratitude journal, I usually wrote first thing in the morning. Perhaps that's why I often ended up with similar entries. Reflecting on the previous day shortly after waking up felt too much like moving backward instead of forward for me. I'm not really a morning person anyway, and giving myself one more thing to do in the morning was not inspiring for me. If I was going to write about different things, the only way this was going to happen for me was to do it at the end of the day.

I also realized that I respond better to audible reminders than visual ones, so I set an alarm on my phone that went off every day at 9pm to remind myself it was time to reflect on my day and write my gratitude. This helped me follow through with what I said I would do.

When Life Seems Like a Big Puzzle

The beginning of 2014 marked a time of big changes for me. I had been running a business for a little more than five years. I'd done all the things business people will tell you to do: make a business plan, write out the numbers, and make goals and action steps to get to those goals. However, when I would do my annual year-end review, I saw I did all the action steps but still ended up far away from any quantifiable goals I may have written for myself.

I was working very hard and following all of the "right" steps I had been told would make things happen for me, but I wasn't satisfied and it wasn't working.

2014 was the year I decided to look at things from a different point of view. A friend recommended I read Danielle LaPorte's book *The Desire Map*, and I took to it right away. In very basic terms it's about changing the perspective from looking at life from a place of quantity to a place of quality. Instead of asking, "How much money do I want to make this year?" or "How many clients do I want to have this year?" it's about coming at life from the standpoint of "How do I want to FEEL when I'm doing anything in my life?"

Something about this really resonated with me even though it was completely counterintuitive to everything I had learned so far. I worked through the exercises in the book and arrived at my top five Core Desired Feelings: limitless, thriving, shining, nourished, and in the flow.

It's not that this way of thinking about life isn't about taking action. Quite the contrary! Instead of taking action by making a list of what I "should" be doing to get from Point A to Point B, it became about taking action by answering "yes" to the question "Does this take me closer to feeling my Core Desired Feelings?"

In addition to the Core Desired Feelings, during 2014 I began to realize that what I want most in life is to be awakened and open – I call these my Greater Aspirations in Life – and they are different from my Core Desired Feelings.

Perhaps it's easier to understand all of this as setting intentions rather than setting goals. When I think about an intention, it's different from a goal; there's not necessarily an end point. It's something I aspire to do every day whether or not I reached that state of being the previous day. It's a continual effort toward a state of being.

When I think about goals I feel they have an endpoint. For example when I set goals it was usually with a quantity in mind, like "I will work with 20 new clients this year." Once that goal is reached, it is finished and it's time to start a new goal. Maybe the difference in using the language of "goal" versus "intention" is really just a shift of mindset, but that's exactly what I needed in 2014.

As I've tuned in to my Greater Aspirations in relation to my Core Desired Feelings, I realize there is a difference between *feeling* awakened and open and *being* awakened and open. To me "feeling" can often be a fleeting moment of emotion whereas "being" implies a state of existence that is more everlasting.

Not that feeling and being are completely mutually exclusive. It has become my sense though that feeling my Core Desired Feelings - limitless, thriving, shining, nourished, and in the flow- are actually leading me into being awakened and open.

I mention all of this because when it comes to getting to the places (or feelings or greater aspirations in life or even goals) we want, I've found it's rarely as easy as going from Point A to Point B. We often expect to go in a straight line, directly from A to B. In reality, the path usually leads us two steps forward, one step back, up in a big loopty loop, two more steps back, four steps forward, down a huge cliff, and who knows what else before we get to Point B.

This can be frustrating in the game of life, especially if we don't see how the detours and side trips actually bring us closer to Point B. What I found interesting about this is that when we try taking the shortest path from A to B, we can get hung up on time and how long things are taking. We then don't see that the detours and side trips made the trip that much more fun and exciting.

The little kid in me loves roller coasters a whole lot more than riding in a straight line anyway, so why not enjoy the ride? Of course, as adults who may be focused on getting results, we're often looking for the most efficient way to reach our goals or intentions. This means things that perhaps we should ultimately be thankful for we end up seeing as setbacks or burdens along the way.

What does this have to do with journaling gratitude for a year? Well, just about everything as I discovered! As I look back at what I wrote for my daily gratitudes, I came to see that a large majority of my journal entries were things that took me closer to my Core Desired Feelings rather than taking me closer to meeting business goals. For example:

4/25/14

I am grateful for my skills to improvise. On my radio show today the guest's connection got dropped and I talked until she was able to get back on the line. Because of my ability to improvise, I didn't get nervous or go into a panic like I might have in the past. I simply shared a story that had happened in my own life as it related to what we were just talking about. [Core Desired Feelings = in the flow, limitless].

8/6/14

I am so grateful for catch up sessions with old friends (especially when they buy my lunch!) because I often miss getting to see (in person) friends who have moved away. It was awesome to have lunch with Steph today and hear about all her world travels. Yes! [Core Desired Feelings = nourished, thriving].

8/24/14

I am so grateful I am able to tolerate the heat better than I used to because participating in outdoor events in the summer is fun. I volunteered at the Plum Grove Tomato Tasting today and although it was quite hot, I was able to deal with it quite easily! Woohoo! [Core Desired Feelings = thriving, in the flow, nourished].

10/5/14

I am grateful for the free herb education walk that I got to attend today at the Gaia's Peace Garden. I learned a bunch about herbs (which is giving me ideas for additional plantings in our back yard!), plus they gave us food and tea as well. It was awesome. [Core Desired Feelings = thriving, shining, nourished].

These experiences I expressed gratitude for had very little to do with my business, but they had everything to do with experiencing what I wanted to experience in my life. However, there were lots of bumps in the road as well. One of the biggest lessons I learned this year was when I asked for transformation in the form of opening and awakening, it meant letting go of more than I could have ever imagined.

During this year of journaling there were three deaths in my family, two of them quite close to me. A group I had been doing spiritual practices with on a weekly basis for two years disbanded. I had to cut ties with a health practitioner who had been a big part of my healing journey for four years.

I had to let go of a lot to move closer to a state of opening and awakening. Had I only seen the individual puzzle pieces, these events could have knocked me down instead of allowing me to open even further. In fact, if I'm being honest, these events did throw me for a loop at first, but as I observed my feelings, I was able to find gratitude.

Our Gratitude Mission

7/25/14

I'm so grateful that my clients were able (and agreeable) to reschedule our appointments so I could attend Aunt Ruth's funeral. It was important to me to be there with our family. It's such a strange transition time for us as the older generation passes on.

8/13/14

I am so grateful to have known Grandma Pierce for the last seven years. She was a spunky old gal who you couldn't help but love the minute you met her. I loved listening to her stories, especially about watching the kids play on the elementary school playground just outside her apartment window. She passed away today and I'm sure she's on her way to climbing trees and sliding down the big slide...

8/16/14

Today was Grandma Pierce's funeral. Grandma Pierce was my husband's biological grandmother, but very shortly after we got married I started calling her Grandma too. Again, I am so grateful to have known her (my gratitude entry for the day she passed), but more than that I am so grateful that I always took the time to give her a hug when we arrived and just before we left any of the family gatherings we were at with her. We usually had Sunday lunch with her once or twice a month.

I always made sure that Grandma Pierce knew how much I loved her through the hugs I gave her, and I'm so glad that I always did. You never know when it might be the last time you get to see someone alive.

4/15/15

I am so thankful to have the time and space I need to be in the grieving process I am already starting to feel regarding Magoo (our cat). Something shifted yesterday and I feel like she is getting ready to leave her body. I am grateful that I have tools we can use to help her be comfortable and feel loved up until she is ready to go.

4/17/15

It's hard to feel happy on days like today. We got bad news from the vet this morning that there's nothing else she can do for Magoo. I am very thankful to learn that there are other options besides just euthanasia. The vet said that when left to die on their own, sometimes a pet will live up to two weeks after they stop eating and drinking. She was able to give us a homeopathic remedy though that helps speed up the dying process to about 2-3 days and should help Magoo be more comfortable during the process.

4/18/15

I am so grateful I got to spend a lot of time with Magoo today – some of it outside, and some of it inside. I can feel she is getting ready to leave and I am so happy to get to spend some quality time with Magoo and Bryan (my husband) today.

4/19/15

I am sooooo thankful for all the support and healing/loving energy that our friends have been sending to Magoo and us during her transition time. It has been really tangible during the last two days especially. Although there is sadness and grief, we have felt held and supported by our friends and higher angelic forces that are here to help Magoo and us during this difficult time.

4/20/15

Magoo passed away yesterday afternoon. I am so thankful Bryan was able to take the day off work today to help with getting rid of Magoo's medications and foods and such as well as help with cleaning of the house to help us energetically move through this time of grief and sadness.

In the end I could see the wisdom of the Universe sending me these challenges (even if I didn't like them) because they did lead to greater opening and awakening for me.

It's interesting to look back and see how much I grappled with letting go of not only the deaths but also the relationships and other things that needed to be released from my life. When I finally did let go, my gratitude journal entries for the time period shortly after seemed to express such relief that it was in some ways hard to believe how hard I had tried to hang on. Journaling what I was grateful for helped me see how these puzzle pieces fit, which in turn helped me be more open and awakened.

Receiving is Just as Good (and Important) as Giving

In our society there is a common saying, "It is better to give than to receive." That statement always bothered me for some reason, and doing this year of gratitude journaling has helped me realize why. I was raised in a Christian household, and from age ten to eighteen I lived in a very conservative, Christian, Midwestern small town. Although I can find several references to this idea that giving is better than receiving in the Bible, I wonder if it's been taken a bit out of context when we hear it used in the world today. I'll explain why.

Since sometime in my early teens I have been quite interested in Taoist philosophy, particularly its focus on seeking balance in life. "Tao" means "the way" — it's a principle and a path for order. Some people think of it as the underlying principle for all of nature. Some people define Taoism as walking the path of wisdom. Something about it has always resonated with me much more than other religions or philosophies I studied in school or have been exposed to.

I feel that what particularly draws me to the Taoist tradition is the concept of yin and yang. Here's the short version: according to ancient Taoist philosophy there are two distinct parts to everything, and rather than being strictly opposites, these two parts are actually complementary.

One side of the coin cannot exist without the other. Light and dark; masculine and feminine; doing and being; water and fire; hard and soft; happy and sad; active and passive. These seemingly opposite things are actually part of a greater whole.

In my observation, the same is true with giving and receiving – giving cannot exist without receiving, receiving cannot exist without giving. One can certainly not be better than the other, they are both part of a whole and both complement each other. Giving could never be better than receiving because without receiving there would be no one to give to.

I was discussing the notion that receiving is just as important as giving with a friend of mine. She told me a story about some people she knew who were insistent on not receiving gifts or kindness; they always had to be the givers. In my friend's view, the situation became a bit of a power play – like they were trying to be the "better person" because they never let themselves receive, only give.

How would you feel if you tried giving to someone and they always rejected it? How does it feel to never have your gifts received? Giving and receiving are parts of a cycle, and if one side is not willing to receive, there can be no giving.

As I look back over my gratitude journaling, I realize that very rarely was I writing about physical items. The things I found myself being the most grateful for were spending time with people I care about, events I attended, the way something or someone made me feel, revelations that came to me, and spiritual work I did.

Not that receiving physical items and having gratitude for them is a bad thing. But as I reflect on what I was grateful for, it *was* gratitude for something that I received, but usually that something was not a physical item. I feel this is something for us all to reflect on, especially in our material world where we often give physical gifts to each other but what we really want to receive is the love, attention and presence of others.

Giving Can Be Receiving, and Receiving Can Be Giving.

Right now, one of the most important things in my life is deepening my spiritual practices – diving in and exposing these hidden parts of myself and bringing them to light. I found that many of the gratitudes I journaled involved revelations I had about myself, my world and the way I have perceived my world.

The concept of giving being receiving and receiving being giving opened up for me while I attended a spiritual retreat for a week in October, about halfway through my 365 days of journaling. The theme of the retreat was "The Upturned Heart, a Crucible for Connection." Little did I know when I registered that this course would largely focus on the concept of giving and receiving and how having gratitude opens up our capacity for receptivity.

As part of our practices we tuned into different situations involving gratitude. We went through a large set of scenarios. Here are some examples we were given to tune into:

How does it feel to be an enlightened teacher (such as Buddha or Jesus) and have a disciple throw himself at your feet and profess unending gratitude in an "I'm not worthy" type of way?

How does it feel to be a parent and receive gratitude from your own child?

What does it feel like to give something from the heart to someone and have them express no gratitude at all?

What does it feel like to receive sincere gratitude from a friend who you consider an equal?

What does it feel like to receive half-hearted gratitude?

What does it feel like to receive gratitude from a parent?

What does it feel like to be an adult and receive gratitude from an innocent child (who is not your own child)?

As I worked through these scenarios with a partner, what struck us most was the type of gratitude that felt best to us was receiving gratitude from an innocent child. There was no expectation on either side of the equation, just pure giving and receiving.

In that instance, the adult did the giving, resulting in the innocent child's gratitude. But when the child expressed his/her gratitude, the pure warmth and sincere place it came from became a giving to the adult.

When we give and receive from a place of innocence and sincerity, what results is an unending chain. The giving becomes the receiving and the receiving becomes a giving. It's really a beautiful loop that can continually renew itself.

And this doesn't stop with gratitude between or among people; this includes the Universe (or God, Goddess, Higher Power, Source, Creator, or whatever word you use to describe the greater force that created Life). From my perspective, the Universe is not some unfeeling, disconnected force that merely watches us humans do our thing. There is giving and receiving that happens between the Universe and us. If we can do it with innocence, warmth and heart-felt gratitude, the Universe is more likely to respond and keep the cycle going.

What could happen, what could open up if we expressed our gratitude like an innocent child? And what if we allowed ourselves to really BE in that space of gratitude? There's a big difference between saying "thank you" out of obligation or unworthiness and saying "thank you" sincerely.

And as I reflect on my gratitude entries for the last year, I notice that frequently I journaled about my ability to give. For example:

10/29/14

I'm thankful to have helped a potential client by giving her a free clutter coaching session today. It feels good to give help in this way even though I know she probably won't end up being a client.

1/13/14

I am so thankful I was able to be there for T. today in her time of need. I had an appointment for coffee reschedule last minute and T. and I were able to connect on her work break. She is going through some rough times right now and I know part of what she needs is someone to be there for her. I am glad I was able to be that person today.

4/9/14

I'm so thankful for the space I was able to hold for P. tonight to deal with and move through the health challenges she has.

When we are thankful for not only for what we are able to receive but also what we are able to give it starts to become a kind of endless loop of gratitude – gratitude for both giving and receiving.

Does a Gratitude Journal Change Your Life?

In my experience, yes and no.

Having a reminder to do it daily for a year helped solidify why gratitude is so important. However, there are a lot of different ways of expressing gratitude beyond just keeping a journal. As I mentioned in my Baseline, I do make a conscious effort to express my gratitude, especially to people I encounter during my daily life. I feel like that is just as if not more important than writing in a journal every day.

I can also see how for some people (myself sometimes included!) having one more thing on the "to-do" list becomes more of an obligation rather than coming from a place of heart-felt sincerity.

There were more than a few days when my alarm would go off and I would find myself doing something else and I didn't really want to stop what I was doing to write in my journal. Often I would jot something down to remind myself to write about it later, but in those moments it felt like obligation rather than being truly helpful.

Writing can also be a very left-brained (logical) experience. And gratitude isn't really about logic. To me gratitude is very much a right-brained (intuitive or feeling) experience. Some people are able to combine the two, but if someone were to make the journaling a purely left-brain activity then the entire purpose of the exercise is lost.

This is not to say that gratitude in and of itself is not good – quite the opposite! What I've found since the end of my 365 days is that it's much more effective and sincere if I express my gratitude in the moment. That may mean sending a thought of thankfulness to the Universe for something that happened, or saying "thank you" to our hostess at a restaurant. Whatever the case may be, expressing gratitude in the moment feels so much better than waiting to write it down and trying to recreate the feeling later.

That being said, probably the most helpful thing this experience revealed to me was how all these seemingly off-course things that were happening in my life actually fit together in the greater scheme of things.

Let's be honest, many times as humans we can be quite shortsighted. We want what we want when we want it, which is RIGHT NOW. It was easier for me to see how the Universe may be putting those pieces of the puzzle together in a way that I never would have thought of, and I can definitely see how this exercise could benefit someone else in the same way.

Writing every day also stretched me to find the variety in things I have to be thankful for. Since we were challenged to document a different expression of gratitude every day, it helped me see how many people, experiences, etc. I do have to be thankful for. It also helped me continue looking for more and more things per day, and almost always coming up with something new.

Will I continue a daily gratitude journal? At this point that's not my plan, but I will make it part of my day to express my gratitude whenever it is true and from the heart.

Lessons Learned

Although it took some planning and time management strategies to stick with an entire year of journaling my gratitude, it was much easier than I initially thought it would be to find something unique every day to be thankful for.

Life can be really confusing, and when our lives go off course it can be difficult to understand why certain things happen to us. The gratitude journal helped me remember that life happens FOR us, not TO us. Even during days of grief and sadness there was something to be thankful for. I was incredibly grateful for the support of friends, family, and higher forces (God, Universe, Source, Higher Power, etc.), especially during the challenges I faced.

Receiving is just as good as giving, and in fact receiving can be an act of giving in and of itself. We need both in our lives. Being in a state of gratitude can help us be open and receptive to all the good things the Universe has in store for us.

Gratitude is more a state of being than a state of doing. Holding and feeling the vibration of gratitude in your heart and body is what I mean by "state of being." There are many ways for us to express gratitude, but in my view, we need to be present in our gratitude before we take action. That action might be writing in a journal, sending a thank you card, or telling someone "thank you." Without the genuine feeling behind it, the action is meaningless.

Terry's Take

I work with Tracy on the Life Coach Radio Networks, of which I am Founder/CEO. I always call her (to myself at least) our "Host in the Heartland" because she lives in Iowa. I very much enjoy working with her, and don't say that about just anyone. I am glad I am involved in not one but TWO projects with her – the "LCRNs" as we call it, and *Our Gratitude Mission*.

I am super grateful to her for finishing her chapter very early! She was originally supposed to be in the next book, but some folks slated for this book were delayed, and Tracy happily filled their slot. Isn't it great in life when someone finishes early, PAYS early, ARRIVES early, etc.? It is a sign of utmost respect, and an excellent way to live.

Tracy's insight about Danielle LaPorte's book is spot-on. About 24 hours after I read the first draft of her chapter, I was in session with one of my Life Coaching clients, and she was saying how she wanted to DO less and BE more. I said, "Oh my God I was JUST reading a chapter in my next book about this. Hold on, let me share it with you!" I read what Tracy wrote, and my client LOVED it. She went out and bought *The Desire Map* and it became a theme of the "new" version of her.

This stuff works! I am proud of the empowering insights contained in our book. Also, we aren't afraid to tell you about someone else's wisdom. I always say I don't have all the answers, but I know where to find them!

Russ Terry

Our Gratitude Mission

Chapter 12

Mark Ferrante

With Change to Spare

Age: 52

Hometown: Trenton, NJ

Current City: Washington, DC

Our Gratitude Mission

I've always considered myself to be fortunate in the ways that matter most in life, thus adopting a practice of gratitude came fairly easily to me, at least as an adult. I grew up an only child with two caring parents and although my childhood was hardly idyllic, I had two sets of loving grandparents to whom I could turn for support and counsel throughout my childhood and adolescent years.

I was a very good student but had few friends in school. From an early age I knew I was different but the word "gay" would not have made any sense to me, so I simply thought of myself as "other." As a young child I was quite extroverted but as I aged, I learned to hide important facets of my personality from the world, fearing ridicule and, at times, even retribution. I slowly began to reclaim the truest parts of myself toward the end of my college years in suburban New Jersey. The extrovert in me came rising to the surface when I was chosen to be the commencement speaker at my graduation. During my remarks, I stressed the importance of maintaining a positive attitude throughout life, whether on the job, at home or elsewhere.

Like most, I have basked in successes and triumphs and have weathered disappointments and stretches that felt as though I had been cast adrift, left at the mercy of the prevailing winds. Through it all, I credit a positive attitude and an awareness of all that is sacred around us with keeping me grounded and allowing me to move forward on the path I have chosen.

It is in that spirit that I began my 365 days of gratitude a little more than a year ago. I could hardly have guessed how much my life would change by the time the year had gone by!

The preceding years had brought new and often wonderful changes to my life. While living in NJ in the fall of 2005, I met the person who would become my best friend, my great love and, in 2009, my spouse, Curtis. I am truly grateful every day for his indelible kindness, his generosity and his never-ending faithfulness and support.

Russ Terry

In 2007, despite the fact that my partner of two years lived and worked in Manhattan, I left my government job in New Jersey to take a leadership position with a not-for-profit in Washington, DC. Although I thoroughly enjoyed my role at the small nonprofit, the entire time I knew that there was an expiration date for my time in the nation's capital. The gravitational pull of life with my partner in NYC, not to mention my parents who reside not far away in central New Jersey, meant that I would need to find suitable employment in "the City."

In the late winter of 2011, a wonderful colleague and friend made me aware of a terrific opportunity to serve as a senior advisor in NYC government. I still remember the day I received the call confirming that I had been chosen for the position. I was immensely grateful, not only for my friend recommending me but that I was being given the opportunity to work for a visionary leader and tireless advocate for children and youth. The next three years provided me with a platform to witness profound changes in the way city departments can provide services to clients. It was as if the stars perfectly aligned to allow us to make the kind of changes that occur perhaps once or twice in a generation.

Now that I had joined my partner as a full-time resident in NYC, we expanded our circle of friends and enjoyed an enviable social life, frequenting the theatre, exploring unique neighborhoods across the five boroughs or tasting the endless varieties of cuisine so readily available within walking distance of our upper west side apartment.

My May 1st journal entry sums up my gratitude for new friendships: "Work colleagues invited us to their Central Park South apartment for drinks and dinner. What amazing views! Two additional friends joined the party making for an all-around fabulous spring evening. The very next night our friends Timo and Pamela tied the knot! The wedding was held at an East Harlem Episcopal church with just a few close friends and relatives on hand. I was so honored to be asked to do the scripture reading and even happier my partner Curtis was asked to play the organ! The service was followed by a wonderful dinner at the Central Park Boathouse set amid picture perfect weather."

Even with so much to be grateful for, we decided to pursue a dream that most New Yorkers can relate to yet many find elusive: adding a little more living space without breaking the bank. In August of 2012, we moved from a studio into a lovely first floor, one bedroom co-op apartment in the heart of Morningside Heights.

I was both amazed and grateful that we had managed to find a relative bargain in a very desirable neighborhood that was essentially turn-key. Less than five months later, however, my "attitude of gratitude" began to be severely tested as we soon realized that the apartment was pervasively cold in winter, a true anomaly in NYC, where owners and tenants alike routinely leave windows cracked even on the bitterest of days to mitigate the influence of over-zealous radiators.

Still, work was fulfilling, and the new space afforded us the ability to host small gatherings once more temperate weather arrived. We continued to meet new and interesting people, who invited us to share with them what they loved best about the City. It was during this time too that a wonderful addition to our family arrived, a little dog named Lucky. A colleague of Curtis' seemed to have one furry friend too many, so we were more than happy to give him a new home. I am grateful every day for his sweet disposition and his protective stance. I even learned to be grateful for his early morning wake up "kisses."

In the winter of 2014, Curtis and I were invited to a Super Bowl party at our friend Gil's apartment just a neighborhood or two north of us. Curtis cares little for football but I enjoy the competitive nature of such events and the camaraderie of watching such spectacles with those who share a passion for the game. It was on that night, in the midst of a Seahawks rout of the Denver

Broncos, that I met Russ Terry and learned of his gratitude journal. Who knew that as a result of that party, I could become a published author?

A few months later, on May 8th, we stopped by Russ' book signing event in Bryant Park. My entry from that night reads "Along the way, we got to chat with three passersby who were very curious about Russ' project and our connection to it. These random strangers were so lovely and upbeat. And, we got a second book signed for my Philly friend Paul!" That night Russ mentioned he was looking for people to embark on a one year Gratitude Mission. I thought, "This is one invitation I do not want to pass up!"

In retrospect, this "chance happening" could not have come along at a better time, as a month or two later my life would begin to change rapidly on several intersecting fronts.

One morning in March, while staying home to nurse a rather nasty cough and cold, I received a call from my boss that he would not be staying in his current position and that my job would likely change. While he expressed optimism for my prospects within the City, he added that this was to be expected with a change of administrations.

It was during this same time period that I started my year of journaling. It was challenging at first, not because there isn't something to be grateful for in every single day, but because I tend to look at the big picture. Thus, focusing on that one moment of beauty or that seemingly insignificant encounter on any given day required a certain discipline I was not used to engaging.

By late summer, it had become increasingly apparent to me that my role within city government was systemically being stripped of its vitality and that I needed to actively pursue other options if I wished to continue making meaningful contributions in my chosen field.

Our Gratitude Mission

Independent of my desire to feel both useful and wanted in my work, I cajoled Curtis into entertaining the idea that we should contact the real estate agent that found us our current apartment to determine if we could recoup our investment or, better yet, turn a profit and find something that would both be cozier and yet offer us a different perspective of the City.

Within two weeks of listing the property and after only one open house, we had an acceptable offer! I was so excited and grateful that the process was moving both quickly and (it seemed) painlessly.

The weeks and months that followed as the calendar turned to fall and then winter proved to be anything but painless. Challenges with work, family and the sale of the apartment tested my resolve and left me wondering if we could, indeed, pull off the "master plan" I conceived of when we met with our broker, Robin, that mellow September evening.

Up to this point in my story, I've made only passing references to my parents, but that is not to say they haven't played an integral role in shaping my world view. My mom began experiencing a slow yet steady decline in her mental faculties in 2007, not long after I moved to Washington DC. By 2012, it was entirely apparent to me, if not to my dad (her primary caretaker) that she would need a level of support he was not equipped to provide on his own. Eventually, in late 2013, he came to accept this reality and placed my mom in an assisted living facility just a short drive from their home.

It cannot be overstated that one of the most precious gifts I've received in my life - and one of the things I am most grateful for - is the unconditional love and nurturing spirit of my mother, especially during my earliest years. While it saddens me to see her diminished capacities - unable to hold a conversation or comprehend the circumstances of her loved ones - I hold cherished memories of the games we played, the songs we sang and the stories we shared as I was growing up.

My entry from Mother's Day: "Though this is the first year my mother is in a continuing care facility, I am grateful she is in a good place with thoughtful and capable caregivers and I am equally grateful that my father has respite after being her sole caretaker for the past five years."

In late September, my dad called me to say that he was going for some follow up tests – including a stomach scan. He seemed not surprised to learn that the tests showed an early onset of colon cancer. Despite the news, he was determined to address it forcefully and in as timely a manner as possible. From the first time I met his surgeon and the dedicated staff at Capital Health Systems, I felt grateful that he was in a good place and would receive first-rate care.

Just a few weeks later, on October 20th, he entered the hospital, underwent a successful procedure to remove the malignancy and actually enjoyed a few laughs with me, his brother and his nephew. It was somewhat challenging for me to travel back and forth from NYC to central New Jersey to see him each day but I was extremely grateful that he came through the operation so successfully and that I could help him during the recovery phase.

Less than a week later, my dad was home and I naively thought he would soon be back to being his gregarious, independent self. I could not have been more wrong. With few friends close by, little follow-up care and with me having resumed my regular work schedule in NYC, what ensued can best be described as a complete "failure to thrive."

Three weeks to the day he went home, I came down to his place to take him to a follow-up doctor's appointment. Truly, I have seldom ever been as grateful as on that day. Were it not for this scheduled visit which resulted in an immediate re-admittance to the hospital to combat kidney failure, dehydration and a precipitous weight loss, I am convinced he would not have survived the year.

Our Gratitude Mission

While it was certainly no fun seeing him spend Thanksgiving in the hospital, I began to see signs of his former self by the time he came home. We now had a game plan for his recovery, which included an additional procedure, physical therapy and increased socialization. In spite of new challenges at work, I was thoroughly grateful that I had the freedom to take personal leave to assist with his convalescence. Whether shopping for his groceries, picking up his prescriptions or just giving him pep talks, I found myself being grateful for these tasks. Although he was not always fully able to express it, I knew he was grateful for my thoughtful navigation of these turbulent waters.

Concurrent with my father's health scare and my nascent search for new employment, I learned all too well the complexities of New York City real estate sales. What began as a cut-and-dried process in the fall quickly turned into a quagmire of open building permits, lost paperwork and phantom signatures. With each passing day, our patience grew thinner yet my ability to be grateful for even the tiniest morsels of progress to chew on remained unchanged.

The period between Christmas and early January proved to be especially frustrating with key personnel on holiday or otherwise unengaged, yet, there always seemed to be at least one person who shared a word of encouragement or the hint of closure to our real estate drama. For these, I was unendingly grateful.

The holiday season brought me an additional gift – an interview with a national nonprofit headquartered in New York. The catch, however, was that the position was based in Bethesda, MD. By this point, I welcomed the prospect of leaving New York altogether (rather than moving to an outer borough). The weeks of anxiety surrounding the sale of our property made me more than ready to see the bright lights of Times Square in my rear view mirror.

When I referred earlier to a "master plan" hatched in September of the previous year, I left out one important wrinkle: taking the profit from our sale of the NYC co-op and purchasing a property in Fort Lauderdale, Florida. With bargains still to be had, a burgeoning gay community and the promise of sunny, mild winters, we decided this could be our little slice of Shangri-La. So off we went, looking at units in several dog-friendly communities, narrowing it down to three possible choices – much like couples on HGTV's *House Hunters*.

Unlike half hour, formulaic programs like *House Hunters*, when push came to shove we were not sure we would be able to land our first choice given we were not much closer to a closing in New York.

Then, within a matter of a few days, the clouds lifted, the paperwork matters quickly resolved themselves and we were free to move forward. The best news of all was that our dream condo was still available and our offer was quickly accepted. Speaking of acceptances, within that same week, I also got an offer letter from my prospective employer and quickly arranged a start date.

It is hard to quantify which outcome I was more grateful for. The rapid succession of February's events left me giddy, relieved and anxious all at once.

Almost as if my 365 days of gratitude was destined to reach a climatic pitch, a dizzying span of nine days in March saw us move into an apartment not far from my new office inside the DC Beltway, close on our Manhattan co-op and purchase our new "home away from home" in Oakland Park, Florida.

It is worth noting that the last transaction was not all sunshine and smiley faces. Our plan to obtain a modest mortgage and invest some of the money from our NYC sale was dashed at the last possible moment, in large measure because of the bank's concern about the newness of my job and the uncertainty of Curtis' employment situation given our recent relocation.

Our Gratitude Mission

Having this particular rug pulled out from underneath our feet left us feeling both exposed and stressed, yet I was grateful that we still had the wherewithal to complete a cash deal for the condo. Knowing that for the first time in my life, I would own something "free and clear" was a resoundingly positive feeling, one that ameliorated the sting of being rejected by the bank and punished for our honesty.

As my 365th day of gratitude approached, my husband Curtis said his own special goodbyes to New York, having lived there more than half his life. He left his job after twelve very productive years on the best of terms, receiving accolades and stellar references. Still, the transition has been a bittersweet one for Curtis and I am immeasurably grateful for his willingness to leap into the unknown in a new city faced with the prospect of finding new employment.

Reflecting upon the entire year, almost nothing is as it was last spring. I have a different job, in a different city and am now a homeowner in still a different state. I learned (anew) to be grateful for the simplest of things yet also for the most important: I am so thankful to have found a workplace where I can, again, have an impact on the policies and practices governing young people who make bad decisions and who, in most cases, deserve a second chance. I am grateful to have a second chance, myself, in the DC metro area, as the first time around felt more isolating and one dimensional, largely because my partner, my family and many of my friends were living three hours away.

I am grateful that my father has been able to resume his normal routine and that we can once again enjoy a good meal and a glass of wine together when I come to visit. My gratitude extends to those who care for my mother each day and that she seems physically healthy and in good spirits. I am grateful to have the condo in Florida. It's a place to run away to, one that genuinely feels like home as soon as we open the front door. Although I miss my friends in New York, I will be forever grateful for the wonderful and uniquely fun times we shared along the way. And, yes, even though it was a bit disorienting and at times dispiriting, I am grateful that my former workplace moved forward without me, thereby allowing me to reconnect with practitioners and policy-makers at the national level. And at the end of it all, it feels as though I traveled to the place I am meant to be and arrived "with change to spare."

Lessons learned

Throughout these 365 days, I learned three lessons:

1. The act of being grateful is a spiritual one. It both lifted my spirits on many occasions but it also grounded me in who I am at my core.
2. Possessing a grateful spirit is a portal to seeing how wonderful life is and can be. It helped me see others in a more positive way and allowed me to imagine myself as a better person.
3. Being grateful isn't simply a momentary experience – it has a lasting effect. It can change relationships, it can alter the trajectory of everyday encounters and it can help shape my experience of the world around me and the people, places and things that matter most to me.

Some of my favorite journal entries that I didn't get to mention:

May 7th – Change can, indeed, be difficult but it was high time I cleaned my office and prepared for a possible move. I was grateful for the help of my wonderful partner, Curtis, who kept me on task as we sorted through and largely discarded three years of paperwork. The office feels clean again and I am ready for whatever comes next!

July 4th – I'm so grateful for our friends Steve and Beckie and the invitation to view fireworks from their lovely Brooklyn Heights apartment. Not only do they have a bird's eye view of the festivities, they are such gracious hosts and we also got to spend the evening with our friends Grant and Laurie.

Our Gratitude Mission

November 27th (Thanksgiving) – Dad is still in the hospital (for the second time this fall) but I am grateful he is doing so much better. He really seems to "get it" this time that he has to exercise, eat properly and listen to his doctors. The release to home last month proved to be perilous but I have a good feeling about his release this time!

December 20th – Tough last minute call not to fly to Mississippi with Curtis to spend several days with his wonderful family. With all that my father has been through, it felt like the wrong time to be relatively far away. I'm grateful to Curtis and his family for being so understanding about my decision to cancel and to JetBlue Airways for giving me a full credit for future travel.

March 18th – "Closing Time" – I've always loved that song by Semisonic but in this case – this was actually our second closing in a week! I've never had the experience before of buying something outright and it felt both scary and exhilarating! Even though our "plan A" did not end up happening, I am very grateful we were able to secure this lovely condo and look forward to enjoying it for many years to come.

August 2015 – Though my year of gratitude ended in April, I wanted to share one last moment of gratitude with you. After something of a roller coaster job search experience for Curtis since our move to DC, Curtis finally received his offer letter from Boston Properties and started his new job on August 24th. We are both very grateful for this new opportunity and for once again feeling productive and valued in the workplace!

Russ Terry

Terry's Take

I am grateful for the Seattle Seahawks! At the Super Bowl party Mark mentions, he and I were seemingly the only ones rooting for them. (I must admit, I do it only because I think my namesake – Quarterback Russell Wilson – is awesome.) We formed a special bond, exchanging high fives and the like. Little did we know at the time that we had gratitude in common too. Thanks to meeting that night and staying in touch, we are on *Our Gratitude Mission* together.

I appreciate Mark sharing his personal stories, especially the ones about his parents. Those of us in our forties and fifties can be faced with parents having more health challenges than they used to. I like that he finds gratitude in the situations that are going on with his Mom and Dad. I experienced this in 2014 when my Mom was diagnosed with breast cancer. I was scared, and sad, but she pulled through it and I'm happy to say she's now cancer-free, including a clean bill of health at her 2015 mammogram. Gratitude helped us during that difficult time, and I know it can help you also if you and your family are faced with similar circumstances.

Our Gratitude Mission

Chapter 13

Nydia Givens

I Did Not Die: Gratitude 365
Enjoying the Journey

Age: 28

Hometown: Charlotte, NC

Current City: Washington, DC

Our Gratitude Mission

Nydia Givens Be Grateful 365 Gratitude Mission

This Year I Resolve To....... "Reflect on my day and my life each night and find gratitude in something, even if it's only my breath, my heartbeat, my LIFE!" The first realization I made that inspired me to embark on my gratitude mission was that if you change your attitude you will change your life. Often, we can't see or focus on anything outside of our current pain and discomfort to acknowledge what we do have to be grateful for; as a result of this mindset we remain feeling and living like a victim to life.

~ Nydia Givens

"I Did Not Die"

Before meeting Russ Terry in early January 2014 and embarking on *Our Gratitude Mission* with him, I had already taken part in a Social Media Instagram challenge in December 2013 entitled "#OperationThreeTen." This challenge required that I document a list of ten things daily on my social media pages that I was grateful for. Completing this daily gratitude mission was motivating because in 2013 I faced some of the most challenging moments of my life emotionally, physically, spiritually, mentally and transitionally. In 2013, I experienced emotions and life events that I never had before. After years of meaningless relationships filled with emotional detachments from family, friends, and significant others, I never thought I would be able to feel and conceptualize the emotion called love. I, Nydia Givens, found myself head over heels in love for the first time.

For all five, yes I said five (maybe six), glorious months I was living inside my own *Eat, Pray, Love* moment filled with trips around the country, delicious food, adventures, spiritual awakenings, and fiery passion. I was looking at life through rose colored lenses. One day however, one of my lenses fell out and I could see the harsh reality of what my heart would not allow my mind to see and accept. I thought I loved someone who might be my soulmate based on what Elizabeth Gilbert once said: "The person who shows you everything that is holding you back, the person who brings you to your own attention so you can change your life...Soulmates, they come into your life just to reveal another layer of yourself to you, and then leave."

After falling in love, I experienced the heartbreak after we parted ways, as I was not destined to be with him for more than a short season of my life. I realized that, in order to get what I deserved out of life, I had to part ways with that person. Pain is inevitable, but suffering is optional and I had been choosing to suffer in hopes that things would change.

Also during this year, I made the important decision to disengage my friendships with two of the most important and long-standing relationships in my life—my best female friend for twenty-one years and my best male friend since high school. I realized that in all relationships I deserved to be treated like more than an option. I wanted consideration and respect for my thoughts and emotions, and I felt those things were not being given. I felt my friendship was being taken for granted. I decided if they could not mutually prioritize our friendship, then I would not be the one to continue doing so. Needless to say, I stopped reaching out and, as a result, we never spoke again.

In an effort to invest in myself and live up to my potential, as I advised others to do, I enrolled in a training course to become a certified life coach. I believe we all are destined for greatness and I want to make it my legacy to help people step into their greatness! To do so, I had to make another change. I moved into my own apartment for the first time, taking a step toward the peace, happiness and independence that I needed in my life. During all of these transitions, I embraced many lessons that I will share with you. The first lesson is that everything is an opportunity for growth. That being said, I decided to put my unpleasant emotions related to certain issues aside, and work toward putting my deficient mindset to rest in 2013. I was ready to embark on a new mission of gratitude for everything that has and ever will happen in my life. It is all a part of my destiny to challenge and mold me into the greatest me that I was called to be.

While I was on this path of emotional reconciliation and peace, a sorority sister suggested that I continue my daily expressions of gratitude. This time, however, instead of doing it for one month, I challenged myself to extend my daily gratitude to a complete three hundred sixty-five days and call my gratitude mission #begrateful365.

While on this mission in early January 2014, I met Russ Terry during my final life coach training class. He was called to fill in last minute as an assistant instructor. During our training Russ told a few of us about the anticipated release of his first book *My Gratitude Journal.* Then he mentioned seeking people to be participating authors in his second project that would document other people's gratitude mission for a full year.

I felt like this was something God was truly calling me to do. I had already been documenting my daily gratitude between 2013 and 2014. I never imagined it could lead to being published in this, or any other book, so early in my career. I was never supposed to meet Russ that weekend, but the Universe made it possible. I had to take advantage of such a great opportunity to share how gratitude was improving my life.

I believe that participating in *Our Gratitude Mission* is part of my destiny. I am grateful for this mission, as it has given me the ability to go beyond my current situations and see something to be grateful for every day. By sharing my gratitude story I hope to inspire others who need my light to shine, so that they might be able to see their way out of the darkness.

"Enjoying the Journey"

In the beginning of my year-long gratitude mission, I extended most of my gratitude toward those like-minded individuals and peers who had really been my support system during my transitions – my classmates in the life coach training class. I am grateful to be blessed with people who give me encouragement and love, and appreciate me for exactly who I am. While studying to become a Life Coach, I learned to be grateful for the process of growth. In growing, I am grateful to be in tune with my life's purpose, which will be achieved in self, relationships, and business. I find gratitude in removing judgment from others and myself, knowing that I can just be in the game of life and not attached to the outcome. I can just let it flow.

"Life is a perfect adventure; a game that cannot be won or lost only played."

– Bruce D. Schneider

"Life was like a box of chocolates. You never know what you're gonna get."

– Forrest Gump

While transitioning into full-time life coaching, I worked for a Mortgage Advocacy agency that shall remain nameless. Because I was very unhappy and unfulfilled while working for this company, I slowly started to learn the true beauty of gratitude. For countless days I would sit at work feeling as if I was watching paint dry, praying for the day of my emancipation. Then I had a thought: why not reframe my thinking and focus on the things I was grateful for pertaining to my job? I created a list to remind myself that anything uncomfortable has its purpose. You can find and show gratitude in all situations, even those you honestly do not like. I hope this encourages people who find themselves in a similar situation to view things from all perspectives, because there is a lesson to learn in anything. My gratitude list reads as follows:

1. Grateful for consistent income.

2. Grateful that I have had the opportunity to create new friendships and acquaintances while enjoying some laughs.

3. Grateful for the opportunity to travel around the country and meet new people.

4. Grateful that this job has pushed and inspired me to have my own business.

5. Grateful that this job has financed my education.

6. Grateful for the chance to make an impact by improving someone else's life.

7. Grateful to know I can become confident and knowledgeable in a field outside of my comfort level and experience.

In working for different businesses and organizations over the years, I often felt pressured to suppress my thoughts and actions to conform to the desires or views of leadership or the masses, neither of which I agreed with. I was never very fond of this way of life. Unfortunately, I also found myself working with people who doubted my abilities. In turn, I questioned my own capability based on what others thought I could or could not do. One day, in reflecting on my gratitude, I realized that I am grateful to know myself enough to know when things are off for me and I'm unfulfilled. I am grateful that God works in mysterious ways, and for the freedom to be myself in my delivery and my ways in order to effectively minister and inspire people. I don't have to be apologetic about my humor, my bluntness, or my inquisitive nature. Some people might hate it, but others might love it, and God uses the things you are ashamed of sometimes to be that ministry tool for others. I was created this way on purpose and I have learned to be 100% happy with it.

For those who doubted my ability to perform and fulfill anything I was assigned to do, I realized that I was prequalified by God when I was called to do the assignment. I was grateful and reassured to know that if He called me, I was already prequalified and did not need anyone else to believe in me or approve my power in my mission. If He said it will be done...IT WILL BE DONE!

Similarly to Moses at the burning bush, you might doubt yourself but know He is not going to call you to do something He does not think you can do. His missions and understanding are so above our human thought process we can only hope to know half of what He is trying to do with and through us. What I'm saying here is do not let anybody, not even yourself, stop you from what God has called and prequalified you to do. Be grateful for the calling.

"It is better to follow the Voice inside and be at war with the whole world, than to follow the ways of the world and be at war with your deepest self."

– Michael Pastore

"Be weird. Be random. Be who you are. Because you never know who would love the person you hide." – Unknown

After confidently accepting my (then) current employer was not the place I was destined to be any longer, I gracefully counted down the days until I would be emancipated from the confines of this institution both physically and emotionally. On the blessed day of April 28, 2014, I was finally granted my freedom with a discharge letter and a severance check. There were not enough words to express the gratitude I felt regarding the life-changing transition that had taken place and the opportunities to come as a result of my release.

Despite not loving it, I was blessed to have a job that opened up my mind and my life to new opportunities. This job showed me that my abilities measure beyond what I knew for myself. My experiences helped me realize I can overcome fear, and that unconditional love and understanding is possible. Also, if you don't stand for something, you will fall for anything! The people at that job pressured me to conform. I didn't want to, and therefore I knew it was time to go. After leaving this job that I held for the last two years, I was prepared, released, and excited that I would finally be able to focus on walking closer to my destiny. No more suppressing anything, but being free to express myself and work as God led me. I was thankful for the few who were honest and true people, accepted me for who I was, and aided in my growth and development. I knew that Destined 4 Greatness Life Coaching was coming soon!

That said however, in May 2014 I was unemployed and suffering from unsettling thoughts about things that happened in my life. Even though I was grateful to be free from a job that left me unfulfilled and unhappy, I still felt like the victim of life's unfortunate or painful situations. They often say, "An idle mind is the devil's playground." The devil has studied us for a long time so he knows how and when to attack us. During my idle time of unemployment, I felt like I was starting to come under attack. The question I had to ask myself is how much time had I committed to studying the devil knowing that he was studying me? I have learned that by studying him, I am able to recognize his attacks, thus enabling me to respond in a more prepared and empowered way.

"Put on the full armor of God so that you can take your stand against the devil's schemes. For our struggle is not against flesh and blood, but against the rulers, against the authorities, against the powers of this dark world and against the spiritual forces of evil in the heavenly realms."—Ephesians 6:11-12 (NIV)

As I sat with an open mind and emotion, I was attacked with various situations that would have normally upset me to the point of crying and breaking down. I quickly reminded myself that what's done is done. What you once had as possessions, relationships, and friendships are now gone! You asked to be set free from certain situations, so now that they are gone, do not allow those things to still have power over you because of what they might have wrongfully taken from you. I had to remember that anything that I lost or was taken from me could be replaced. I didn't need to reinvest my emotions in places, situations, or people that were no longer in my life.

Worrying about what they "did to me" was useless because it was over now. The lesson here is this: if you want your life to change, your mind must change first. You can win against the devil, but you must prepare your mind to do so. I am grateful THE DEVIL LOST THAT DAY!

"Tell my mind and myself that it is ok to focus on something else that is not your memory of the past and to enjoy the possibility of new opportunities."

–Nydia Givens

"The only thing that makes it part of your life is that you keep thinking about it."

–Unknown

I was grateful I didn't allow the devil to leave me feeling defeated over the things that I felt life had not given me or had taken from me. We often get so caught up on the people who don't do for us, or appreciate us, or are not in our lives, much more so than we acknowledge and show gratitude to those that are in our lives and do for us and appreciate us. I had to realize that, when we do the former, we put our energy into the wrong people and we also do a disservice to the latter: those who do supply our needs. I am grateful for those people who think about me consistently and reach out just to see how I am. I am grateful to people who invite me to things, instead of always waiting for me to contact them first, which I experienced in the past. I'm also grateful for those who reach out on holidays and birthdays, regardless of if we talk on a consistent basis or even not at all. I have learned people don't always treat you the way you treat them and that's life, but I need to acknowledge those who are there and reach out more because they deserve it. They deserve more time and energy than what I put into those who are not here or not good at cultivating a friendship.

~~~

Our Gratitude Mission

Here are a few noteworthy expressions of gratitude from this past year. I want to acknowledge those who have been a consistent blessing in my life...

July 15, 2014 "Feels So Good Loving Somebody When Somebody Loves You Back."

We often grieve about the things we do not have, and who left our lives or who we had to get rid of. I know I do. What I have learned is that we should spend more time and redirect our thoughts toward what we do have, and who does treat us right, and utilize those relationships more. I realize this is what I have with my life coach training colleagues from iPEC, the Institute for Professional Excellence in Coaching. Last year around this time I made one of the most impactful decisions of my life and after three years of consideration finally enrolled in school at iPEC to become a certified life coach. During this journey I made trips to Washington, DC, where I have met some of the greatest people ever. My peers and I have grown together, cried together, laughed together, and most importantly loved together. These people have shown me gestures, love and words of affirmation that I did not even know were possible. Being with them was the most enjoyable time of my life. It is the greatest feeling to be around people who understand you, and accept you for who you are. I am most grateful that in meeting them I have learned that I do have a group of people who honestly believe in me like no other, even on those bad discouraging days when my low self-worth comes in. I always have a reminder in my room and as my screen saver of all the wonderful things they have said to me to tell me how much they care about me and how I have inspired them. Feelings and words like this no one can ever take away from you, and I am forever grateful that they have given me these things to hold on to forever.

October 8, 2014 "My Provider"

"It's handled." —God

I woke up today with a positive hopeful spirit that things are about to turn around as I have new ideas and a new outlook. A few minutes later it was brought to my attention that my unemployment had been cut off. Shockingly enough my first reaction was not fear or sadness, but to laugh! I laughed and said "Oh, well isn't that something?" I continued to my task at hand. In my next task I checked my Gofundme.com/eips1k page to find that I had received my first donation! I became overwhelmed with gratitude and started to cry tears of joy as I thanked God for the blessings he had bestowed upon me. For the last six months I have believed that God would honor the patience I had with my former employer and the faith I had in my unemployment. In doing so, I was able to follow the vision He gave me to start Destined 4 Greatness Life Coaching. I know I am destined for greatness and I know the road won't be easy but like any road there is a destination and I will make it. I thank everyone for their support. For those who believe in my vision and in me, I pray that I am able to bless and uplift them daily with my words and my journey.

At the start of and throughout my gratitude mission, I was in an emotionally vulnerable place, trying to overcome various situations. By pausing every day to be grateful, I saw my growth – in multiple areas – over the last year. A coaching session with a peer validated this for me. We were going over an assessment I took in December 2013, right before embarking on this gratitude journey. As I reflected on my feelings at that time, I realized I did not want to focus on all that was unpleasant. Not that the negative stuff was bad to go through. Quite the contrary – I now see why it happened and I am grateful for its purpose in my life. I also realized that I was now able to tap into coping skills and thought processes that I was not aware I had. This coaching session confirmed to me that you always have everything you need inside of you to get through any situation in life. Those things will come out of you exactly when you need them to. Sometimes you need to experience certain things so that you can learn. This growth may not come when you want it, but it will happen exactly when the Universe wants it to. I am grateful that even though I am not exactly where I want to be yet, I am not where I was, and now I know how to accomplish my goals and dreams. I'm grateful I broke those chains and connections to things, habits, and most importantly people who I often relied on or trusted more than myself. I thank God for the loss of: job, friends, family members, relationships, and money, because I realize if you have everything, what else is there to gain and have faith in?

In concluding my year-long gratitude mission, I know that no matter the situation there can be a silver lining and you can find gratitude in anything. You have to take the time to reframe your thinking. If you change your attitude you can change your life. If you believe everything happens for a reason, spend more time thinking about that reason and less time dwelling on your emotions about what happened. That would be more fulfilling because obsessing over the obvious will not change the outcome of what was. How could I be happy with God about one blessing and then upset if something else does not work out? Sometimes you have to be grateful for the blessings of yesterday and when all else fails know that THIS TOO SHALL PASS.

....

My 10 Favorite Expressions of Gratitude

1. April 20, 2014 "Grateful for the Sacrifice of Jesus"

    So I was watching *The Ten Commandments* earlier, becoming a little frustrated with the ungratefulness that the Israelites demonstrated toward Moses. Moses left his family, parted the Red Sea so they could walk across to freedom, destroyed the person who held them captive, gave them food, water, and protection, but yet they still turned on him, complained, wanted more, and were never satisfied. Jesus healed people, devoted his earthly life to teaching and helping, and then suffered a painful death just so people could be forgiven from sin and have eternal life and not suffer. As I sat in acknowledgement and gratitude for all that Jesus has done for me and continues to do for me, I realized that we often take advantage, abuse our bodies and the life we were given, sometimes showing what would appear to be ungratefulness for what Jesus did for us. If I took a bullet for someone else, yet they shot themselves in the head anyway, how would that ultimately make me feel? Be mindful of what we do with our body, and most importantly with our lives. Show gratitude and respect for what was done for us.

2. May 24, 2014 "Thank God I Know God"

So again today I was watching the reality series *LisaRaye: The Real McCoy*. She was discussing her battle with trying to find religion and a relationship with God. Hearing her story and her questions and concerns about what it might require to be a Christian and how to really "let go and let God" made me so grateful that I know The Lord and have a personal relationship with Him. I have matured in my knowledge and my faith so that I do not question or fear as much as those who are infants in their walk might. This process takes time, patience, and understanding; however, the rewards of our faith are so worth it.

3. May 29, 2014 "Enjoying the Journey"

"You're single because God is preparing you. The question is ... are you learning?"

Some of my sorority sisters (or sorors for short) and I JUST had this conversation today. People are sitting around so worried about who everybody else has, and why they do not have anybody, they are missing the lesson and the growth experience that comes with the single life. There are too many other areas of our lives that we need to focus on, instead of sitting around being "thirsty" and complaining about what you have not received from someone else. A better path, in my humble opinion, is to find the love in yourself!

I am so grateful that I have never been one of those people who always feel like I have to be in a relationship. The question remains however, is that you? I am grateful that I have chosen not to compromise my self-worth and what I believe in just to have someone in my life. I am grateful that I can be happy for other people finding love even in my singleness, because I know that what God has for me is for me and He will give it to me when He is good and ready and "we" are prepared. Did you catch that? I am grateful to be wise enough to know that you need to learn how to enjoy the journey.

4. April 10, 2014 "I Was Here"

"Success is: liking yourself, liking what you do, and liking how you do it."

— Maya Angelou.

I am grateful that most importantly no matter how I feel when I go to sleep at night I know that even if I never see another morning I have fulfilled my destiny. I have lived, learned, and was here. I have seriously done something in almost every area of life I wanted, and done more than I ever thought I would. To the point that if it was over tomorrow my impact speaks for itself and I can say I was here because I lived a life to help more than just myself. What we have done for ourselves alone dies with us; what we have done for others and the world remains and is immortal. As I never even imagined life after high school, I now have a passion to inspire people, most importantly children, to look and work toward the future. To live in one's purpose will provide a plethora of things to be grateful for.

5. June 23, 2014 "Grateful to know it is possible!"

"Looking at my future self and knowing that I can have more than what is expected"

Today, I was advised to watch a motivational speech by Les Brown titled *"It's Possible!"* In it, he is discussing how we can do anything we want because most things we desire have already been done before, and someone has provided us a model to use as our guide. The most inspiring thing to me that he discussed was the growth process of the Chinese Bamboo Tree. This is a tree that, when planted, shows no outward signs of growth until its fifth year, when it then grows to more than 80-90 feet in only six weeks. The lesson speaks about the tree, but it also speaks about our goals. They have to be nurtured, watered, and we MUST have patience. Our patience is tested when starting any new venture as we wonder if our efforts will be rewarded. Like the tree, things might be slow to show progress. But when things finally do flourish, they will prove to be bigger than you ever imagined! Our roots are like the tree, growing a strong, sustainable foundation during our development process, which will be needed once our businesses or whatever aspirations we are working toward are manifested. I am grateful to know that, regardless of what my business or my life looks like right now, I believe without a doubt it will manifest into what it was destined to be in its perfect timing. Moral of the story is: do not give up! You must remain persistent even while you are unable to see any growth on the surface, just like the Chinese Bamboo Tree.

6. July 8, 2014 "This too shall pass"

"The ability to know that with all the emotions I am feeling right now this too shall pass; grateful for finding enough in me to express my gratitude even in moments of sadness."

Sometimes we have those days where we want to be alone or we are feeling not-so-great about life and it can drag us into a sad place of discontent. Well, today I am grateful I don't have those days as often anymore. I praise God for renewing my mind and my spirit in a way that, even when things are not going the way I would desire, I do not let these feelings of discontent linger and overtake me into some type of depression. All things are possible through Christ who strengthens me. When things are not going all that great, remember this too shall pass!

7. June 12, 2014

"Life becomes easier when you learn to accept the apology that you never got." – Robert Brault

One thing I am learning in life is everything does not need to be fixed! Some things just are not for us and when we can be ok with that, we can start moving forward in the right direction and making more investments and opening up more opportunities for those things that are for us. I am grateful for the best things I never had because I know now that the best things that are for me to have are still out there. You can see very clearly when the rain is gone so the question is how long do you want to stand outside in the storm? Some of us are still choosing to do so; grateful I stepped out of the rain!

8. July 27, 2014 "What I Learned in My Twenties..."

Today, I had the chance to watch the web series *Everything I Did Wrong in My 20s*. The show depicts a 35 year old woman who is depressed about all the things she wishes she would have done in her 20s and her unhappiness with the current state of her life in her 30s. While watching this show, I was grateful that some of the things she would have told her 20 year old self are things I feel like I am telling myself now. I am grateful that in my 20s I have grown in so many ways, and made the decisions that benefited me and supported my dreams. Even though I have taken jobs I didn't like, had relationships I didn't like, and found myself in many unpleasant and unfulfilling situations, at this moment nearing 30, I would not say I did anything "wrong" in my 20s. I lived life the best way I knew how with the knowledge and experience I had, and I do not regret it. I know everything has its purpose, good or bad, right or wrong, and I am looking forward to my 30s and reflecting on what I have accomplished. Enjoy the moment you are in, where you are supposed to be, and if you do not like it...change it.

9. March 26, 2014 "My Inspirations to be Young, Gifted, and Black"

I want to take time to show gratitude for those people who inspire me to accomplish more than I would have previously imagined for myself. These are just a few individuals whose work ethic, creativity and accomplishments I admire, including musician, producer, songwriter, and bandleader Harvey Cummings, actor and model Benz Veal, and the late and forever inspiring journalist, teacher, and entrepreneur extraordinaire Clayton Perry. These three men are a few notable people who have in my opinion successfully sought after and accomplished so much at a young age, more than most people ever do in a lifetime. In reflecting over this today, which would have been the 30th birthday of my brother's best friend Clayton Perry, I realized that in such a short amount of time this man accomplished so many things ... clothing lines, teaching, journalism ... the list goes on, and I can't help but think and admire the fact that he might not have done everything he sought out to do but he did so much and most importantly he did what was fulfilling to him and impactful to others. The only thing that you can leave behind in life is the stuff you have done. Be inspiring! I want to thank these people for being an example of success. Keep rising to the top.

10. August 17, 2014 "Grateful that I DID NOT DIE!"

In 2013 and 2014, I went through some of the most trying but eye opening experiences of my life! I was a person who literally could not fathom or conceptualize the act of being 100% or even 50% fearless and vulnerable to another person, action, or idea. I was once challenged to do an exercise in which I had to walk blindfolded, relying on the words and faith in one person to guide me to my destination. In the challenge, I had to take on one of my biggest obstacles – FEAR – and work toward identifying it and overcoming it. My biggest fear was that I would open up and then somehow fail at things, and as a result I did not take on certain challenges. What I learned to realize is, even if you do not get the outcome you are looking for, or do not succeed in the way you desired, YOU WILL NOT DIE! Things do not always work out how you want, but you will survive them. They will not break you, and if they do, it is only because you let them. I was scared of the vulnerability and uncertainty of love. I took a risk, opened up, and fell in love. It did not work out due to deception, but guess what? I DID NOT DIE! I put my trust and loyalty into family and friends who ended up stealing from me and/or dishonoring me but guess what? I DID NOT DIE! I put my all into a job for financial security, took on more financial responsibility, and lost the job but guess what? I DID NOT DIE! You can do it all and none of it might work out the way you planned or hoped for but guess what? YOU WILL NOT DIE!

....

Lessons Learned

Here are some lessons I learned in my year of Gratitude:

1. "Knowing that sometimes God has to take something away from you in order for you to be open and available for something better to come into

your life. Sometimes you have to give up what you want in order to get what you deserve."

April 15, 2014 – Around this time last year, I was in a totally different space. I was coming down or "crashing" from an emotional high I had never experienced before. I don't regret any action or feelings I have had in the past, because it was only preparation for helping me toward what is to come. All of us - men and women - have our lonely days, but we have to learn how to enjoy the journey and keep ourselves focused and maturing in the meantime. No relationship or situation happens by mistake. But know that not everything is meant to stay around long term. Accept the lesson and move forward toward what is especially destined for you.

2. "Knowing that my value is not defined by how others value me or how I perform at something."

   February 7, 2014 – I'm learning to respect the process of life, no matter what it looks like when I'm going through it. Also, letting God be God by not overthinking Him, His abilities, or His plan but realizing we will never fully know His plan. This is ok because if you trust the process everything is going to work out the way it should.

3. July 20, 2014 – Recently, I have begun thinking about the concept of nature vs. nurture. In other words, from the time we are born, we develop traits which are shaped by the environment we grow up in – the "nurture." Throughout life we grow and start releasing and weeding out all those traits that are not good for us, or are not beneficial to remain inside of us, because of where we are going and/or because we won't need these traits anymore. This process is needed to tap into our individualized innate "nature," unaltered human traits we get genetically and biologically through our parents, so that we manifest into who we really are. It is similar to the metamorphosis of the butterfly. It might have

started one way - as a caterpillar - but it was always meant to be a butterfly. I am grateful that I understand this process and am going through it. There are no obstacles, only opportunities. Remember you are exactly where you are supposed to be, and if you don't like where you are, figure out if and why you need to change it.

4. "Take the time you need for yourself because ain't nothing going anywhere."

June 10, 2014 – "Take Me Away" So I had been doing really well in emotionally handling my transitioning in all areas in life, but today I snapped just a little. I became annoyed with the repetitiveness of the job application questions. Like if I turned in a resume why do you still need my work history? Also, I do not remember my old supervisor's number! Leave me alone! I just had to make a decision to say NO! I am not going to do it. I put what I knew and submitted it. Then, when my brother asked me for money and I said NO, he got upset. I said, "Oh well be mad and go on then." After all was said and done, I just had to push everything away and go watch the new season of *Orange Is the New Black* to take my mind off things. It helped me escape and there's nothing wrong with escaping sometimes. We cannot allow other people and life to overwhelm us. Today, I am grateful for my escapes. I am also grateful to realize that I cannot wait until I work for myself and never have to fill out another application again! It is ok to not feel bad about saying no. It is important to worry about yourself. People have to learn how to be resourceful without you.

5. "The only thing standing between you and your goal is the bull s*%$ story you keep telling yourself as to why you can't achieve it." - Jordan Belfort, *The Wolf of Wall Street*

April 8, 2014 – Let's be honest. We all have the potential to be great and do great things, but for some of us, we don't always push ourselves, due to self-doubt, laziness, etc. I think sometimes the reason we do not do what is necessary to change is because we are afraid of change. We are afraid that things just might work. We are afraid we will come out of our comfort zone, and we will be successful at something we only hoped or imagined for ourselves. Regardless, I will be the first to admit that it is all an excuse, because in the end where there is a "will" there is a way. Let's destroy our excuses so we can get to our will and then to our way! I learned today in a surprising way that I can do anything with preparation and sticking to being who I am. In being authentic in my endeavors I can succeed and be confident in anything I desire to do.

6. "Make sure you are not falling in love with the POTENTIAL of someone. We must know the difference between loving people for who they already are vs. loving the idea of what they COULD be. Make sure you love him for who he is today. His potential should be the icing...not the cake."

—Jada Pinkett Smith

September 17, 2014 – This has to be one of the best pieces of advice I have ever received or read. It opened my eyes to realize that, in order to have a healthy and fulfilling relationship with a person, you have to be able to love them unconditionally. Also, you must ask yourself: "If this person never changes, and never grows into the person you think they can be, will you still be able to stay with them and accept them for where they are RIGHT NOW forever?" I once told myself and someone else I would be able to do that. I realized I was wrong and it was the best thing I ever realized. Don't go into anything trying to change someone or focused on what they can be, especially if that is not where they desire to be, because things probably won't work out as you would hope.

7. Sometimes you have to encourage yourself.

    March 23, 2014 – This morning I woke up, looked in the mirror (with no makeup or anything) and the first thing I thought to myself was "You look beautiful!" As women, we often go through those days where we do not feel at our best or we feel "fugly" as I say it, but sometimes you just have those days where you feel like "dang that girl is bad (Fine)!" I once told a random girl I met, who expressed her issues with low self-esteem, "On those days you feel beautiful you have to hold on to that moment. Take a picture if you have to, because nobody can EVER take that moment away from you! Beauty, along with happiness and anything else, starts from a love you must acquire from within. Once you are solid in that, nobody can break you but you!"

8. *"'Tis better to have loved and lost*
      Than never to have loved at all."
    – Alfred, Lord Tennyson. This line from his poem *In Memoriam A.H.H.* resonates with me because I never felt it was possible to love at all.

9. We are all both the teacher and the student. God will send anyone and anything in your life to teach you a lesson and vice versa.

10. Never give up! You have everything inside of you to do anything you desire. You just have to tap into it and keep moving.

11. Stop beating a dead horse. When the student is ready, the teacher will come.

....

Final Thoughts

The gratitude mission of 2014 was a long year full of ups and downs, additions to my life and major subtractions, and I am grateful for every last one of them.

Russ Terry

I am grateful to those people who showed me what friendship and companionship was not, and I am grateful to those who showed me what it is! I am grateful for the jobs that provided an avenue for me but showed me that it wasn't a road to be traveled long term. I am grateful for my new attitude, which has allowed me to sustain in the toughest times. I am most grateful to God as He has showed me in this year, seriously, that all things are possible and that He is the provider of all things. I would be nothing without Him and I am thankful that I know and have a relationship with Him.

What I hope people take from my gratitude story most importantly is every day we are given a second chance. Make the rest of your life the best of your life. Do not ever limit yourself. Live, give back, be selfless, and love yourself most of all. It is my hope that you utilize this gratitude mission for what it is and you remind yourself that, even at your lowest when it seems like there is nothing good in existence and you feel all alone, you still have something for which to be grateful. Make the best of it; don't let it take the best of you. Be inspired!

Terry's Take

Words cannot express how grateful I am for that serendipitous weekend in early January 2014, when as Nydia said the two of us were not supposed to meet. I was called in literally the afternoon before, because the Assistant Trainer who was supposed to co-Lead the training got shingles at the last minute and they could not find a local replacement near the DC/VA area. Not only did I meet Nydia that weekend, but also Donna Newman-Robinson, who you heard from earlier, and TWO of the authors slated to be in *Our Gratitude Mission 2*. I had such a great connection with so many of the dozens of students that weekend, that at the end when I had to say my final thoughts, I was doing the "Oprah ugly cry" (from when she was surprised on her show by her idol, Mary Tyler Moore). It's a great example in life of being spontaneous (I said yes even though I was teaching all day Tuesday to Thursday in New Jersey) and "going for it." I am so happy I did!

As for Nydia's year, I am grateful to her for sharing her challenges, and being so incredibly empowered by everything that she was faced with. I am inspired by her. The advice she shares in here is relevant for all of us, whenever we are faced with difficulties. I am glad I did a workshop in Charlotte while she was at that job, before she got as she says "emancipated." It was good to see her during her workday. I felt like taking her out to lunch brightened her day, which made me feel nice and happy. As we have said throughout this book, giving is receiving and vice versa.

Russ Terry

Our Gratitude Mission

Chapter 14

Alex Long

365 Blessings

Age: 40

Hometown: Washington, DC

Current City: Houston, TX

Our Gratitude Mission

Over the course of the past year, I have experienced tremendous blessings in the way of family, friendships and career. Every time there seems to be a challenge, God sees me through the storm and offers a blessing. My year of gratitude has highlighted this for me, not necessarily because I received any more blessings than in previous years, but because I was focused and in tune with what was happening. I took the time to stop and truly appreciate what I have, and not concern myself with what lay ahead or with what I did not have. Stopping to recognize what might seem like an insignificant event, such as a random act of kindness from a stranger, a show of appreciation from someone for something you've done, or a moment of peace during a walk, can have such a positive effect on us. Taking the time to stop and recognize these events made me realize just how truly blessed I am. We all are. That's the easy part. Recognizing the blessings in the dark times, well, that is not so easy. But, I believe that is what will carry you through your hardships. Most importantly, being a blessing to others, even when you don't feel like there is anything to give, will help you have the necessary perspective to appreciate your circumstances. It is, after all, the challenges in life that give us the courage, wisdom and the fortitude to press on.

> March 28, 2014 - Yesterday my husband, kids and I made the trek from Houston to Washington, DC to attend my step-brother's wedding. Today marks our first official day in DC and our first stop was to meet an old colleague and friend, Russ Terry, for breakfast. Turns out, Russ is also in DC for his first official book signing for his newly released book *My Gratitude Journal*. After meeting with Russ and hearing that he is working on his next book, a compilation of other gratitude journals, I felt compelled to sign up for the challenge. The thought of taking time to reflect each day on something I am grateful for, for an entire year, felt like a wonderful exercise. A BIG thank you to Russ

for presenting me with this opportunity to participate in his next project!

When I learned that Russ was enlisting authors for his second Gratitude book, I immediately knew that I wanted to be a part of it. What a fantastic way to share how important gratitude is. It can be life changing when you alter your perspective to see life with a spirit of gratitude first. I strive to be a blessing to at least one person every day. I may not always succeed in doing so, but my intentions are there and my greatest sense of fulfillment and purpose is when I can help someone else. I truly believe that this book will touch the lives of those who read it. If I can make a positive impact for at least one of those readers, then mission accomplished.

This year of journaling was so important because it highlighted areas of my life that got me to where I am today. It reminded me of difficult times and situations I endured that helped shape me into the person I have become. As I thought back to my childhood and adolescence, I decided to base my writings not just on my year of gratitude, but also my life's journey.

We get so consumed with what appears to be missing from our lives but, in reality, we are all blessed in ways we don't even realize. This notion of gratitude was first highlighted to me during a high school mission trip to Banica, Dominican Republic. As background to emphasize the lesson of gratitude I learned, let me first share what was happening in my home life when I went on the mission trip. I was seventeen, and experiencing a rather difficult time at home with my father, who was enduring some financial hardships. As a self-employed single parent, for many years he juggled caring for a young daughter on his own while managing his construction business. He always struggled to have steady work and manage his resources well. When the recession of the early nineties hit, so were we. We entered a period of darkness; we slowly lost our comforts, and eventually our home. Not many people knew what was happening with us, as pride kept our reality a secret.

Our Gratitude Mission

As for my excursion, after my junior year in high school, I had the opportunity to volunteer on this mission trip and I knew I wanted to be a part of it. The goal while we were there was to help some of the local community members build thatched roofs for their homes. The experience was a humbling one. We lived for a week with the local villagers in their homes, slept in their beds, ate meals with them, and even used their outhouses. For one solid week we lived without all of the comforts we American teenagers were accustomed to.

What stood out to me the most during my trip was that the same people we were there to help, who were living in extreme poverty, were also happy, carefree, and very appreciative of the help we were there to give. I never once heard a complaint or a grumble from any of the locals; rather, they were excited to have us there as guests. They wanted to share their gratitude with us, as well as their culture, music and food. What little they had, they wanted to ensure we were given the best.

As a young adult, that was an incredibly eye-opening experience: meeting people who had fewer material things than I did, and yet were so happy with what they did have. Their focus was not on the house they lived in or the clothes they wore, but on laughter, fellowship and life. That event, I believe, prepared me for the season just after that, when we lost our home. The experience opened my eyes to circumstances seemingly much worse than mine, and yet gave me an entirely new perspective on how to deal with my own losses and accept my reality.

Looking Back….

I grew up in the Washington, DC metro area with my father, who emigrated from Brazil back in the late sixties. He came to visit a friend and that visit turned into a permanent move. He quickly got a job, then a green card, and the rest is history. He then brought my mom to the US to start their lives in a new country. It was just the two of them, with both families remaining in Brazil.

I was born in 1975, and was raised an only child. I grew up without any of my extended family and no immediate siblings, so I grew accustomed to being by myself. When I was around eight years old, my parents separated, and shortly thereafter my mother moved back to Brazil. It was a bitter separation and I was torn. I ended up staying the US with my dad. It was a real challenge for a single father to raise a daughter on his own, but he was determined to do it and was not about to let me go.

For the next several years, it was just the two of us. I learned to cook and clean at an early age, but most of all, I learned to be by myself. Many times, I forgot that I even had a mom. The distance made it difficult to communicate frequently; this was before the technological advances that make it so easy today. Quite honestly, though, as a young girl, forgetting just made it easier to deal with. I would occasionally get letters in the mail from my mom, but for the most part, it was just my dad and me.

The physical distance from my mother undoubtedly created an emotional chasm between us. Years of living apart in different countries and a very bitter separation for my parents led to a strained relationship that took several years to mend. While I missed this time away from my mother, I now recognize that it was necessary so that other people would come into my life and play a very important role for me.

One of these people was a wonderful woman named MaryAnn, whom I met at the age of nine. MaryAnn and my father worked together for the same construction company at the time and became friends. She wasn't married and didn't have any children. We quickly took to each other and got very close. She became the person that I went to for everything, and answered all of the questions, problems and concerns a nine year old girl would have that a father could not address. Having lost her own mother at a young age, she understood me. As a teenager, MaryAnn was my voice of reason and my sounding board. She was quick to tell me how it was, even when I didn't want to hear it. She taught me how to think for myself, stand up for what is right, and be vocal about it. I owe much of my savviness, sense of humor, independence, self-empowerment and the lens with which I see the world to her. I referred to her as my American mom.

In 1993, when my father and I lost our home, I went to live with MaryAnn. She wanted me with her, end of discussion. It was a period of transition. I was about to enter my freshman year of college, I was working a job in retail so that I could pay my own bills, and I also had an internship, which I felt would eventually help me secure a job in my field of study. While all this was going on, my mother returned from Brazil with my younger sister, who was born there and is thirteen years my junior. My mother was an in-home nursing companion for the elderly, and always worked the evening shifts. This meant I needed to help care for my young sister during the evening hours. All these duties started to take a heavy toll on me. I stopped going to class as a means of rebellion. I was spiraling out of control emotionally and was dealing with it in a very passive way. I had too many responsibilities and thought I had to stay strong. I was also dealing with a lot of pent up resentment toward both of my parents for a variety of reasons. It was incredibly selfless of MaryAnn to take me in at that time, and deal with me and all of the baggage that accompanied me. Looking back, I realize that she had a tremendous amount of patience. I lived with MaryAnn for about seven years, until I was able to buy my first home.

The separation from my mother, while incredibly difficult for me, turned out to be a gift, because it allowed me to meet and cultivate an incredible bond with MaryAnn. It seems odd and counterintuitive that you need to experience a loss in order to experience a gain but it's very true.

MaryAnn passed away from a long, dreadful disease in 2005. While I was very sad, the time away from my mother helped me to deal with losing MaryAnn. It also helped the year before, when my step-mother Ana (my father's second wife) passed away. The step-parent/step-child dynamic can be a tricky one to navigate, but Ana was always so wonderful to me. I am grateful I had her in my life. I may have had a lot of time away from my Mom, but these two other special ladies helped to make sure I was nurtured and had positive, adult women role models.

Despite all of the emotional turmoil I experienced in my childhood and teenage years, I know my father did his best to raise me, and I love him very much for that. I wouldn't change one day of my life, as it has made me the person I am today. That's really what gratitude is: knowing that no matter what your hardship may be, there is always a positive side to it. Sometimes you just have to dig deep to find it.

Family

My mother and I began to re-establish our relationship around 2006. I had gone to live in New York for a period of time and was engaged to be married. We had a number of discussions (and falling-outs). I got my thoughts and feelings out in the open. I would be remiss if I did not mention that my wonderful husband Joe worked behind the scenes through prayer to reunify us. Joe and I married in 2007, and that event inadvertently brought my mother and me closer together. I relied on my mother to help me plan the wedding and entrusted her to help me be less anxious about one part of the big event: It was at my wedding that my mother and father saw each other for the first time since their separation in 1983. I carried a tremendous amount of anxiety for my parents' impending meeting and even asked that they meet beforehand to diffuse the awkward or even bad situation. They never complied with my request, but in the end, everything turned out well and my parents were both quite civil to one another.

After the wedding, my mother and I continued to grow closer as a result of our combined efforts. We got to know one another better and I learned to forgive in order to make it work. When my daughter was born in 2009, my mother was fully present. She went above and beyond the call of duty to help me with my new baby. I finally had the mother I missed all those years. It's funny but children really do have a way of bringing family together; since I became a mom, my mother and I have become much closer. As a young girl, I yearned to be close to my mother, and part of a larger, close knit family unit. Now, I have both and feel blessed beyond belief. I am so grateful to have her close to me.

My parents have also come around in terms of how they interact with one another. I never thought I would be able to host both my parents in my home at the same time, but that is exactly what has happened. Since our oldest was born, every year my dad visits Texas for the kids' birthdays. It was an odd moment when during one of those times, I was sitting on the couch with my mother on one side and my father on the other.

Around the time I started journaling, my mother started talking about relocating to Texas. She wanted to be closer to us and help us with the kids, since my husband and I both work. I never actually thought she and my step-dad would leave their comfortable surroundings in Florida and relocate. About six months later, they did just that! I am so thrilled to have them nearby. Not only for my kids, as they will be able to grow up with a set of grandparents who are active in their lives, but for me as well. I am spending more time with my mom now than I ever did, and she is present in a way that I hadn't yet experienced. I am so grateful she's in my life again, and that my children get to experience having a close relationship with their grandmother. It is a gift that I never thought to ask for, and yet I received. Here are some of my gratitude journal entries relating to this big moment in our lives:

> August 6, 2014 - I am so grateful that my mom is moving here to Texas to be near us. She just closed on her new home, which is down the street from our house. What a blessing to have family nearby! The kids

are beyond excited and I am happy that we will be close to them in case they ever need us (and vice versa). Family is such a blessing and, because I grew up without my family close by, I feel very grateful to have them near me and more importantly, that my kids will grow up with at least one set of grandparents geographically close. Can't wait!

September 5, 2014 - Mom and Allan are here for good! It is a bit surreal, but I am thrilled. Oh and the kids are too! How wonderful, to finally have family close by again. I am so very grateful for this. I know it will be life changing.

September 20, 2014 - Mom and Allan have only been here for a couple of weeks and today I had an opportunity to go to the Houston Fine Arts Festival with Allan. This was special to me for two reasons: 1. I don't really get a chance to hang out with him one on one in a neutral setting, and I knew that he would really enjoy the event and 2. It is also rare that I get the chance to see artwork in an exhibit or museum. It was special to me that I had the opportunity to do that. I am looking forward to more occasions like that!

There are very few friends that I grew up with whose parents remained together. Despite having this be the normal model of my youth, I very much value and admire the sanctity of marriage; I hope to not become another statistic of divorce. My husband Joe's parents are still married to this day and I aspire to be like them. I want my kids to grow up with two loving parents in the same home, and not have to ever decide between their mother and father, the way I did with my own parents. I very much admire my in-laws.

Our Gratitude Mission

They are a wonderful example of what marriage should be. Even though they live in another state, I always cherish their visits and am so pleased when the kids get to spend time with them.

> May 2, 2014 - Today my mother-in-law came in from Greenville, SC to spend a week and a half with us while I go on my business trip to Calgary. I am so very glad she is finally coming to see us; she hasn't been to visit us since we moved to Houston and I know that she and the kids will all really enjoy spending time with each other. For that matter, my husband will get some good quality time with his mom as well and that is priceless. We are blessed to have both of our parents living so that our children can have memories of their grandparents.
>
> July 7, 2014 - Today marks seven years that I married my wonderful husband, Joe. Hard to believe those seven years have already passed. So much has happened during that time. We have lived overseas, relocated states twice, 2 kids, 2 dogs and a few jobs. I am so blessed to be with such a good man! I love him with all my heart and I know he loves me too. I pray that we have many more years together on this earth. Also thankful that my dad is another year with us, today he turns 67—our wedding day was on his 60th birthday and we celebrated with a cake for him during our reception!

As for my father and me, we remain close to this day. I love him very much and know that he always does his best with others in mind first. If there's one thing I have learned from my father, it is the notion of selflessness when it comes to giving. He has always had a huge heart and gives freely (to a fault sometimes), but it is admirable to see how he cares for others. He is an easygoing guy, who always has a good disposition. I believe this is something that has helped him immensely in life as a means to cope with his challenges. My hope is that one day, my father will be closer to us geographically as well, so that our kids have the opportunity to be closer to their grandfather and get to know him and the wonderful person that he is.

Friendship

> December 1, 2014 - I am so happy to have met so many wonderful people here in our neighborhood. It is amazing how many friends I have made both individually as well as collectively with my husband. We have really bonded with the friends that we have made.

Good, lasting, authentic friendships don't come easily. I'm talking about the kind of friendships when your friends have your back no matter what and are always there for you when you need them. I have met some wonderful women over the course of my gratitude year and have developed some beautiful friendships as a result. In fall 2012, we relocated to the Houston area from Florida for my work, so establishing these connections has been important to my integration in a new city. They have made me feel part of a community. In early June, I met two of those friends at a birthday party for one of my daughter's classmates. They were chatting in Portuguese, which I am fluent in, and I approached them to ask if they were Brazilian too -- to which they responded "yes." We exchanged numbers and the rest is history. Carolina and Karen have become close friends with whom I share mommy nights out, many laughs and even holidays. I have also met some wonderful neighbors who have become good friends too. We have formed close bonds with some special folks.

Our Gratitude Mission

I was also blessed to reconnect with old friends. Twice in my year of journaling I traveled back home to DC, and reconnected with friends. Each time I go, I make it a priority to see as many of those people as possible, because it is so important for me to maintain those ties.

> April 3, 2014 - My trip to DC, while tiring, has been wonderful. I have had the opportunity to visit with so many friends and family. The test of true friendship, I believe, is that no matter how much time passes, you can still reconnect and pick up where you left off. My friendships range from grade school to college and even work. I love them all and am so happy that I had the chance to visit with everyone that I did. Each person means so much to me and is such an important part of my life. I also got to see extended family from my dad's second marriage at my step-brother Danilo's wedding. It was a beautiful event and quite emotional as well, as we recalled my deceased step-mom, Ana, whom I adored. The speeches were beautiful and my best friend Karen E. and I danced the night away … we had a blast.
>
> June 12, 2014 - Today marked the start of the World Cup, the only sporting event I actually follow. My friend Karen R. invited a group of ladies over to her house to watch the game and hang out. What a great time we had and I enjoyed meeting new folks in the neighborhood. I'm grateful to her for opening up her home to all of us rowdy soccer fans!
>
> September 13, 2014 - Joe and I met some great neighbors last night, and tonight, one of them invited

us over to hang out. It is so wonderful to meet people that are close in age and are like-minded. I am very excited to get to know them better! It is events like these that make me confident in our decision to move to Texas. This is starting to feel like home!

September 19, 2014 - Today I got to have lunch with a group of girlfriends. It was such a nice break in the day to have the opportunity to do that. I am fortunate to work close to home and near my family and friends, which gives me the flexibility to indulge in these types of things. I know it won't last too much longer, so I will take advantage of it while it lasts! I also am grateful to have had some quality time with my friend Carolina; we had a lovely dinner and great conversation, as usual. I adore her!

November 27, 2014 - My dear friend Kimberly is visiting from Tampa for Thanksgiving. I am so happy that she chose to come and spend the holiday with us. She is one of the few good, lasting friendships I made while living in Florida and someone who I know will continue to be a part of my life for years to come. We have had a great visit; lots of laughs and wine!

December 5, 2014 - Our dear friends Karen E., Ed and their son (my Godson) David arrived from DC for what I hope is their annual visit! It is so wonderful to have them here with us. We consider them family, and I really appreciate the quality time I get to spend with Karen. I miss her.

Our Gratitude Mission

Career

Over the course of the past fifteen years, I have worked in the International Human Resources field for various companies. The last few gigs in my career have included some hard knocks. I learned tough lessons and developed through challenging clients, adversarial teammates, and a few horrible bosses. Those experiences crushed my self-confidence and made me doubt just about everything I did. I constantly questioned myself and my abilities. I knew what I was capable of, but I let the caustic environments I was in get the best of me.

One thing helped me to stay grounded and was a constant reminder of my self-worth. No matter where I was or what I did, I always tried to be a blessing to others. I would seek out any opportunity to help someone else and I would give whatever I could, be it time or resources. This was critical to my sanity and was a good reminder for me of who I am, and what my greater purpose is. I always try to pay it forward, whenever I can.

When I began my year of gratitude, I was quite unhappy in my career and feeling very unappreciated and underutilized. I was brought in to clean up a mess. I had inherited a group of about forty very disgruntled employees and it was my job to make things smooth. Not to mention I had an extremely difficult and highly critical boss, and an unsupportive senior leadership team. I spent two and a half years in this environment, constantly questioning and doubting myself and my abilities.

Prior to that role, I worked for other large well-known financial institutions in the same capacity and had similar experiences. There must be something about big corporate environments that just doesn't agree with me. Either that or I was purposely put into situations that would challenge me in a way I wasn't quite prepared to handle. I worked for a large investment bank in New York, where my abilities were constantly questioned and I felt as if I was working in a pressure cooker. I then went to work for a large accounting firm, which relocated my husband and me to Florida. This was a particularly dark period in my life, during which I struggled with anxiety and postpartum depression. While difficult, it was also necessary. I had to deal with much adversity at work and try to prove myself as a valued member of the team. Needless to say there was a lot of competition and the backstabbing that went along with it. Over the years, my self-confidence took a downward spiral. I was so beaten down that I questioned my professional ability and at times, my worth.

Midway through my journaling year, I was courted by two prospective employers for roles much larger than the one I was in. I was quite flattered that I was even being considered for these positions, especially since they sought me out. It was a pivotal time in my career and I knew that I needed to make a decision as to which opportunity I would take. I prayed about it, and asked God to direct me on the right path. I was unsure which direction to go in, as the two companies were quite different and I had to choose if I wanted to go to a very large, structured environment (been there, done that), or a smaller, unstructured one. The latter had much more potential in terms of opportunity for growth but at the cost of less direction. The lack of structure would afford me the opportunity to build my space, apply what I know and be the leader of a team, a goal I had for a long time.

I opted for the latter role and am so glad I did. It has been a phenomenal step in my career and has allowed me to flourish in a way that I hadn't thought was possible.

As I assess my year of gratitude, I take note of my career progression and the blessings I received. While I experienced some challenges and disappointments, in the end it was necessary in order to experience the blessings that were about to occur.

> July 24, 2014 - Today was a double whammy of good for me. I had an interview in the morning that went really well, and ended with the hiring manager telling

me that he would love to have me on his team...what? It is never that easy! The fact that this is a stretch job, big promotion, more money, and was by far the easiest interview that I have ever been on, in terms of format and ease of discussion, is mind blowing! I am feeling extremely thankful for that and quite humbled by the experience. Then to end the day I met my new group of girlfriends for a girls' night out dinner and we had a blast. We continue to bond with one another and I feel so blessed to have met and built this wonderful friendship with such a great group of women.

August 11, 2014 - Today was a particularly difficult day at work. Despite my continuous efforts to position myself to grow and take on more, I have come to the realization that the organization I am in just does not want me to continue working there. This afternoon, however, I received an email from a prospective new employer indicating continued interest in me. It was perfect timing. I really needed some good 'work' news, and it has lifted my spirits!

September 16, 2014 - Today, my new manager, who has only been in her role for a few weeks, is visiting from our corporate headquarters office in Canada, where she is based. I am extremely grateful that she took the time and effort to come and see me. My previous boss, who was my superior for two years, (and also based in Canada) never came to visit with me, not once. During the new leader's visit, we had an honest discussion about my job and future with the company. She gave me some very candid feedback, which isn't always easy to hear, but it was constructive, and I appreciate it. She is tough and fair and it is unfortunate that I won't get a chance to work with her longer term. I know that my future here is on borrowed time, and I need to plan my exit strategy. It's time to move forward.

September 17, 2014 - Got a call today from two job prospects that they are interested in proceeding with the interview process. After the visit with my boss this week, I needed the boost and confirmation that I am still needed and wanted. I am feeling a bit dejected, so it's nice to know that my potential prospects are still on the table and there may be options for me to move forward. Tomorrow is my last interview with one of them.

September 30, 2014 - Today I received an offer of employment from one of my suitors. I am so happy, grateful and relieved. To have options is an amazing feeling. Also, to be recognized for my abilities and my experience is great feeling. This process has been a good reminder to me that I haven't advanced this far in my career in vain—I know my stuff and it's time to regain my confidence!

November 3, 2014 - Today was my first day with my new employer! I am so grateful to have this opportunity. I finally feel like I am being given a role which will allow me to grow myself professionally, add value in my area and work in a meaningful way. I have been held back and felt quite stale. It's time for a change and I am so excited!

Paying it Forward

To paraphrase a well-known bible verse, "To whom much is given, much is required."

This is my mantra, the words which I constantly remind myself of. At the forefront of my gratitude is giving back. It doesn't need to be material; it can be time, compassion or even a smile. You never know the effect a kind gesture will have on someone who you encounter, no matter how brief.

> September 3, 2014 - As a treat, my husband and I picked up the kids from school and took them to one of their favorite spots for dinner. When we got to the register to pay, a very nice lady who works there, Anjelica, gave us two free meals, just because! She said we are good customers and that because we come frequently, she wanted to give us that. Wow it's amazing how small, random acts of kindness can make such a difference in our lives! I'm very grateful for Anjelica and her kindness.

I am at a place in my life where I can truly appreciate the person I have become, through the lessons I've learned and the hardships I've endured. I try very hard to always be a blessing to those around me, and believe in giving freely. I always remember where I came from and, despite my struggles in life, how far I have come to where I am today. It is up to each one of us to help make the world a better place! It's not going to happen on its own.

> July 11, 2014 - One of the things that people sometimes miss out on is having perspective. Perspective is critical

to how we see the world and our own lives. I try not to get too WOUND up about silly, insignificant things, because I know that there is always something bigger, more serious out there that could impact my world. I am blessed for everything that I have and am. I pray that I continue to keep my focus on my path, and not allow the outside world to distract me.

September 6, 2014 - Today I am grateful for the things we often take for granted, like taking a walk, or being able to walk for that matter. This morning I took my dogs for a walk, and as I often like to do, I noticed the environment around me. We can get so caught up in our daily grind and struggles that we tend to forget how much more difficult it would be if we didn't have our basic faculties. Also, I am so grateful to live in a tranquil environment where one can walk freely and in peace without fearing for our safety. With everything we hear about on the news happening in other parts of the world, where basic freedoms are limited and even restricted, we tend to forget just how blessed we are to live in a country where we are free to be who we are.

September 22, 2014 - "New beginnings" I am very thankful for the opportunity to start fresh. Lord knows I'm not perfect. Like many of us, I am a work in progress as I like to call it. I get caught up in a rebellious pause of action and harm no one other than myself. Today I choose to do something about it, and turn my awareness into action. We all have a responsibility in life to improve ourselves, and I thank God for giving me the wherewithal to do so.

Our Gratitude Mission

Gratitude is something that is often overlooked and certainly underestimated. The power of gratitude, be it recognition and humility for what you have or an act of someone demonstrating gratitude toward you, is an incredibly powerful thing. My life hasn't always been easy; I've had my share of difficulties and hardships. But I wouldn't change any of my life events, as difficult as some of them may have been, for they have shaped me into the person I am today. These challenges have also helped to give me a perspective on life, which can often be overlooked by those who aren't forced to deal with adversity. I am so appreciative of what I have, yet I struggle with how to impart the life lessons I have learned to my children. I want them to appreciate what they have without having to go through some of the hardships I endured. I take my past as a constant reminder of what was, and what could always be. It is foolish for us to think that we are not immune to loss.

Today, I consider myself beyond blessed. Despite my challenges in life, I am a smart, accomplished, well-rounded person who gets a kick out of being a blessing to others. I have my health, a loving family and wonderful friends who love and support me. I have a great career and a beautiful home. Above all, I have a relationship with God.

Quite some time ago, I developed a daily habit. Every morning when I wake up, the first thing I do before getting out of bed is to give thanks. I thank God for the day, the ability to wake up and take another breath, to be able to plant my two feet on the floor and to have the opportunity to make an impact in someone's life. We are not promised tomorrow, so all we can do is be grateful for today and make the most of it.

This year has reinforced my practice of gratitude. The lessons I have learned these last 365 days have been impactful. The most important of those lessons that I will walk away with is that no matter how difficult a situation or season in your life, you eventually get through it. Coming out on the other side, and being grateful for that experience, is what matters. Someone once told me that failure equals success. I didn't completely understand what that meant until I started taking inventory of my journey and the losses along the way. You have to experience loss to truly appreciate the gain.

I have come out of this experience with a heightened awareness of the blessings I have, and more determined than ever to help others in need. I would like to eventually redirect my talents and embark on a career that will help that population, and provide opportunities to those who may not have had a chance otherwise. I will teach my children the importance of living a life of gratitude as well as respect, tolerance and kindness. We are all on this planet for a purpose and I truly believe that mine is to be a blessing to others. After all, I only have 365 days a year to do it.

Here is one final entry from my year of gratitude:

> November 10, 2014 - Today was my first day riding the bus to work downtown at my new job. A very nice lady named Stacey sat down next to me on the way into town, and we proceeded to chat for almost the entire ride. She gave me very helpful tips on commuting via bus, and even showed me where to catch it on the way back. Funny enough, we work in the same building (though for different companies), so when she got off at her stop I was able to follow her. I was so relieved to have met her and so grateful that she was kind enough to show me the ropes.

I have been doing most of my writing on the bus commuting to work, as it gives me an hour of uninterrupted time where I can focus on my writing. That last entry I found to be quite apropos; as I am finishing this chapter, Miss Stacey is sitting beside me. Thank you!

Our Gratitude Mission

November 2015- As an update to my journey, I was laid off from my job this month due to the downturn in the company's industry. While the timing is not fantastic from a personal perspective, this occurrence has been a blessing in disguise. I am finally going to take the opportunity to assess my career path and work in an area that brings me greater satisfaction and a sense of fulfillment. I am a firm believer that everything happens for a reason and this is no exception. This is just one more blessing to be grateful for, and I will make the most of it!

Terry's Take

I am so grateful that Alex and I met on a business trip for our firm in San Jose/San Francisco. It's interesting that she, Mari Ryan (who you heard from earlier) and I all were having challenges at our related jobs there simultaneously! As I mentioned in my Terry's Take at the end of Chapter 2, from my standpoint, the firm is otherwise a great place to work. Anyway, that night at the group dinner, Alex and I sat near each other, and I was instantly drawn to her. She's just so darn funny!

It was also excellent to catch up with her in person in Washington, DC early in 2014. Our nation's capital is such a pivotal place for many of us involved in this book. That's where I met Nydia Givens and Donna Newman-Robinson. Mark Ferrante moved there during his year of gratitude, and of course Alex is from there originally and we happened to be visiting there at the same time! What are the chances? I love serendipitous moments like this. They make life so much more enjoyable.

My Mom always says, "You never know what goes on behind closed doors," meaning many families have drama or struggles that we don't know about. A number of our authors share them, and Alex is no different. Reading her story makes me (and hopefully you) grateful that I grew up in the same country as both my parents, and that we were not homeless at all! There are so many things in life we take for granted, and when we stop and think about them, it automatically gives us a plethora of people, things and experiences to be grateful for.

Chapter 15

Domonique Lewis

The Key is Within Us

Age: 52

Hometown: Newark, NJ

Current City: Paris, France

Our Gratitude Mission

My name is Domonique. I was born happy, whole, complete, resilient and confident. As a child, listening to my mother's pronunciation of my first name was music to my ears. It reinforced my self-confidence, and as a child, this made me feel special. When my mother would introduce me to other adults, she would say, "This is my daughter <u>DO</u> <u>MO</u> <u>NIQUE.</u>" I adored how she could just be so proper at any given moment. She pronounced my name in the same way those beautiful fingers glided gracefully across the piano. She loved to sing, and was a very talented singer. While I may not be an accomplished singer like my mother, I am grateful to see where the artistic talents I do have come from.

Living with alcoholics, things would become dark very quickly. Growing up, I listened to my aunts and uncles sing and I watched those adults playing cards and drinking. It would seem like everyone was having a ball until the violence broke out. Despite the tumultuous and impromptu storms of my youth, I survived.

When I was a little girl, I felt most alive dancing. During the calm moments with the adults, we would have fun doing a "Soul Train" dance or there would be a dance contest amongst the kids. At the age of 18, I took my first dance classes, ballet then modern dance. I dreamed of becoming a professional dancer, but was haunted by lack of self-belief and worry that I could not earn a living as a dancer.

Sometimes, it felt as though the harder I tried to advance or to succeed in one domain or another, the more the harsh insults from my relatives (not my parents) would resonate in the back of my mind. They were not deliberately being mean or spiteful to me; it was not personal. I forgive them for the pain they inflicted on me and I forgive them for not giving me the love a child needed. It would be very easy to continue to blame them and remain a victim for the rest of my life.

Russ Terry

In their own way, they wanted to ensure that I allowed my inner brilliance to shine bright. We are all enlightened spiritual beings having a human experience. They were helping me to rise above the secular realm and use my interior light to heal my life. I am here to recognize my own magnificence.

At age ten, I went to live with my father. My parents had a pact that if my mother could not care for me, then he would. When I was with my father and grandparents, I felt secure. No alcoholic fights or bouts of hunger. I could feel the energy shift and I began to recover.

In hindsight, I am grateful for the role my relatives (not my parents) played, as I have come to realize that others' opinion of me is not the reality of who I am, nor the person I have become.

I was introduced to Nichiren Daishonin's Buddhism in 1988, thanks to my best friend from my youth who shared the Buddhist practice with me. There was a day in particular, in which I distinctly remember this woman, Pat, had visited my friend Yvonne. I was impressed and moved by Pat's warm words of encouragement toward Yvonne. Yvonne was in the midst of immense personal struggles as a single mom, searching for steady employment and faced with financial difficulties. Her self-esteem was at an all-time low. Pat said to her, "What is important is what you do from this moment forward; the past is over." Her words resonated with me, and this story has stuck with me always. This would set me on a new spiritual path to inner transformation.

In 1990, as part of a fresh start, I left New Jersey and moved to Washington, DC. It is there that I would meet my future husband. From the marriage, we brought three wonderful sons into this world. We enjoyed many adventures followed by a transatlantic move to Paris, France. The move would initially be for two years to get to know his family, the French language and culture. Many say Paris is the most romantic city in the world. However, the weight of various factors eventually was too heavy a burden for him and me. We separated in 2003.

Our Gratitude Mission

After the split from my husband, for logistical reasons, I chose to remain in France to raise my sons here. I wanted to keep the boys close to their father and vice versa. Despite my well set intentions, in the fall of 2003, he returned to the USA indefinitely. In spite of his return, I decided to stay. I didn't want to disrupt my young sons' lives any more than we already were.

This decision did not sit well with my father, who I was very close to. He was not particularly pleased to learn that I would stay in France, without my sons' father or family of my own. Moreover, I was still learning the language. My father's concern was, "How would I manage alone?" Thanks to my ex-husband's return to the United States, I had to learn the language and fend for myself.

Since I was clear on my decision to remain in France, my father changed his home phone to International calling service so he could call me from the USA, at any time. An example of that: I was in Mali, West Africa, on a mountaintop of a village, and I received a call from my father. Modern technology!! I am so grateful that he did change his service, and appreciated his calls and his efforts to stay connected. It was important for him to know that his "baby girl" was safe, even though I was on another continent.

My father passed away in October 2008 followed by my Mother in May 2010. While they were alive, I made many transatlantic trips with my sons to see their grandparents, and also to accompany them in their transition from life to death. My father will be most remembered for his "joie de vivre" (cheerful enjoyment of life, in case you don't know French), smile, strength, compassion and sense of humor. I carry all these characteristics with me. I am profoundly grateful to my Mom for her very sincere expressions of gratitude toward everyone and for everything. She spent her last 25 years in an extended care medical facility. She would be over the moon when family visited, no matter how long or short the stay.

Russ Terry

Thanks to my colorful past experiences, not only could I reconstruct my life, but I have been able to encourage other women and young ladies who have been through similar situations to do the same. Our discussions brought them relief in knowing they were not alone and they could survive.

I am grateful for the journey and circumstances that led me to France. If the father of my children had not brought us to Paris, we would not have had the experience of living International lives in both the United States and France. I also would not have had the occasion to slow down and see what I was truly made of. As a divorced mother, raising my sons alone, in two cultures and two languages, I have done my very best to instill the following in my sons: integrity, self-love, self-respect, and the importance of education, family and the pursuit of their dreams. I can see how I have been so much more than that little voice inside of me ever wanted me to believe. Along the way, I have been establishing a new relationship with myself and showing myself more self-love, acceptance and consideration. At my essence I am pure divine spirit. It is all of who I am.

When dancing, I could be who I wanted to be. In my new town, I signed up for African dance classes. I could hear that little voice saying, "You are inferior to the other dancers." The subjective feelings of "inferiority" were only in my head. I pushed those negative thoughts out of the way and got to the business of dancing. Simultaneously, I was making friends with other women and creating a circle of heart-centered friends. I would later be invited to dance with a group of musicians and three other dancers with whom I have created infinite treasures of the heart. We would perform in and around France and Luxembourg. We still perform today. When I perform, I communicate with the audience in a way I am not able to express with words.

On two separate occasions, my passion for African dance would take to me Mali, West Africa. My low self-esteem would cause me to self-sabotage, but when I let that go, "I" began to dance. I am still learning that the most

Our Gratitude Mission

important person is "ME" – how I feel about me, right here, right now, not the past, the future or the opinion of others.

It feels good when we can look back at how far we have come. The young girl from Jersey is now living abroad, raising my sons with integrity and speaking two languages. Now that is something to be grateful for!!

When I began the Gratitude campaign, I had already done a few things to change how I see and feel about myself, independent of my external environment.

First, one of the hosts on the Life Coach Radio Networks invited me to share my journey from the United States to France. This was done, live, on the radio. What an honor! The platform afforded me an opportunity to let others hear my story, especially the part about staying in France with my three sons after the divorce. I felt the fear and did it anyway!

I was touched and surprised when a guest from the show sent me a message to say "Thank you" for sharing what I went through. That person's teenage son was inspired to learn French when he learned of my sons' journey. He felt that if they could do it, so could he and he did.

I truly appreciate my heart-centered family and friends, who were at my side when my father's health began to fail, then when I lost both my parents, and through the transatlantic journeys as a result of it all. Thanks to the person I am, I naturally created a supportive circle.

To celebrate my rebirth as I constantly fought those false beliefs, two years ago, for my 50th birthday, I threw myself a party; I organized everything: I invited the French-African drummers and dancers with whom I have performed, and we gave an impromptu show. I also hired a DJ, two singers and a guitarist. The hall was beautifully decorated in leopard prints (my favorite) and we had a catered meal, wine and champagne. The highlight of my party was the presence of my in-laws, from whom I had felt estranged. Their presence closed the gap. My cherished friends, from the town I used to live in, came too. My very close friend drove down with her family from Holland to be present. She also stunned the crowd with her rendition of Bill Withers' "Ain't No Sunshine When She's Gone".

It was a wonderful feeling to have been surrounded by heart-centered friends who made it a memorable event and journey, commemorating all our time in France. This was also a reminder of what I am capable of doing.

"Choose an ambition and, with full force, expect that it is possible and that you can make it happen. Give constant attention and committed effort to your dream, and your motivation will perpetuate itself. Demonstrate a positive attitude as you strive for great things and take care to create a supportive environment around you that amplifies your motivation."

By Brendon Burchard in *The Motivation Manifesto* page 67

This gratitude project has enabled me to course-correct by fully learning to treasure my life. I am in charge of my life and have been put on this earth to be the leader of my own life. Our minds are like a computer that has to be reformatted, thus taking our lives to a new dimension of awareness. From this place of calm, I can see how truly magnificent a woman I am and the awesome life I lead. By appreciating all aspects of my life, I will influence all areas of my life. I will let go of the past and soar, reaching new heights. Validating and approving of myself from the internal core of my being, and never looking externally, is where I am headed. I want to do great things in this world, but first I must be the change I wish to see in it.

Our Gratitude Mission

Pivotal Moments of My Year of Gratitude

My Sons

With permission from my oldest son, Pierre, I am sharing his story with you. He feels that people should know about his mistakes and bad choices.

It is April 2014 and unbeknownst to me, I have taken a backseat, from across the Atlantic, to watch my son's life go off course.

Back in June 2012, my oldest son returned to the USA to be with his father and sign up for university. He was accepted at an established Art School in Washington, DC to study Graphic Arts, in which he has a natural talent. He enjoyed school and his teachers. Without warning though, things take a downward turn. His father is no longer present for supervision.

It appears that he is on a path of self-destruction driven by anger, disappointment, and low self-esteem.

Things continue to go from bad to worse:

- Suspended from school
- Lost his wallet with his French ID
- Fired from his part-time job
- Evicted from his apartment
- Both French and US passports gone.

Surely, this is a comedy. My son is "officially" an alien in his country of birth, the USA, with no means to return to France as he has no passport. You ask yourself, how does one go from being a citizen of two countries to an alien in one of them?

I express gratitude for the situation as I could clearly see that all was in the hands of the Universe; all was unfolding exactly as it should.

Upon reflection, I wanted to control the situation, run to my son's side, and doubt myself. Where did I go wrong? What am I going to do? This is what I wrote in my gratitude journal when I learned of his situation:

<u>April 13, 2014</u> - *Pierre has been evicted from his apartment and his passports are gone for good, but he has his Buddhist Gohonzon (scroll), which is safe. Anger wells up, yet I tell myself, "I do not own this. He chose not to follow my guidance or advice and there is not much more I can do." I offer prayers for his protection and safety.*

Gratitude wells forth as I pray for wisdom in a time of crisis, and trust that it will work out. First, putting myself through an endless ordeal of internal questioning, replaying certain events over and over in my head, negating myself ... none of these were creating value. It is ok to feel the pain but not to allow unhealthy perspectives to settle in and replace my confidence in myself, and my faith.

Second, no longer in a place of fear or panic, I feel confident in what I have done for my son, all that I have given him and the straight roads which I have led him down. He chose to go in another direction and this can happen to anyone. Does this mean that I failed as his mother? By no means! This is his life experience, which will shape his character and encourage other youth. The rest of his travels are about self-discovery, independent of what he has been through thus far. I like to put it this way: if we do not hear the warning that life puts before us, life forces us to stand up and be accounted for, through its experiences.

The President of our Buddhist organization very eloquently put it this way:

"Those children who cause the most pain and suffering to their parents will inevitably grow and develop to lead lives of value and become an inspiration to others." Daisaku Ikeda

Our Gratitude Mission

Had he not gotten off course, he would not have gotten to know his Aunt Frances (my sister), who took him in. This brought her and me closer together.

This homeless stint of bouncing from sofa to sofa lasted only two months, but it was the longest two months of my life. At the same time, other Buddhist members would send me photos to say they have seen my son, that he is attending meetings with the youth division and sharing his experience. I am thinking "That is my son!" He has his mother's fighting spirit.

This is what makes us unique. Here what I journaled:

April 27, 2014 - I feel emotionally exhausted today. Got a Facebook message from Pierre to say he is ok and has found a little job. A Buddhist member from DC sent me a message to say, "He attended the 'Soka Gakkai International' meeting in New York and this is where he shared his story with hundreds of other members." How powerful!!

At that moment, I saw how much my son was protected and that his life was being guided in the direction it was to go.

In December, I returned to see my son, and sister, over a three week period. We reconnected and bonded. I saw the harsh winds of life had slapped him around, yet I was able to rest knowing he was with my sister, making daily efforts on his personal development.

In one of our conversations, he reminded me that he can do whatever he puts his mind to. As my son put it, "Being in the United States has helped me grow and have a clearer understanding of life." Everyone has their own path they must walk and cannot be controlled. Whatever the lesson that life has in store for us, we will get it.

Life was also moving forward for my two other sons:

Russ Terry

My middle son, Idriss, who is 20, practices gratitude and we enjoyed seeing the fruits of his labor. He signed a contract as an Electrician with the Town Hall near our home. He was grateful to land this job, which corresponds to his high school studies, and also helps to finance his driving lessons. (In France, you must go through a Driving School which is very costly). The job also helped him put money aside for a car.

In December 2014, he passed his driver's permit. January 28, 2015, he had his first car accident and my car was totaled. It was the end of the day, I was leaving work, when I got this call "Mom, I was coming around the roundabout in second gear, lost control of the car and hit a tree." My stomach dropped. I asked, "Are you hurt?", "No, I am so sorry, it was an accident." He and the tree were unscathed (smile).

I wrote this in my journal:

January 28, 2015 - What protection!!! Life loves us. This accident could have happened at any other time, any other day, but it did not. It happened where it was supposed to, near his place of work, near the house, with no other vehicles or passengers involved. I'm profoundly grateful for divine intervention.

My youngest son, Claude, who is 17, also expressed his gratitude for having been accepted into a two year Culinary Program in Versailles, with the third year in Pastry.

Prior to that, I was pleased to have been home to accompany him as he terminated junior high school. I am grateful I could be supportive of his decision. He found an employer, which is a brasserie, in Versailles near his school. Generally, in the first year, the interns do not get to do much cooking. Fortunately, in his case, he is grateful to have a young chef who is teaching him more than the basics. He also had one of his tarts served to a customer.

Our Gratitude Mission

I am grateful to have a cook/pastry chef in the house (laughter!!)

It warms my heart to see each and every one of them choose the direction they would like to go in and work to realize their dreams and desires.

<u>My Health</u>

By the end of 2013, I had set into motion my professional/personal objectives. However, my best laid out plan would not stand up against what the Universe had in store for me.

January 2014 rolls in and my health issues would constantly get in my way. I was determined to not let my back problems get the best of me. I needed to be at work, because I had already taken too much time off for sick leave, and was not fully present to handle the workload I was responsible for to support the team.

After that, I got a flare up of tendinitis in my left hip, which was a throwback from falling down the stairs a few years ago. No, I can't deal with this! The doctor gave me pain medication and prescribed a week off. Guilt set in because I couldn't be present. I asked my doctor for only two days off, so I could get back to my office. By the end of the week, both the tendinitis and slipped disc were wreaking havoc on my body. I pushed through but things got worse.

At the end of January, the pain intensified, which meant I could no longer focus. I was falling behind and had left lots of tasks undone. This would later come to haunt me.

By mid-February, my doctor put me on sick leave. Another MRI confirmed the agitation of my slipped disc. This would inevitably keep me behind the eight ball. It was like going up a slippery slope, which is very difficult to do. Nonetheless, I had to accept where I was and go deeper.

My self-worth was displaced. The events were not happening to me but through me. I was telling myself that, "I am worthy," "Show up for you," "Others' opinion of you is not your business, nor is it important." The Universe was trying to get my attention.

While on sick leave, I was able to participate in a Time Management online training with Russ Terry, who suggested I look into Brendon Burchard, a New York Times bestselling author and an expert on Time Management. I followed him on YouTube as well as obtaining his book *The Motivation Manifesto*, all in an effort to feel good about myself. I was also setting the stage for my return.

Thanks to the training, I was looking forward to going back to work to put into practice what I took away. Time management is important for professional projects, development and to avoid being overwhelmed.

When I was grappling with health issues, my mind was running rampant with abundant self-negation. However, I was learning to forgive myself for the situation I found myself in. It was not my fault. It was serving a purpose, although I could not see it due to the blinders on my eyes.

Louise Hay, author of *You Can Heal Your Life*, says hernias signify "ruptured relationships, strain and burdens" and "incorrect creative expression." We can affirm: "My mind is gentle and harmonious. I love and approve of myself. I am free to be me."

My return to work was repeatedly postponed due to my slipped disc. I could not walk nor stand for long periods of time, so I constantly thought how and when would I get out of this situation? Through it all, I was so grateful to be in France with the ability to receive good medical care, and have my bills taken care of.

Our Gratitude Mission

While on sick leave, I took the opportunity to deepen my faith, through studying more Buddhist teachings, meditations and other spiritual practices. I was inspired by this quote:

"*Those who embrace the Lotus Sutra, however, can turn all this around. Hell becomes the Land of tranquil Light; the burning fires of agony become the torch of the wisdom of a Thus Come One of the reward body.*" - Nichiren Daishonin

Being on sick leave for an undetermined period was hell. However, awakening to my Buddha state was the reward. In other words, I was exactly where I was supposed to be, going through exactly what I was to go through. I would get through this. Although at times it felt as though I was at the end of the world, I was not. Just let go of the reigns and let the Universe do its job.

May 9, 2014 – *I am grateful to be pushing beyond my self-imposed limitations and creating expansion for me. Thanks to my disability, I am discovering and doing that which I have never done before, such as: exploring the healthy aspects of nutrition, voice lessons, learning trades to start a business, and participating in online courses.*

I always wanted to sing. I sang in the choir and fully admired the gospel singers. In the back of my mind, there was this voice that would say, "You'll never sing like them, you do not have what it takes," while another part of me was saying, "You'll never know until you try, what do you have to lose? Besides, time is on our side."

I am grateful that I listened to my higher self because I used the time daily to practice breathing, and took voice lessons offered online. I called my dear friend Lucie Itela, who runs her own music and dance association – *ArtMajik*. I have danced and taught dance with Lucie over the years. We have great appreciation for one another. However, my proposition on this day would be different. I shared with her what I wanted to do – sing! She invited me over, listened to my voice and said, "You have a lovely voice" and "I would love to do a duet with you." We planned a date in May – when *ArtMajik* would participate in the celebrations marking the abolition of slavery.

What a glorious feeling!!! So, we began rehearsing with a guitarist. Did I tell you what my real prompt to want to sing was? I was actually inspired when I first heard Clarence Milton Bekker (playing for change) sing "Stand by Me." It was something about the lyrics that spoke to my inner being. I needed to sing the song too. Decision taken, I would sing this as a solo. I did sing it as a solo. Surprisingly enough, there just so happened to be a voice coach who came up to me to compliment me on the "melodic tones" in my voice. Wow!!! I am so grateful for this experience because I can see my many hidden talents bursting to get out.

As I mentioned earlier, I am grateful to Russ Terry for many, many reasons, but especially for introducing me to the teachings of Brendon Burchard while I was on sick leave. I knew that once I returned to work, I must overcome my limitations, and learn better time management skills, so I would be assigned more projects and taken seriously. When I resumed work in September 2014, I was armed with Brendon's advice and resolve to become the professional change I would like to see.

Once I released myself from various toxic situations, relationships and burdens that I had been carrying like a trophy, a spiritual shift occurred and I began an inner healing.

January 4, 2015 - Yeah!! What a blessing to be here with all of you. My perception of my life, professional and personal, changed so drastically in 2014, as the stage was being set for a new mindset to show up differently in my life: to allow me to step into my authentic self despite how uncomfortable it felt, and to stand up and say NO, this is not working for me. I survived numerous situations including the loss of an intimate relationship in the midst of what seemed like unsurmountable difficulties. But these events did not happen to me but through me as I view it from the grand scheme of things. So, I say thank you to the Universe for the various challenges I faced. You see, strangely enough 2014 started off on what seemed like the wrong foot, but it didn't, it went exactly the way it was supposed to. Yes, I have grown in leaps and bounds this year thanks to being a part of this project: discovered latent talents, participated in numerous trainings and have been accepted to start a nine month Professional Coach training program in June. So as I sit here in the airport upon my return from visiting my son in the USA, I say thank you. I, and my sons, have made it and we are stronger and wiser. I look forward to seeing the flowers bloom this year and beyond.

January 6, 2015 - 3 am, sleep evades me. I got back from DC only two days ago. Grateful, I went to my Buddhist altar downstairs. I have this quiet place to pray without disturbing the household. While praying, I visualized me behind my son, Pierre, supporting him always. Grateful knowing he is safe on his journey through life.

Love and Relationships

During my year of gratitude, the time had come to step out of an unhealthy relationship. I am actually grateful for my decision, which was not an easy one. In light of where we were in our respective lives, it was best for both parties. I remember a relationship coach say, "You cannot fall in love with potential." Boy, did she hit the nail on the head with that expression. Through prayer and guidance from the Universe, I could see how the ego can cause a relationship to self-destruct based on our limitations, expectations or barriers. When we remove the blinders of illusion, we open our eyes to what's clearly in front of us.

Let's take a step back and look at my childhood. My mother was not emotionally available. Neither were any of the other adults; they were prisoners to their addictions. One day they may be available, the next day not. We are souls first, persons second and always expressions of divine spirits.

Back to present day, a few months after the breakup, I was eating lunch with a close friend who had last seen me right when it happened. On this day, she said, "Something has changed. You look surer of yourself and stronger." I was!! I had been reciting my Buddhist prayer and doing my inner work.

I'm a big fan of President Ikeda, the President of the Nichiren Buddhist Soka Gakkai, which is the largest of Japan's religious movements. He is poetic when it comes to matters of the heart. He says, "What is most important is that we become absolutely happy no matter what, continue to polish your inner mirror day and night. How do we do this? By chanting NAM MYOHO RENGE KYO and a transformation will naturally occur."

I am grateful for a very memorable and heartwarming friendship I have nurtured with a gentleman. We will call him Craig, to protect his identity. We met 11 years ago, when we were both separating, respectively, in different countries. We were looking for a friendship and dialogue, no more. With mutual respect, we shared the evolution of our lives. The years pass as the seasons. We were there to support and encourage one another through the various stages of divorce. It truly is a blessing to have someone, like Craig, with whom you can confide. And that we did! Divorces finalized, children getting older, parent or parents lost, a virtual shoulder on which to lean, a few jokes and smiles to get over the next hurdle, all in two different countries. Without warning, we had become an integral part of each other's lives; we always knew we could trust each other.

In 2010, six years after our first virtual meeting, two months after the passing of my mother, with the help of some divine intervention, we finally met in person. It wasn't that we were meeting for the first time, but the virtual energy we shared all those years was waiting to solidify. You know how when you long to see your best friend, or a lover, you are filled with excitement.

Our Gratitude Mission

That is exactly it!! As friends do, we took each other in, and then laughed hysterically. "It's really you!" "Yes, it is really me" followed by Colgate smiles. We also were able to enjoy each other's company, marking the 10 year anniversary of the passing of his father. How mystic is that? I trust the mutual respect as Heart-Centered Friends. It will always be until the Universe deems otherwise.

As I contemplate what's next – or in this case who's next – there remains a shield around my heart. It's healing so many of my heartaches from the past. That said, I look forward to the future with a huge smile.

Intimate relationships for me used to be like a dragon's fire, but I can happily say that's now down to a flicker. This is a truly valuable learning curve as I have decidedly chosen to work through my issues to heal all of me.

I give myself permission to forgive those who have hurt me and to forgive me for all the many times I have hurt myself. We are all victims of victims. Let's get on with the show!

I am not saying I won't ever be hurt again or even afraid to open my heart and allow myself to be vulnerable. What I am saying is that I will be able to say, "Thank you for this opportunity to be a better person today and tomorrow" and I shall keep moving forward.

<u>May 4, 2015</u> - I have been too much in my head and thinking about all the things I feel I could have done differently, or should have, or why didn't something turn out this way or that. But the fact is it's no longer important. We cannot rewrite the past; however, we can continue to write beautiful stories in the present, which is for our future. The moral of the story is, "What matters is what we do from this moment forward." We keep showing up for our lives. Onward and Upward!! I am grateful for this insight as our personal development is a daily practice, as is our faith. Blessings to you all!

Russ Terry

Here are some other noteworthy entries from my year of gratitude:

March 28, 2014 - Today, I begin to note what I am grateful for – SO many things: I am grateful to be a part of *Our Gratitude Mission* with other like-minded individuals. I have less pain and I am able to sit up longer in prayer. My youngest son Claude's chocolate cakes will be on display today, in two different places: the bakery and at Metis Tropicale, a French West Indian Restaurant. Last but certainly not least, I am grateful for and truly appreciate my sons' help, no matter how big or small.

April 1, 2014 - Abundant gratitude reigns in my heart. My second son, Idriss, signed his first job contract with the Mayor's Office near the house. I am so proud of him. He was searching high and low for a full time job based on his studies.

April 28, 2014 - While at pool therapy for my back, I met an older man from Benin, West Africa, who felt so honored to have met me, an African American woman in this French suburb of Paris. He expressed gratitude for our encounter, knowing what Black Americans endured in the USA as slaves etc., and that Africans were taken from Benin to the USA. Wow!!! I was left speechless and profoundly touched by his heart.

May 20, 2014 - I'm grateful that I am at home, on sick leave, to deal with my emotions in private regarding Pierre's current situation. This is my time to turn within and heal me, and also to give him the emotional support he requires.

June 15, 2014 - My youngest son has been accepted to culinary school just at the same time he found an employer to hire him for an internship. Thank you, Universe.

July 4, 2014 - Grateful that the various pieces of information that I have put before my sons have helped them make informed decisions. My lesson here:

Our Gratitude Mission

Let go! Whatever the outcome, they will make the best decision for themselves at that moment.

September 12, 2014 - My fear of standing out caused me to hide, and not show up for my life, or allow my authentic self to shine. Armed with Time Management tips from Russ Terry's training during my sick leave, I will succeed.

I am grateful for this awakening. I am pushing through my self-imposed limitations so I can be a role model for my sons. I could not have had this epiphany without the time off, prayer and inward reflections. The ethics I pass down to my sons are that we are paid to go to work. We have a responsibility to show up and be conscientious of our behavior and interactions in the workplace.

September 14, 2014 - It is now that I have and want to create a name for me, to become the kind of person/woman/mother/Buddhist that people genuinely refer to with pride, as someone who has touched their lives. I thank the Universe in advance for the millions of lives I want to positively impact on this earth.

September 15, 2014 - Grateful for the "WhatsApp" message from a friend of mine, who lives in Holland, but was visiting Japan, who happened to run into someone who knew me from Washington, DC. My name came up in the conversation, and here is what the woman in Japan, originally from DC, had to say about me: "Domonique is awesome and courageous, I am so proud to have known her and her family." That was mind blowing and brought tears to my eyes especially when you look at my post of the day before.

September 22, 2014 - I'm grateful for my daily prayers to push through my fears and show up for work. My back hurt and the old me would have called in sick. This time though, I said no. I can do this; I am on the mend. By the end of the day, I felt better physically and, just as importantly, empowered!

Russ Terry

October 1, 2014 - Appreciated the very positive comments from a few colleagues. One person expressed how she looks up to me as a role model. Grateful I could make her feel better about herself in some small way.

November 11, 2014 - Just wanted to share that I am so grateful to be grateful for ALL life has to offer and it loves me.

November 21, 2014 - Woke up feeling so blessed for being alive and my life as a whole.

November 22, 2014 - "Upgrade Your Life" weekend in the Network Marketing Industry. Friday was spent with Women Entrepreneurs. Exciting!!

December 11, 2014 - I have completed my "Assessment Skills Evaluation," which was paid for by the company. It offered new insights into my character. I was surprised to learn that I am a natural born leader. Wow!!! Not quite in line with it at this moment, but it feels good to hear. There is a place in me that says, "Yes, you are!"

January 17, 2015 - I'm grateful for the positive feedback from my youngest son's manager at the restaurant where he is an intern. He said, "Your son is very motivated and always on time."

April 4, 2015 - Grateful for friends with whom we share good times and sometimes not, but always leads to even better times. My girlfriend drove down from Holland with her son so we could spend Easter together. A four-and-a half hour drive became eight hours due to traffic. Funny how we both brought to each other a bottle of Chardonnay wine from South Africa. Hilarious!! Great minds and shared tastes go hand in hand. We bought the same white wines in two different countries in Europe. How cool is that!! Happy Easter :-)

Our Gratitude Mission

I hope you enjoyed my chapter and learned something from it. I leave you with my favorite Inspirational Quotes, which are mostly about gratitude with some other life lessons sprinkled in:

- If you want to turn your life around, try thankfulness. It will change your life mightily (G. Good)
- I would maintain that thanks are the highest form of thought and that gratitude is happiness doubled by wonder (G.K. Chesterton)
- Reflect upon your present blessing, of which every man has plenty, not on your past fortunes, of which all men have some (Charles Dickens)
- Hope can be found in some of the darkest places (author unknown)
- If you count your assets, you will always show a profit (R. Quillen)
- Things turn out best for people who make the best of the way things turn out (J. Wooden)
- Gratitude turns what we have into enough, and more. It turns denial into acceptance, chaos into order, confusion into clarity ... it makes sense of our past, brings peace for today and creates a vision for tomorrow. (Melody Beattie)
- Gratitude is a fullness of heart (D. Chopra)
- The future belongs to those who prepare for it today (Malcolm X)

This past year has been about going within to see my inner transformation, to a place of being omnipresent and grateful. By noting daily that for which I have been grateful, I jump for joy.

If it was not evident before, I am already complete, divine and a lovable human being.

Looking for validation from the outside is done via our ego, not from a place of divinity. It keeps us prisoners of the past versus pioneers of the future.

Russ Terry

This gratitude campaign, for me, has been sheer magnificence. My soul is opening up, thanks to this more profound insight. I look forward to the many joys life has ahead of me for the rest of 2015 and into the future. First, I am recovering nicely from my back issues, and I am giving myself more love. Second, I am developing professionally. I can't wait, but I will, to see what else awaits me on the professional horizons. Third, I am getting back to my number one passion, "African dance," as a teacher and student. I am opening up to the idea of seeing myself as an entrepreneur. There are several projects on the back burner and I am working to bring them forward. One example is becoming an independent black travel tour guide for Black Americans coming to Paris, to show them a Black Paris. This is so me! I am crazy excited about it, although fearful at the same time, so I must become more knowledgeable and sure of me. The upside is that I have gotten my feet wet by giving personal guided tours to a few referrals in 2014. In the near future, I hope to get funding to finance my Personal Development Coach training. Lastly, I want to bring into reality my book entitled *Voilá,* an account of my journey from America to France and my life thereafter.

As for my sons, Pierre is getting back on his feet. I'm grateful that he is pushing through his false beliefs, and for his decision to make more conscientious choices. His daily drawings are his "art therapy" and they're also keeping his artistic talents sharp. Perhaps he will return to France within the next year to rejoin his family. He is grateful for his experiences over the past year and looking forward to finishing the year on a more fulfilling note. His goal is to become a graphic artist and perhaps an architect.

Idriss continues to develop as a dancer. This is his dream to become a professional dancer and he has passed several exams toward this level. His time is invested in his full time work, with plans to return to school next year so he may develop professionally, and become certified as an Electrician too.

Our Gratitude Mission

Claude started his second year of culinary cuisine in September as he reflects on making his school year 2015/2016 a concrete year. He will also have exams to prepare for. His long term goal is to become a private chef.

In closing, I am grateful that I can see how my being grateful has impacted those around me. I would like to take as an example someone I know. This young lady on many occasions expresses her gratitude toward me. Here is what she said in particular, "When you come in, there is so much light, joy and energy. You make people feel good. You make me feel better about myself. You are very compassionate and a good example of how to overcome adversity. I am so lucky to know you." Thank you from the bottom of my heart.

Russ Terry

Terry's Take

It's so cool and inspiring that Domonique has transformed herself from "the girl from Newark, NJ" as she says to a global woman living in Paris and speaking two languages. I live in Jersey City, which is just 15 minutes from Newark. I do some work there at Rutgers University, and feel a special connection to the city and its students, many of whom come from the surrounding area. Newark and its residents have had their share of challenges, but hopefully our book will inspire those in inner cities (and others) that anything is possible!

I have met so many of the authors – and their families – in person, but have not met Domonique yet. I look forward to that happening someday. We Skype, but nothing can replace that in person interaction. Maybe I'll get to meet her sons too. They seem like they're up to such cool stuff in the world. I give her a lot of credit for raising them on her own in a 'strange' country. Based on what I have seen, she did an excellent job. I would bet money that all three of them are very grateful to her and for her.

Our Gratitude Mission

Epilogue

There you have it! 5,475 days of Gratitude: 15 people multiplied by 365 days. Before *Our Gratitude Mission* began, many of the authors were at least a bit intimidated by the task ahead of them. Look at them now though – all finished the mission, and all were able to find a *different* expression of gratitude every day for a year! I am incredibly inspired by their stories, and hopefully you were too.

Want to connect with those of us involved in the project or join our Gratitude Group Coaching Program? Email me at russ@russterrylifecoach.com. To continue to see what we're grateful for in years to come, Like us on Facebook and follow us on Twitter:

- www.facebook.com/MyGratitudeJournalByRussTerry
- https://twitter.com/Gratitude4aYear

Now that you are done the book, what's next for YOU? Are YOU going to keep a gratitude journal? We hope that in some way we have motivated you to do so, and given you the tools necessary to make it happen.

If you have a child (18 or younger) who wants to keep a gratitude journal and be part of my fourth book (tentatively titled *Grateful Kids*), please email me at russ@russterrylifecoach.com.

Lastly, I love hearing from fans of my books! I'm immensely grateful for all the nice feedback and support. See below for how to add me on social media:

- www.facebook.com/russterrylifecoach
- www.twitter.com/RTerryLifeCoach
- www.linkedin.com/in/russterrylifecoach
- www.instagram.com/russterrylifecoach

Our Gratitude Mission

Made in the USA
Middletown, DE
21 February 2016